# ROYAL BOROUGH OF GREENWICH

Follow us on twitter  @greenwichlibs

Blackheath Library
Tel: 020 8858 1131

BL

## Please return by the last date shown

05/16

1 6 JUN 2016

−1 FEB 2018

# Being Luis
## A Chilean Life

Luis Muñoz

First published 2005
by Impress Books Ltd
Innovation Centre, Rennes Drive,
University of Exeter Campus, Exeter EX4 4RN

© Luis Muñoz 2005

The right of Luis Muñoz to be identified as author of this
work has been asserted by him in accordance with the
Copyright, Designs and Patents Act 1988.

Typeset in Amasis and Folio by Keystroke, Jacaranda Lodge,
Wolverhampton
Printed and bound by Short Run Press Ltd, Exeter

British Library Cataloguing in Publication Data
A catalogue record for this book is available from the British Library

ISBN 0–9547586–3–3 (hbk)
ISBN 0–9547586–1–7 (pbk)

To the thousands who were silenced forever

# Contents

Contents

# Preface

Much has been written about the Chilean political movement, the social conflicts and the history of the people's struggles that ultimately led to the election of the popular socialist government in 1970. But little has been written about the personal experience of people living in Chilean society during the sixties and in particular the youth and university students' movement.

The media had reached the far corners of the country. At the beginning of the sixties there was a campaign to make radios available to every family in every town and every village in the country. This campaign was not only a government plan to inform and educate, it was an economic plan of the Christian Democrat government of Eduardo Frei.

When Frei was elected in 1964 he promised radical economic reform, which was to boost heavy industry and the powers behind it. This was the new rich investors fiercely competing with the old agricultural economic powers. These new economic groups were dynamic entrepreneurs who supported Frei's campaign, which was mainly directed to attract the middle classes and young professionals. The accelerated development of heavy industry would bring several benefits to the country as a whole. There was the potential for every household to own a fridge, an electric or gas cooker, a heater, radio and television. For the more affluent, there would be cars. Yes, cars would be cheaper because Fiat, Renault, Citroën, Datsun and other car manufacturers had promised to build assembly plants in Chile. This would bring even more benefits. Many car parts would be manufactured in the country, bringing more industry and more jobs.

These ambitious plans were widely and rapidly implemented during the first few years of the Frei government. More houses and roads were built. Labour reforms were introduced to protect worker's rights. Attempts were made to unionise the *campesinos* (peasant farmers), and token land reforms were introduced. As a consequence, production increased and nearly every household in the country did have a radio and domestic appliances. But what would easy access to broadcast information for the country's illiterate bring? Although Chilean-manufactured electro-domestic products reached Peru, Bolivia, Ecuador, Uruguay, Paraguay and other Latin American countries, the bubble could not last and it burst in a tragic way.

In the socio-political arena, information flooded in about the Cuban revolution, the Cuban missile crisis, the war in the Middle East, the independence movement in the ex-colonies of Africa, the Algerian independence war, the Vietnamese independence war and the Russian invasion of Czechoslovakia. All these events, in one way or another, gave a sense of solidarity with peasant workers in Vietnam or Algeria, for example. For the first time, perhaps, there was a sense that, even in the Andean mountains one was not alone, that there were brothers and sisters on the other side of the globe with similar interests to fight for.

What was true for a peasant or a factory worker was also true for the youth and student movement: university reform was demanded, initially, from Argentina to Mexico, France, Italy and Chile. The wind of reform would reach almost every corner of the world. The students' demands were for democracy, participation in the decision-making process and joint student–academic government. More importantly, to open the universities to the people and to make them accessible to the working classes.

It started at the University of Cordoba in Argentina in 1967. The students occupied the university campus and soon, little by little, different sectors of society joined in the protest. White-collar workers followed manufacturing workers until there was a general strike. The students' demands for university reforms were superseded by higher demands for the entire province, to the point of demanding independence from the central federal state. Soon the repression was unleashed. Cordoba was surrounded by armed forces and the beating, shooting, imprisonment and killing started. University reform was finally achieved, but the price Cordoba had to pay was high.

The students' revolt continued in Mexico. The National Autonomous University of Mexico's students gathered at the University of Tlatelolco. This time the government and its repressive forces were not caught by surprise and what became known as the massacre of Tlatelolco followed: the repressive government forces massacred the students, without mercy, in broad daylight for everyone to see. More than four hundred students were killed. It was March 1968.

In May 1968 it was France's turn to have its student's revolt, but with one big difference. France was a developed country with a reputation for tolerating dissenting opinion – at least inside its own territory – and a developed culture and intelligentsia. The De Gaulle government understood that it could not afford to follow its underdeveloped counterparts in South America and so did not send troops to 'persuade the students'. What started in Paris would eventually paralyse the entire country. 'Everything was put into question', even 'the question' itself. To a lesser extent, other universities of the developed world were affected by the aftershocks of the Paris '68 revolt.

These events would have an enormous impact on the generation of the late sixties and early seventies. The worldwide student revolt not only questioned the establishment and its political and economic power, it brought with it a sexual revolution and peace movement. These events, from what I witnessed and experienced as a member of that generation in my country, greatly influenced the way we acted.

For a start, we genuinely believed that we were making history. It made us believe everything was possible. That there were people in other countries, in other parts of the world, who shared our feelings, our concerns, our aspirations and our dreams; that we were not alone in our pursuit. We believed that if we were erecting a barricade in the streets of Santiago, another barricade had been erected in a street of Chicago, Rome or Cairo. They would know our purpose as we would know theirs.

This sense of oneness gave us a feeling of omnipotence. We were unstoppable, indestructible. What did it matter if one lost his or her life in the attempt to change the world if there were millions of people ready to take your place in the long battle? Millions of minds were tuned in to the same wavelength. In the meantime, the aspirations and dreams of the young generation of dreamers were being fuelled by the ordinary aspirations and dreams of the young everywhere. The instinctual desire to impress girls, parents and peers at an age of vulnerability found its theatre in the turbulent and, more often than not, bloodied confrontations with the status quo of the time. There was an element of bravado that sometimes developed into arrogance.

I am not proposing that the things we did, the triumphs and the defeats, were wrong, or that I would not do them again. Nor am I suggesting that because you rebel, you deserve to be punished, tortured, made to 'disappear' or be killed. The students of Paris rebelled and none of them were killed for it. They, too, might have felt omnipotent and even arrogant; however, they achieved a momentous thing – a revolution. When I look back at our lives in those years I can only think of the frankness, the openness, the honesty, the nobility of everyone's intentions. How much trust was given to the notion that ultimately everyone would understand that. Everyone would see the necessity and the inevitability of the changes to come. They were intense times – and our lives were intense too. Relationships were loaded with profound meaning. In retrospect it seems as though we reached maturity earlier than normal; that we had to take a social responsibility too early in our lives. Maybe that we were sensitised too profoundly by the injustice, inequality, abuse, discrimination, poverty and hunger around us.

★ ★ ★

I remember the first time I visited Chile after twelve years in exile. It broke my heart to see little children, barefoot in the streets, selling sweets among the cars, running, trying to avoid being hit in the heavy traffic. I was with my eight-year-old daughter Diana having a drink, sitting outside a restaurant. I hadn't seen her beautiful face for four years; four long years since her mother, Eugenia, took her back to Chile, and away from me. A little girl came to our table to offer her sweets and asked whether I would like to buy some for my little girl. I looked in my pocket for some change, with the intention of giving her some money. But I could only find a large bill and so told her that I did not have any change. At that moment a waiter arrived to hush her away and she ran off. My daughter was furious and asked me why I did not give the little girl any money. I explained to her that I had no change. 'Why didn't you give her the note then?' she asked. Ashamed of myself I took my daughter's hand and ran into the street after the little girl. She was not there but there were a few boys around. We asked them where the little girl had gone and they pointed into the distance to the other side of the wide, dual-carriageway called Providencia Avenue, which runs through one of the richest neighbourhoods in the country. They shouted her name and, not without difficulty, zigzagging in the traffic she crossed the avenue to where we were. The other boys were asking why we wanted the little girl and why we didn't buy the sweets from them. Filled with emotions and memories, I could barely talk. The little girl asked us what was wrong but all I could say was 'my daughter wants to give you this', and I placed the big bank note in her dirty little hand. She smiled sweetly, speechless. I hid my tears.

'What's the matter papa?'

'Nothing, I'm just a bit sad, and you?'

'I'm happier now,' she said.

This was twelve years after I was 'asked to leave' Chile and seventeen years after the Pinochet coup. Seventeen years after the Chicago School economic policies had been implemented. There were hundreds of small, barefoot children in the streets of Santiago begging, most of the time, not for money but for some of the food people were eating or for the leftovers. The look in those children's eyes will never leave me.

We had left our blood and flesh in the torture chambers. We had generously given our lives, lost our most dearest and loved ones. All because we did not want to see the heartbreaking scenes of children of such a tender age begging for food in the streets. And here they were, in their hundreds, during the day and in the middle of the night, sleeping in the entrances to the big stores. How could I ever return to Chile, like many exiles had done, to live in 'peace and reconciliation' when the children of Chile were unable to sleep, abandoned on the streets of the big cities, among lavish opulence, with empty stomachs?

'I will come back some day my sweet darling,' I told my daughter when she asked me to stay in Chile with her. But you will not see me, my precious, because I know I could not bear to see what I have seen so far and adopt the 'peace and reconciliation' slogan. I could not forget the past and declare myself blind to the present. This unbearable heartache would probably drive me to pick up a cobblestone and throw it at some unsuspecting soldier. Or I would paint a furious placard to protest against injustice on behalf of the hungry people. Or I would try to confiscate the food from the larders of the rich and arrogant people.

# Acknowledgements

I would especially like to thank Sara Bursey, my wife and mother of my two precious boys, Pablo and Orlando, for having the patience of a saint in our adventure together and during my worst moments.

Thanks to Helen Bamber for her persistent encouragement for me to write this book and John McCarthy and John Furse who both read early drafts.

Thanks to Julie Watson who took it as a personal challenge for this story to be printed.

Thanks to Richard Willis, Julis Willis, Colin Morgan and Briony Frost of Impress Books for their persistence and encouragement.

Following pages: me, aged five, and my sister Lucia, aged seven, proudly wearing our new school uniforms.

# Coup

8 a.m., September 11, 1973.

Already dressed, Diana switches the radio on. The music on the station, on all radio stations, is military. What we have feared for so long has finally happened. There has been a coup. Every now and then there is an announcement, read by a military voice, advising people to stay at home: 'The armed forces are in the process of taking control of the state structure and are dealing with some minor pockets of resistance.' The Popular Government has been deposed.

We look at each other and embrace for a long time. Time to wake up. 'We have to go,' we say simultaneously. No time for breakfast. We jump into the 2CV and head for the centre of Santiago. The streets are almost deserted and I leave Diana on a street corner where someone is already waiting for her. We look at each other not knowing when we are going to meet again, if at all. I head towards an apartment near the University Arts Faculty, in the centre of Santiago, to a pre-planned emergency rendezvous with other comrades in the event of a coup d'état. In the Plaza Italia there is a group of soldiers with a huge artillery piece pointing towards the San Cristobal hill. There are also several 50 mm machine guns placed in different corners of the square shooting at anything that moves. It seems so unreal, shooting everywhere, dozens of people lying dead in the streets, and I am still moving, as if my 2CV were invisible. The soldiers look at me and ignore me or direct me to continue. Suddenly a group of three soldiers direct their guns straight at me and order me to stop. I then realise that in the car there are a number of political books from Diana's work. I stop and they ask me where I am going and what

Diana, aged twenty, while a university student at Santiago.

is in the car. They look at the books and then let me go, telling me to return home or I will be shot dead. It all seems like a bad dream.

It is still early in the morning and around the Arts Faculty the shooting is fierce. I see tanks for the first time and it looks as if the police are still loyal to the president because the army is shooting with heavy artillery at the police depot on Santa Lucia hill. I park the car on a deserted street and walk to the apartment trying to make myself invisible.

There are two comrades in the apartment and the mood is sombre. My throat is dry and my chest heavy. Rapidly, some information and orders are given: 'Not everything is lost; there is a column of special forces loyal to the president marching towards the centre of Santiago.

We must meet them and give them instructions.' I am entrusted with the mission.

I decide that it will be safer to walk to the meeting point. It is about twenty minutes away and I have the feeling that the main avenue, La Alameda, will have more people and cars on it. As it happens, I am right. Again, as at Plaza Italia, it is like walking through a dream. I am able to pass, without hurrying, amongst the soldiers shelling the telecommunications tower and government buildings in Plaza Bulnes, the civic centre of Santiago. Further west there are more soldiers and officers shouting orders. I need to reach Plaza Brasil, towards the west, where I believe the troops still loyal to the president will assemble. I would later learn that the commander of these troops was captured before he could get out of his bed, savagely tortured and then hanged the same day at the barracks.

I carry on walking slowly, observing the troop movements and actions as if I am indestructible. I arrive at Plaza Brasil and wait for about half an hour while the world around me falls apart. But there is no sign of the loyal troops. Where are they? There are more hostile troop carriers, tanks and other military vehicles travelling at high speed in different directions. Soldiers are running and shouting at people and to each other. I feel as if I do not exist, as if nobody can see me. I decide to take advantage of the situation and walk back from Plaza Brasil to where the car is parked near the Arts Faculty; a long walk in the middle of gunfire.

The gunfire is persistent and there are many bodies on the ground; women and children are crying while other civilians are being marched away with their hands on their heads, followed by soldiers with machine guns; but everybody miraculously decides to ignore me. By the time I reach Plaza Bulnes again, planes are flying low overhead in the direction of the presidential palace. Huge explosions follow – smoke, flames and more bombs. There are people running everywhere in panic.

I keep on walking fast now, turning around every now and then. There are still many people, mostly men, running in all directions, trying to find shelter from the bullets and grenades. Soldiers are running and shouting towards what seem like pre-arranged targets. The telecommunications tower is no longer under fire, as it was when I passed the first time. There are bodies everywhere now; passers-by painfully carry the wounded. There are no ambulances; the coup organisers do not care about wounded civilians. The presidential palace is in flames and still under fire from the tanks and artillery surrounding it. I am hurrying along with a group of civilians while soldiers pursue us, threatening us with their guns. I am without fear, living in semi-reality, as if I do not belong to the crumbling world around me. The day has grown warmer and there is hazy sunshine.

I discover that walking on my own posesses less risk than in a group; I attract less attention from the soldiers and, taking a zigzag route, I manage to get to the car. I decide that the military are unlikely to exercise the same kind of ferocious attack against the population in the rich neighbourhoods that I have been witnessing in the centre of the city. So I make a mental map to get to a pre-arranged safe house in the western suburbs.

Avenida Irarrázabal is quite busy, people hurrying, trying to reach safety. I stop at a traffic light and notice that a man is looking at me. I look back in disbelief as he starts to approach the car; it is my father. What is he doing in this place, at this time? He is the last person I would have expected to meet on the day of the coup, and almost at the hour of the curfew. He looks very sad and afraid. 'Where are you going?' he asks me. The child in me does not know what to answer. It is as if I am about to do something naughty and he has just discovered it. Do I have to tell him the truth, that I have just been through a battlefield trying to contact the troops loyal to the president? That I have just been stopped and searched twice, with safety-catches off the machine-guns and nervous fingers on triggers? That the presidential palace is in flames? That I left Diana early in the morning to join her comrades, to make who knows what desperate attempts to stop the coup, to resist, and that I will probably never see her again? That I am going to meet my closest comrades at a safe house and wait for weapons and orders? That nobody who is alive will sleep tonight?

I want to tell him all these things, but I do not. He won't understand but only disapprove and get angry. Again, more anxious this time:

'Where are you going? There is nowhere to go, let's go home.'

'Do you need a lift?' I say.

'No.'

I look into his eyes and I see something I do not remember seeing before: concern. He is sincerely worried about me, his son. 'I have to go, dad,' is all I can say. He steps away from the car, looking sad and lost. We both know; all those arguments, in my late teens, about change, justice, equality, dignity, revolution, and now the time has come, the historical time, the time to pay with our blood for the audacity to dream. Bye, dad. I extend my hand and he grabs it for a second, maybe two.

Fifteen months later he would slowly walk towards what was left of me, a skeleton inside an oversized concentration camp blue fatigue, trousers tied up with rope, tufts of grey hair, at the age of twenty-six, and huge purple bags under my eyes. He avoids looking straight at me, as though I am too painful a sight for him, his son turned into a walking cadaver by monstrous treatment. He cannot bear it; he looks like a desperate man, and does a desperate thing. When he sees the opportunity, he comes closer to me and whispers in my ear: 'Tell them that you did not do it, tell them that you would give up everything, that you were just a bit silly, and we will walk away from here, together, right now.'

Poor dad. I do not know if he is prepared for my answer.

'Who do you think I am? What do you take me for? Do not insult me! Do not make me feel ashamed of you! What do you think I have been doing here, imprisoned for three months? What do you think we are all doing here, dad? Negotiating our escape? What I have been doing, what Diana was doing, and all the others before us and after us, dad, is resisting, and all we have got is ourselves, our bodies, our lives to fight back with until we draw our last breath!'

A friend of my father's manages to visit me in the camp one day. 'He got himself arrested a couple of times, your dad. After you disappeared, he used to go to the gates of the military barracks and shout: "You have taken my daughter-in-law and now you have taken my son, you bastards! Give them back to me! Give me my son back!" He was drunk and they beat him up.' This revelation leaves me with a strange feeling. I am proud because I never expected my father to do anything like that, but I also feel terribly sad. Whenever he could, my father brought me little avocado and ham sandwiches and a few almonds. After his visits, I would watch his back as he walked away towards the camp's gate, his long old overcoat dragging on the ground, a defeated man.

I had watched the same back many times before. As a boy I used to follow him everywhere as he walked around the enormous fruit and vegetable wholesale market in Santiago. He was hoping for a bargain that would turn our fortunes. I would follow him for hours, my empty stomach beginning to ache, through the huge maze of the market, full of all kinds of people and voices, until everything else would disappear,

# Family

2

My mother must have been nineteen when she married my father. She was not easily persuaded; he had to bring presents and serenade her in front of her bedroom window while my grandmother heaped abuse on him. She was extremely beautiful. There are a couple of photographs, taken by one of her admirers who was a photographer, which we still keep. I do not know which of my brothers has the original, but we all have copies because she looks so beautiful.

It is difficult to put the pieces together and to know for certain my mother's story from before she married because I guess she felt uneasy with what happened to her. After her death in 1995 I tried to put the pieces of her life together. Talking to my brothers and sisters did not help much because everyone has different accounts of the same events. Besides, everyone feels a bit ashamed and shy of sharing a piece of mother's history and comparing it with a sibling who is bound to question it on the grounds that she told him or her a different story. There is a fear of being robbed of something one has been hanging on to as the only, privileged child, depository of the true story of mother.

What has in any case emerged is quite sad. She was born in 1925. Here we are already faced with a discrepancy: was it September or October? There are two entries for the same person: one provided by her mother and another by her father, each giving a different year. Her mother came to Chile with her Spanish immigrant mother. Her father, Hipolito Eyraud, was a Frenchman who emigrated from France to Argentina and then to Chile. He was a university lecturer from Marseille who taught sculpture and painting at the University of Chile in Santiago.

My mother, looking glamorous.

He had two sisters who were nuns and lived in a school and convent in Viña del Mar, near Valparaiso.

It is not exactly clear what happened, but my mother ended up, as a small child, living with her father's sisters in Viña del Mar until she was about eleven. At that time, her mother attempted to recover custody of her daughter and the matter ended up in court. My mother was left to decide which one of the parents she wanted to live with. She, having had enough of the nuns who spoke to her only in French and treated her like a servant, decided to try her fortunes with her mother, in the process ignoring her father's pleas and promises of a life of glamour in Paris where she could study painting, dancing or singing and where they would live together happily. My mother did not budge. She chose a life of poverty and deprivation with her mother and grandmother. When she married my father she was working as a laboratory assistant.

My father was eight years older than my mother and at the time they met he was working as a metal engineer for a British mining company. His father was a civil servant from a Spanish-Jewish background and his mother and family were so extraordinary as to really deserve a chapter of their own. Zoila Valdes Oyarzun, my father's mother, was the eldest of eleven brothers and sisters. Their mother was a healer and shaman, the daughter of a Mapuche (native of Chile) and a Chilean-Spanish aristocrat whose three brothers and sister fought for Chilean independence against the Spanish with Simon Bolivar of Venezuela and Jose de San Martin of Argentina. They wanted a United States of South America. Zoila had red hair, dressed like a Victorian lady and had a very strong character. My father lived in fear of her. She had three boys and died giving birth to her fourth little boy when my father, the second son, was only ten years old. Following a Jewish custom, grandfather married Zoila's sister Elena and had one daughter, Aunt Raquel.

Before I was born, my father's elder brother, Luis, a paramedic, died of tuberculosis after he had volunteered to help the victims of a devastating earthquake 400 kilometres south of Santiago.

Soon after I was born, my grandfather died.

My father, being the eldest surviving son, ended up supporting and living with his step-mother, Elena, his step-sister, Raquel, and his aunt Dominga, together with my mother and her two children: my sister Lucia and myself. His younger brother, Rene, had also married and had a son and a daughter. Uncle Rene was a metalworker who lived modestly with his family and came to visit us almost every weekend. So we were an extended family of seven children, five boys and two girls (Lucia, myself, Eduardo, Raul, Irene, Arturo and Fernando) and five adults (mother and father, grand-aunt Dominga, grandmother Elena and Aunt Raquel, in her late teens when we first lived together).

I was born a few weeks prematurely, a weak baby. I had what the doctors called a 'primary complex', a combination of various illnesses and handicaps. These included weak lungs and a weak stomach. The story goes that the family doctor, who was half German and very fond of my mother, had a baby son born more or less at the same time with the same health problems. His baby did not make it and died a few weeks after it was born. The doctor became obsessed with my survival, but I was so poorly that after a time even Dr Moll gave up and told my mother to take her baby home to die. The 'grannies', Dominga and Elena, were not so easily defeated, however, and when the comatose baby landed in their hands, they set themselves to use all they could remember from the teachings of their healer mother, the shaman. They prepared potions and beverages, using carrots, red peppers, cow's blood, donkey's milk, lamb's liver and dozens of herbs. They chanted, prayed and rubbed the baby, who would never cry. In his best moments, he would only stare at them

*Family*

My family. From left to right: Eduardo, me, mum, Irene, Fernando, dad, Arturo, Raul and Lucia.

with his huge eyes. It worked; centuries, or maybe even thousands of years, of healing came to fruition. But the grannies could not declare victory yet: at four years of age I contracted TB; this time, though, they had to allow antibiotics to help. With a weak immune system I could not run the risks of vaccination and I had to manage without, acquiring every childhood illness around – measles, chickenpox, mumps – every time scaring the elders stiff.

It is no surprise that, when grand-aunt Dominga was dying at the age of ninety-five, completely lucid, her last breath was reserved to ask the remaining adults in the family to 'please, look after Luisito.' I was eight, looking out of the second floor window at the summer night sky, without understanding why she had to die. I was also a bit taken aback by her final words, because, as far as I knew, I was not her favourite child. I thought she preferred my brother Eduardo or sister Irene. I felt bothered somehow, as if she knew of something dangerous I was going to do in the future that I needed to be protected from or be prevented from doing. I started to cry in my silent way.

My father's wages, which could have comfortably provided for a couple or even three children, became insufficient for the number

10

of people depending on them. So he then decided to leave his job with the British mining company and join his cousins in a small metal construction factory. We became more relaxed financially and were able to move to a bigger house with a big garden. It was not rented; dad bought it new in a development in the southern outskirts of the city. Everything smelled new and it was very quiet since beyond our house there was only a canal, fields and orchards. There was also a small swimming pool and a chicken pen.

I remember being fascinated by the chicken pen, which was quite big and had special compartments for the hens to lay their eggs at the back, so one could slide open the little doors in the morning and get the warm eggs for breakfast. I would spend hours watching the chickens and the turkey, fascinated by the suddenness of their movements, as if they had been hit by a powerful kinetic force, their way of walking like marching soldiers, and how improbably they could balance their huge bodies on their disproportionately small legs and feet. I was four or five years old at the time.

The house itself was big, with high ceilings, a bit dark, with no hot water and my dad was always trying to improve things by acquiring the latest invention to heat the house and bath-water cheaply. The heating devices were dad's own inventions – different designs of paraffin-burning appliances which he built in the metal factory. For the shower, there was a more revolutionary alcohol-burning device that would go up in flames more often than not, leaving the water perfectly cold in the middle of a shower. 'People should learn how to use it properly,' he protested.

Cooking, heating and hot water was supposed to be provided by an inefficient wood-burning stove in the kitchen. When dad decided that enough was enough he bought a huge electric cooker and boiler, banishing the wood-burning stove to the garden. Grandma then invited me to give it a good clean and asked me to chop some wood. 'Only bad taste and unhealthy food can be had from such a huge box of white metal, my boy.' And she was right. So whenever she could, and with the help of one of the children, she cooked outside on the old stove and bread, roast beef, chicken, corn or tortillas continued to have the lovely taste of eucalyptus firewood.

Little by little, as I grew up, the grannies taught me the whys and the wherefores of the adult world. They would also talk about the mythology of the mountainous country where they came from and the stories of the

Me dressed as a pirate in *Pirates of the Caribbean*, the school play, aged five.

elders. By touching, cuddling, embracing and caressing they taught the language of love and care. By the way they cooked and treated food they taught respect for nature and the earth; to accept the beauty, fragility and anger of the elements.

In contrast, my father was an angry man and, for that reason, not a good father or husband. People used to say our family was so big because dad loved children. I felt confused when I heard this because I only knew love from my grannies and Aunt Raquel. Dad wasn't a remotely loving father; in fact we were frightened of him most of the time. He dominated my mother. They were both non-believers and when they got married at a civil ceremony my father persuaded my mother not to use her maiden name, against custom, because it was a 'foreign', French, surname – Eyraud. So my mother became Mrs Gonzalez-Gonzalez, her mother's surname twice. He also forbade her to visit her mother and half-sister.

Due to the fact that I was physically weak and, at one time or another, developed this or that condition, our visits to the doctor or the hospital were quite frequent. Afterwards, there was always a cake and a soft drink for me. I remember the cake and the drink, bought at a kiosk inside the hospital gardens, because the mixture of the vanilla-flavoured cake and the cherry-flavoured drink melting in my mouth was delicious. It is something I have tried, in vain, to find and replicate ever since.

I do not know for certain if all of these visits to the doctor were necessary or not, but it was certainly an excuse for my mother to get away from the house, to visit her mother or go to the cinema. I do remember, though, being blind for few months, suffering from heart murmurs another time, having my tonsils and appendix out and undergoing two operations to a splintered elbow. On one of those hospital visits my mother took me to the park where the Arts Faculty is situated. We were wandering around and there were people coming and going up and down the steps of the grand entrance to the university. Suddenly a man in his fifties appeared, walking down the steps; at that moment my mother said to me: 'Look at that man, he is my father.' From where we were, he looked like an ordinary middle-aged man, bold, slender and agile. At the time I did not think much of the situation but, looking back, my mother seemed sad, like a little girl wanting to make contact with her father but afraid at the same time, eager though for me, her own child, to recognise him.

When I was eleven, my father fell out with his cousins and finished working with them. He decided to become self-employed and sold the house we were living in to move to another one he had bought some years before, which he had been renting out. This house was in a middle-class neighbourhood in the west of Santiago, at the foot of the Andes in the Macul district. The house was, and still is, a beautiful bungalow with a big garden and lots of trees. I loved the area and still do; it gives me a sense of stability, with the Andes within walking distance.

My dad tried various small businesses that failed. His savings and the proceeds from the sale of our previous house ran out. In the end, almost in desperation, he bought an old pick-up truck and started buying and selling vegetables in the market. Without the knowledge and experience of the business, things did not go as planned and he continued to lose money.

I remember the day, after a row over money with my mother, that he told my younger brother, Eduardo, and me that he could no longer support us and could not afford to pay for our schooling. If we wanted to continue with our studies we would have to work and pay for it ourselves. We were supposed to work with him in the fruit and vegetable business. I was thirteen and my brother was twelve. We decided to work in the morning before school, buying at the wholesale market from five thirty onwards and starting school at eight thirty. Very often we were late, the school gates were shut, and we had to try our luck gaining entry through one of the gaps pupils used to escape from school. I would often fall asleep in class. After school we took turns in going back to the market and helping my father there.

Things went from bad to worse. It seemed that in a matter of a few months we went from a family that was financially comfortable to one living in complete misery. Soon there was not enough to pay the electricity and gas bills. Food, apart from fruit and vegetables of course, became scarce, as did shoes and clothing. We had to resort to using candles at night and kerosene for cooking and heating. The old truck kept breaking down and, with no money for repairs, I was unofficially appointed the truck's mechanic and maintenance man. My father not only had no idea of how a motor vehicle worked, he also could not drive. He acquired his driving licence through a friend in the licence department. Thus I was also the co-pilot, in charge of the gear stick while father drove, since he was unable to coordinate all the operations at the same time. This state of affairs resulted in three road accidents, in one of which the vehicle turned over on its side. We ended up with minor injuries, shocked and with the entire cargo of fresh, free-range eggs plastered all over ourselves, the truck and the road. I felt completely humiliated, defeated and desolate; I assume that my brother and father felt the same way.

One day the twenty-five-year-old truck's gear box broke and my father ordered me to repair it. I borrowed tools from a neighbour and began to dismantle the transmission system and the gear box, marking with a piece of string and paper every single nut and bolt. I had never seen the inside of a gearbox before so, after taking the transmission shaft off,

I lifted the back wheels and, with the gear box open, I ran the engine. Using my fingers I moved the pinions backwards and forwards and discovered first, second and third gears, forward and reverse. It was the second gear that was the problem because it was worn out. I introduced a thin ring of metal to tighten the second gear pinion and hold it in place when engaged. It worked and after a week or so all the children in the neighbourhood came out one afternoon to help the 'mechanic' push-start the truck down the road and then have a noisy and jubilant ride in celebration. But not even the encouragement and joy of the neighbourhood children could lift the deep sadness that had engulfed my family and me. My father never thanked me for my hard work and ingenuity.

Childhood and teenage years ended abruptly for my siblings and me. No more hockey, no teenage parties, no holidays and, most disastrous of all, no more school for my brother and me. After a while, though, we managed to enrol at an evening school that finished at eleven at night.

One day my father decided to rent a small grocery shop in a rich neighbourhood, selling quality produce at competitive prices. The rich neighbours were not interested, however. They bought in bulk from big suppliers and only sent their servants to our shop for things they had forgotten or for emergency supplies. The small grocery shop was yet another failure, so my two younger brothers and I had to work harder. It was not long before food started to become scarce even at home, something that had to be hidden from the neighbours in spite of the fact that they probably already knew; we had had no new clothes for three years and had outgrown our old ones many times. My father had started to drink heavily by now.

The lack of proper food, the winter rains and the cold, together with long working hours, opened the way for illness to take hold on our young, developing bodies. As always, it was me who got the illness first, passing it on to my brother, sisters, mother and father. First I contracted mumps, then a succession of bad colds and bronchitis. Grandmother Elena died, in great pain, in one of those years.

★  ★  ★

It was New Year's Eve; father had to go to the city on business. He left precise instructions for me not to close the shop and leave before he returned. My younger brother was allowed to go home before me. We knew very well that when father said he was coming back to collect us after one of his business meetings that he would be back after midnight and completely drunk. This time, though, he took the pick-up; he would not drink much if he had to drive.

I was left on my own in charge of the shop. Every now and then a customer would walk in to buy something they had forgotten. It was a hot, summery night; the shop looked attractive, well lit and clean, with the goods neatly displayed on the shelves. It was getting late, nearing midnight, and there was no sign of my father. I started to feel miserable, thinking about other families gathering for their 'last supper' of the year. After their meal there would be fireworks and drinks. At midnight people would embrace and wish each other a 'Happy New Year' and become emotional, forgiving each other all the grievances of the departing year. Then the neighbours would arrive, with embraces, good wishes and toasts going on into the night.

It was a wonderful time for us, even more important than Christmas because the embracing, kissing, forgiving and good wishes were even more meaningful than Christmas presents. There was also a sense of family and community togetherness, and children were allowed to stay up all night if they wanted to. They would have had a long 'siesta' the previous afternoon so they could stay up after midnight. If somebody was asleep, or absent for another reason, there was a sense that that person, whether adult or child, would not be able to make it in the coming new year.

It was an exciting time for children too. The New Year embrace was something special. It would have been a grave offence to refuse a greeting and embrace, even from a person you did not like or you were on unfriendly terms with. It was a time of forgiveness, peace and recon-ciliation. So, for boys and girls, this was an opportunity to embrace and kiss any pretty girl or boy regardless of whether you were liked or not. It was a wonderful experience to realise that the girls would respond to your embrace and kiss with the same eagerness, feeling their lovely perfumed cheeks and their pert young breasts pressed against one's chest. All the girls in the neighbourhood and beyond! The best time was obviously New Year's Eve because, although the embracing went on for nearly two weeks afterwards, enthusiasm and eagerness started to wane, making it more of an embarrassing experience.

As it neared midnight, customers stopped coming to the shop and the streets became more and more deserted. I had a small radio for company, although the festive mood of the broadcasters made me feel more lonesome and miserable. People were already settled in their homes waiting for midnight. I longed for the old days, when our house would be full of people: Uncle Rene and his family, friends of mum and dad and their children, neighbours, plenty of delicious food, an assortment of drinks and fireworks, and a fun, festive mood. Everything would be beautifully arranged and there would be happiness in the year to come. Instead, the atmosphere at home now would be sombre, the same as last year and the year before. There would be no friends or relatives, little food, no drinks, and no desire to be up waiting for the New Year. The neighbours had already noticed that our family was out of sorts and would not visit us. Only their children, unprejudiced and compassionate, would come to greet us for a brief moment.

It was forty-five minutes before midnight according to the shop's small radio when a vision appeared at the shop's entrance. There, framed by the door, stood the most beautiful girl in the world, dressed like a princess. I had seen her before, of course, several times a week; she would pass the shop on her way to school while I was unloading the pick-up in the morning. She was in her navy blue, Santiago College for Girls' uniform. Sometimes she would come into the shop for an ice cream and be very polite, just like the other girls were from this part of Santiago where most of the country's wealth was concentrated. I knew, through their maids, two or three things about these girls' families. The maids were instructed not to reveal their masters' family affairs, but hers had already told me that she was an only child, her name was Antonia, she was fourteen and her father often travelled abroad. Every time I saw her my heart would leap and my head spin, believing that a smile from her would cure my pain and my misery.

'Hello,' she said walking towards the counter very slowly.

'Hello Antonia, what are you doing here? Why aren't you at home with your family?'

'It's just adults . . . and I wanted to see you. When we drove past earlier on, I saw you and I guessed you would still be here.' She was so confident, so in command of herself, unlike any ordinary girl, or myself for that matter; but she wasn't an ordinary girl, was she?

'You know, I like you,' she said standing in the middle of the shop, looking at the shelves with her hands held at her back. My heart wanted to play tricks by thumping very fast and embarrassing me, but I decided to pay it no attention.

'I like you too,' I said in disbelief.

She started to talk while pacing around the shop. 'I always look forward to seeing you in the mornings when I walk past on the way to school, and I love the times when I come in with the other girls after school to get an ice cream and you serve us. I am a bit sad when you are not here. I also think about why you have to work so hard when most of us just go to school. Would you like to be my friend?'

'Of course I would,' I said. I told her that father had decided to sell the shop and that I would not be working there for long.

'That is a pity,' she said. 'Anyway, I think we are going away for the summer holidays, so I won't see you anyway.'

Antonia became visibly sad, her eyes moving rapidly around the shop between glances at me.

'Your family may be starting to miss you by now; soon they will be looking for you in the neighbourhood.'

'I don't think so; they do not care much about me. But, you are right, I had better go.' She looked very sad now, and then she asked me straight: 'Do you have a girlfriend?'

'No,' I replied, which was the truth. I had always wanted a girlfriend, or just a friend, but I thought nobody would be interested in me.

Suddenly, I found myself saying: 'Do you like that big box of biscuits on the top shelf?' I pointed to a big, coloured metal box.

'It looks pretty,' she said.

'I want you to have it,' I told her.

'No,' she replied, 'you are going to get in trouble.'

'As a present from me; don't you worry, I won't get in trouble. We will leave while you are on holiday and we will probably never see each other again; you can keep the box and remember me sometimes.'

'It would be better if I could see you; you are a nice person,' she said. I climbed on the step ladder to reach the metal biscuit box and gave it to her. She took it, smiled at me, then hurried to kiss me and leave the shop quickly. She turned around and waved.

I could not believe what had just happened. It was as though I had been dreaming, which wasn't an uncommon experience for me. My brother would not believe me when I told him what had happened; he would surely think that I had been fantasising. I did not know what to do with this feeling, I knew I had to do something or my chest would burst; I could hardly bear the pressure.

Suddenly I became conscious of the radio. There was shouting and loud music. Midnight had just passed; we were in a New Year. I wanted to run after Antonia and give her a big hug; that would ease my chest. She won't be there, I told myself. She is gone, forever, most surely. Go and look, maybe she felt the same and is coming back! I ran outside. The street was deserted, not a soul around. Misery struck me then. This was my first New Year's Eve on my own, and I had to be the only person on their own in the universe tonight. I burst into tears and cried for a long time. It is not fair, I thought.

'This is not fair!' I shouted.

My father arrived at about one in the morning; he had been drinking. No one had come into the shop since Antonia. I never saw her again, but her vision lived on in me for years, giving me company and comfort, helping me to overcome the hardest of times. I hoped at the time that I did the same for her, being good company in bad times. Most probably she remained unaware of the effect her innocent act had on the heart of a miserable boy.

★　★　★

Father decided to sell the small shop because it made no money and we had to work in the big fruit and vegetable wholesale market, which at the time was a cruel place for adults to work in, never mind for a fifteen-year-old. I learnt many things about the miseries of life and people's battle against hunger in that cursed place. The bonds between my younger brother and me were forged trying to adapt and survive in a place where, one day, we almost ended up in a knife fight over a piece of chorizo and bread.

One day, while my brother and I were sitting on a kerb eating our bread and hot chorizo, a loner, nicknamed 'Satan', due to his devil-like face, came to us and asked for some of our food. 'I haven't been able to work today,' he said. Without hesitation I gave him my half, not because I felt threatened by him, but because I saw frankness in his face and detected a plea in his voice. He had also said 'please'. He thanked me and sat down to eat in silence, every now and then glancing at us. I felt a sort of friendship was sealed between the three of us.

Satan was feared among the outcasts that worked loading, unloading and stealing goods in that place and by the vagrants we shared the kerb with at eating times. It was said that he was the quickest with a knife. Satan became our protector. He threatened a man who made me drop two tomato boxes I was carrying by grabbing my backside; if he did it again he would face Satan's knife. He would also steal from the merchants for us and so we would sell sacks full of lemons, oranges, green beans, peaches or whatever was available and in season. We would look for him in one of the wholesaler's stands where he was working at the busiest time, around six in the morning. In the confusion he would half fill my sack with produce, then serve somebody else, then come back to me and shout: 'What are you buying? If you are not buying move on please, we don't need onlookers here, come on!' I would leave the place without paying, with half a sackful of whatever; about ten kilos in weight. A few minutes later, my brother and I would go back to 'buy' something else. This method of thievery was never planned or talked about between Satan and me, and my brother never understood what was going on or how the system worked. On the contrary, he never moved fast enough and I always asked him to wait for me outside. You had to be able to read Satan's eyes, the gestures of his face and his body language, sometimes to read his mind too, as he was not a man of many words. Actually, he would grunt rather than talk. He would decide when the moment was right, when the controller was not looking, the precise time of utmost confusion and shouting: 'c'mon, make your mind up, they're the best and cheapest in the market. How many? You! Pay over there! Take this man's money! Please, move, move on!' That was all. Done. Sack full.

Later, at about midday, if you could find time for rest and refreshment, away from the eyes of the merchants, guards and police, among the outcasts, labourers and thieves, sitting on kerbs in the sun, Satan knew we would be waiting for him with hot chorizo and bread or fried fish with chilli sauce wrapped in newspaper. One day, my brother wondered: 'Have you noticed Satan has no friends? That we are the only ones sitting and sharing with him? Don't you think it looks bad that we are liked by him?'

'Look,' I said, 'I don't think that God, if he exists, has helped us in any way, and that could be one of the reasons we have ended up in this hellish place fighting to survive in the first place. Isn't it then a good thing that we get a little help from Satan? It seems that Satan is more caring than

God. And, after all, if you haven't noticed, he is the boss in this place and as long as he is on our side, we are safe.'

Looking back, the whole situation was quite ironic. Abandoned by God, as it were, my brother and I had allied ourselves with the Devil in order to survive. I do not know why that man, who, by all accounts, was a thief, an outcast, living at the very margins of society, working in a place where carrying a knife was a necessity, took pity on me and my brother. Or why he decided to ally himself with two kids. Maybe the advantages were obvious.

In this huge wholesale fruit and vegetable market, where there were auctions before sunrise and tons of produce would change hands, sometimes many times in a matter of hours, there was not a day when at least one big fight, usually involving knives, took place. This was on top of street robberies, fist fights among men and women (also carrying knives) and muggings. It was a tough environment to be in, but one in which, once you had learned the rules and learned to swim in that sea where hunger mingled with an abundance of food from the earth, where failure and misery walked side by side with success and happiness, you could survive, as long as you kept yourself healthy. There were plenty of examples where the slightest disability would signify a certain premature death. Illness and disability were incompatible with life in that place.

I learnt quickly: to select the still-edible fruit or vegetables from the vast waste piles left for collection by the municipal workers in the afternoon; to choose the most nutritious ones in every season; to find the cheapest places to eat, from people cooking on a brazier on the floor to the ones frying on an oil drum on wheels, to the stalls with seats and tables.

Having failed as a merchant, my father decided to try and make a living by doing deliveries in the old truck and took me along. Most of the time I spent the long hours of the night in the freezing windowless truck waiting for my father to return. It did not take long for the truck to break down and I ended up working as a labourer in one of the factories we made deliveries for. I found that it was pretty hard work, especially for my young, weak body. At the end of my first week I was paid less than the other workers because, I was told, 'You are under age and we cannot pay you the same.' This infuriated me and I protested, but the owner warned me to take it or leave it. It was the time of the war of independence in Algeria; the French were withdrawing and burning everything in the process. The owner of the factory was very happy about this fact, telling the workers that the French were doing the right thing for if they found a deserted and barren land and transformed it into an agricultural paradise, then it was right to return a desert back to the ungrateful Algerians.

On the long bus journey back home from the metal factory, where I had to turn an enormous and heavy wheel all day, I felt envious of the boys and girls in uniforms who filled the bus at that time. I longed to be like them, normal school teenagers, with normal mums and dads. Some boys and girls were holding hands, a sight that would make me feel the loneliest boy ever. I would get home, wash myself, eat a fried egg and a piece of bread and leave for evening school, finishing at eleven, home at about midnight, up again at six.

I was desperate for friendship, to feel liked and to love a girl, to make life easier. Since I did not know how to approach a girl, I followed what I had seen other boys doing. If it worked for them, I thought, it will work for me. One evening, on the bus back from work I decided to ask a girl who was getting off the bus if I could walk her home. The bus was full and there were many pretty girls on it. I chose one girl with long dark hair and fine features. She was on her own. The bus was becoming emptier and the girl seemed unconcerned that we were nearing the end of the route. I started to panic, since I had no money to pay for an extra bus fare back home and we had already passed my stop. About two stops from the end of the route, the girl stood up from her seat and went to the back door, and I followed. When we got off the bus, she started to walk fairly quickly and I had to follow her almost at a trot. I found her even more beautiful now, walking in front of me with her bag on her shoulder and her long hair blowing in the evening breeze. I have to act quickly, I thought, before it is too late and she reaches her destination. I hurried my pace and when we were shoulder to shoulder I asked her, timidly and with my best smile, 'Would you like me to walk you home?' Without stopping or looking at me she said: 'Leave me alone!' I was shocked and stood there on the spot feeling rejected and hurt. It had not worked and I wanted to cry. I was miles away from home in a completely strange neighbourhood and I had to find my way home on foot.

It was a two hour walk to get home and I had plenty of time to think. I had failed and I should not have done it. I now thought it to be an odd thing to do; not only embarrassing but somehow unfair on the girl too.

I had offended her and she had reacted accordingly. Why did I think she was going to say yes anyway? I felt awful and decided that I would never approach a girl that way again. Another thought: what would I have done if she had said yes? I did not know but it would have been nice to have had the opportunity. She may have noticed that I was not well dressed. I do not know.

# Love and politics

3

When I was seventeen a neighbour whose husband worked at the Via Sur coach company approached me, gave me their address and advised me to go there early one morning and ask for her husband. She was sure he would see me, direct me to the right people, and I might get a job. This I did and was given a job in an office in the centre of the city, helping to coordinate passenger transport and parcel deliveries. The only problem, I was told, was that I needed my father's consent because I was still a minor as far as the law was concerned. At that time in Chile one was recognised as an adult at the age of twenty-one. My father, seeing that if I no longer worked with him I could become independent, refused to give me his consent. I explained this at work and they told me they would make an exception for the time being.

At work I met Oscar Haute. He was twenty-eight years old, eleven years older than me and a rebel, always complaining about work, pay and exploitation. We would work from six in the morning to four in the afternoon or from one to nine or ten in the evening, longer if a coach broke down and it was late. It was hard work, standing and loading or unloading all the time. Although the payment was the minimum for a white-collar employee, when I received my first salary at the end of the month I could not believe it. I had never had so much money before. Soon afterwards I noticed that the other workers, about ten others in their late twenties or early thirties, married and with children, were not very happy that a seventeen-year-old kid was earning the same wages as they were. In fact my father was by then in a deep depression, in bed most of the time, unable to get up and look for a job, and there were my six brothers and sisters and my mother to feed.

Although I was happy to continue with things as they were, after a few months Oscar persuaded me that I needed to spend some of my wages in purchasing decent white-collar worker's clothing. He had already heard comments about my scruffy appearance. I had had my navy blue jacket since I was nine. My mother had altered my trousers from some old ones of my father's many years before. I only had two decent shirts which had to be washed the night before I went to work.

I became very close friends with Oscar. He took pity on me, whether on my naivety or innocence or my sadness or silent perseverance, I do not really know. Soon I met his wife and three children, and we were discussing politics, religion, art, theatre, music and poetry. He was a very knowledgeable man, the only son of a Chilean woman and a Frenchman. At the time he was an alcoholic.

Oscar was one of those people who do not fit in with their own generation but are able to see what is coming, what is brewing in the heart of the young, especially students. He could not believe that a seventeen-year-old like me could have such a keen perception of the world or as he put it, 'an innate revolutionary consciousness'. I did not tell him then that my 'innate revolutionary consciousness' had been acquired, not in the fashionable university education of the time, but during five or so years of struggle, practically on the streets, silently fighting hunger shoulder to shoulder with my younger brother and my father.

I had no perception of my 'innate revolutionary consciousness' in those days. All I knew was that my mother, brothers and sisters desperately needed my earnings. I could not bear the sight of my younger brothers Fernando and Arturo and my sister Irene, then nine, eleven and thirteen, with their eyes sinking in their faces, cold, hungry and without understanding what was happening. Why, and so suddenly, was there no light, warmth or food in the house? I calculated my wages in the kilos of bread and packets of butter that it was possible to purchase every month. Every time I glanced in a shop window and saw some new clothes I would like for myself the same equation prevented me from wasting precious bread and butter. The real trouble for me started when the equation appeared, even when I needed to buy lunch for myself.

I asked Oscar to come with me to a department store to buy, on credit, a suit, a shirt and a pair of shoes for myself. It was approaching Christmas, the busiest time of year for our company. Apart from the postal service, which was very inefficient, this was the company most people used for the transportation of letters and parcels. It was faster and more reliable than the national postal service, although more expensive. We were working overtime, often from six thirty in the morning until ten in the evening and the management had promised to pay us overtime and a bonus as reward for our efforts.

When our wages arrived, just before Christmas, the overtime had not been paid and there was no bonus. About fifteen of us complained to our manager, who told us that he would make sure we received the money. Payment did not arrive. Two days before Christmas we decided to go on strike. There was no response from the management. One night after work a group of employees had arranged to meet at a restaurant to discuss our strike action. On the way to the restaurant I began to suffer unbearable back pain, to the point that I was almost unable to walk. Oscar and another two of my colleagues decided to take me to casualty.

After examining me the doctor informed my colleagues that he suspected tuberculosis; he injected a powerful painkiller, probably containing morphine. He advised me to see a specialist and said X-rays of my lungs would be needed. There was nothing he could do at that time of the night and the treatment was likely to be expensive.

The painkiller had made me feel a lot better, if a bit dozy, and so I insisted on going to the restaurant meeting, especially since I was very hungry. At the restaurant the waitress said that she would not serve me since I was clearly drunk. I had to show her the doctor's certificate before I could convince her that my state was not alcohol related. With a lot of effort I put across my point of view and position on the strike action. Soon afterwards, Oscar went outside and called a taxi for me. 'You need to go home and have a rest,' he said, handing me a small collection he had made to help me with the taxi fare; it was past midnight.

When I got home it was difficult for me to get into the house without making too much noise since I could not avoid stumbling, the effects of the drug still being very strong. It was dark and I did not want to wake everybody up by putting on the lights, but my mother woke up and came to the door as I was still struggling through the corridor. When she saw the state I was in, she told me that I should be ashamed of myself, wasting precious money on alcohol and who knows what else. I tried to explain to her about the meeting and that I was planning a strike, but she would not listen. 'Just like your father, wasting your wages in getting drunk.' I could not speak, my mouth was so dry and I felt so sad, sad that my mother could so easily mistrust me, that she should assume that I had been drinking too much when I had been in such excruciating pain, fighting for a little bit more money for Christmas, money I had worked so hard to earn but that the company wanted to keep.

I did not want to tell her about the doctor's diagnosis; that would alarm her, I thought. I did not want anyone at home to know; they would reject me and isolate me. Tuberculosis had such a stigma in those days and it was thought to be highly contagious. Hadn't Uncle Luis died of tuberculosis? Didn't I suffer from tuberculosis when I was four? I could not speak and showed my mother the certificate, which only stated that I had been injected with morphine derivate for severe back pain. Without much conviction, she led me to the room I shared with my brothers who were fast asleep.

I do not remember how I managed to go back to work the next day, the day we closed down the shutters. Our manager read to us his letter of resignation in protest at the appalling behaviour of the company towards its employees.

'I am not a slave driver,' he said. 'I asked the employees to work hard, promising them that they would be justly rewarded. I now feel ashamed and dishonoured in front of my employees. I have no alternative in the circumstances but to resign.'

It was, by all accounts, an honourable act. We could not persuade this young, handsome man from a high social class not to resign. His name was Henrique Huerta y Corbalan. Nine years later this man would give his life, alongside President Allende, defending the presidential palace from the assault of the Chilean armed forces on 11 September 1973.

Later that day, we closed the shutters to the public and refused to load the coaches. My back pain had come back by then, so I was persuaded by my colleagues that I was exempt from picketing duties and went home to rest. Panic started to set in: if I had tuberculosis, it would be necessary for me to take precautions so as not to infect members of my family. For this I would have to isolate, without the others noticing, cups, dishes and cutlery that could only be used by me. I would also quarantine the second toilet for my exclusive use. But first of all I had to get a prescription for antibiotics. This would not be easy, as I would have to pay for a doctor's consultation as well as the prescription.

A young doctor and his family had recently moved across the road from us. He had examined my younger brother when he had rheumatic fever and his charges were not that expensive. I went to see him. I was relieved when he told me that he was pretty sure my condition was a severe pleurisy, mainly affecting the right lung, and not tuberculosis. 'This is not less serious,' he said. 'You could also die of pleurisy if it is not treated promptly.' To be absolutely certain of my condition, a series of examinations, including X-rays was necessary. 'You will have to go to hospital. Have you any medical insurance? In the meantime I'll give you a prescription.' The antibiotic he prescribed was chloramphenicol, banned ten years later for its damaging effect on the central nervous system. The prescription advised two capsules every eight hours. To accelerate recovery, I doubled the prescription and decided on two capsules every four hours and forgot about the hospital and the X-rays.

My first act of public rebellion ended in triumph: we were paid the overtime and bonus before New Year's Eve. Although I was happy and had prescribed myself a double dose of medicine, I was far from feeling better and developed a nasty cough. That New Year's Eve was a sad one. I had to work late, but I managed to get home before midnight with a big roast chicken. My mother and my sisters had made salads, and there was a bottle of wine. My father, who was often in bed with depression, was up and in a good mood.

My younger brother Eduardo was slowly recovering from the devastating effects of rheumatic fever, which had nearly killed him. A few months earlier, lying on a dirty bed in a hospital for the poor, I had seen him lifeless, dying, his heart pumping at twenty or less beats per minute. The nurse had told me that they expected him to die any moment. He was sixteen and I felt an incredible anger and frustration at the unfairness of the situation. I knew that it was a question of money. If I had had the money I would have been able to take my brother to a good hospital, give him the best treatment and save his life. I remembered the hard times we had shared, how I had looked after him. Maybe I should have protected him better from the cold, I thought. I could have got a thick coat for him.

Absorbed in my thoughts, just outside the room, with tears running down my cheeks, I had not noticed the nurse calling me back. Eduardo's heart rate had gone to one hundred and twenty per minute and he was bleeding heavily from his nose and ears. His heart was out of control and his temperature had risen to fatal levels.

'There is no point keeping him here,' the nurse had said, 'he will die regardless; you had better take him home.'

'But at least you can give him oxygen here.'

'It will make no difference.'

That night, in the back garden of our house, eyes fixed on the stars, I cried out to my dead grandmother and great Aunt Dominga. I told them I was desperate but that I knew they could do it. They had cured me and they could cure him now. I told them that life would be so empty, so terrible, without my brother; told them that he did not deserve to die, that he was so good, so innocent, so young.

I asked them to caress him with their sacred hands and to hum the way they used to when I was ill; to give his body the power to fight back, to win this time, to live and carry on being my companion in the harder times to come. I promised them I would look after him. I would buy him the best coat to protect him from the winter cold.

He did not die. We went for long walks in the Andes and trips to the desert over the years. He became a sculptor first, then a restorer and archaeologist. He is now a university lecturer.

Shortly after New Year I began to find it very difficult to keep my eyes focused and started to lose the ability to do so. Next, my speech slowed and I had a strong desire to lie down and sleep, although I would be unable to do so during the night. Of course I did not associate any of this with an overdose. I thought I was just tired from working ten hours during the day and then going to college in the evening.

Not sleeping and talking all night worried my elder sister who contacted a childhood friend of ours who was a nurse in a military clinic. Her father had been a Welsh immigrant who worked for the army. Glenda English, for that was her improbable name, persuaded me to see a doctor at her clinic. The doctor, who was a psychiatrist, began by asking me why I had tried to commit suicide by taking an overdose of antibiotics. I explained to him what had happened, about the pleurisy, my panic and all the rest. He found the whole thing very strange, but referred me to a hospital for tests and X-rays.

I thought that the hospital was beautiful and welcoming, although I did not know how I was going to pay for their services. After a while the doctor called me in to give me the result of the X-rays and tests.

'Good news and bad news,' he announced. 'Due to your intensive antibiotic treatment, the infection and the inflammation are almost gone.

We still have to extract some fluid from the right lung though. The bad news is that there is a big scar of membrane surrounding the right lung. Now, this is the same membrane enveloping the heart; during the healing process the membrane has stretched itself to the right, bringing the heart with it in the process. The result is that your heart has shifted to the right in your chest and is under lot of pressure. It is what we call a 'retractile' process. This explains the noise when you breathe and the pain. More tests and X-rays are needed to accurately assess the effects of this process. Book an appointment with the nurse.'

The nurse indicated that in order to book more appointments, I had to pay for the X-rays already taken and the doctor's consultation. The total amount was the equivalent of one month's wages, which I could certainly not afford. Fortunately for me the payment counter was in front of the hospital's exit. I left the hospital without paying, never to return. What happened to my lungs and heart is anybody's guess. What is certain is that it did not affect my politics: my heart remained firmly on the left. Time healed my lungs.

★   ★   ★

When I was six the family had moved to a new house in a development on the south-west of the city. To the south of our house, two or three blocks away, there was open countryside. There was a river nearby where we would go with my grandmother, often to collect medicinal herbs. There was fennel, good for the heart, and silver herb, good for the stomach. There were also different kinds of mint and many other plants whose names I do not remember.

To the west, beyond the river and about fifteen minutes walk away, was the southbound railway line. Since the country is so long and thin, the railway lines in Chile run north–south, apart from the line to the port of Valparaiso. As children we used to go and play on the lines, placing nails and other small metal objects on the rails to collect them after the wheels of the train had run over them, leaving them flat, shiny and hot. Like most children, trains were an incredible source of fantasy for us. This was the mysteriousness of the far south, where the world ended, near Antarctica. Looking at the northbound trains, nearing their last station in central Santiago, they seemed covered in a cold and icy cloud that we thought had accompanied them from the South Pole. In later years

I learned that the trains never went further than the mainland, over 1,500 kilometres to the south of the capital, to Puerto Mont. After that, there are hundreds of small islands.

My older sister and I went to a private school that was far from our house, so we used the school bus. On the bus I noticed a girl of my own age who lived nearby. She was very pretty and I was fascinated by her, mostly because of the way her father treated her: carrying her in his arms, kissing and hugging her, laughing, as if she was the only love of his life. Well, she was an only child and I was envious of her being the sole object of her parents' attention.

Soon she came to our house to play. I must have been obsessed because my mother and my aunt started to make comments about this girl being 'my girlfriend'. I felt embarrassed and hurt. Although I did not know the meaning of 'girlfriend', I wanted her to be my friend. We became quite fond of each other and I loved her.

When we were nine, her father, who was an army officer, was posted to the south and the family moved. I was heartbroken; I watched from our gate as the removal van drove off and they left, I thought, forever. I cried and cried; she didn't even turn around to wave goodbye. Later I would wonder about this part of my life: falling in love with a girl so young and feeling heartbroken for the loss of her, all at nine years of age.

Later, when I was eighteen, working at the transport company and attending college in the evening, my sister told me that she had met Delfina – that was the girl's name – while shopping in the city centre. They had talked and Delfina was very interested in seeing me again. I had seen her once, briefly, after we had moved to our new house, when I had caught sight of her riding her bike. Unknown to me, her family had moved back to Santiago, and by coincidence was living nearby. It was a painful experience for me because I was a small boy for thirteen and she seemed to me to be grown up. She was taller, with developed breasts, and was, disgustingly as I thought, interested in older boys. Accompanying my sister to her birthday party – since I was not invited – resulted in the most unbearable embarrassment for me. There she was, the most beautiful girl around, dancing with boys that were probably sixteen or seventeen. I remained seated in the same chair the whole time, unable to move or talk to anyone. She laughed at me with the other boys for not knowing how to dance. At the end of the evening, she sat at her piano and played a piece of a piano sonata; everybody clapped. She was the star, the princess, the queen, and not the slightest bit interested in me.

It was different now: we were eighteen. I pretended not to be interested when my sister told me of her eagerness to meet me.

'I invited her on Saturday. Will you be around?'

'I don't know; I may have a meeting after work,' I said.

Of course, on Saturday I was very excited, thinking non-stop. Will she be taller? Will she like me? Does she have a boyfriend? We are poor now and the house does not look nice, will she still like our family?

After work I went straight home and arrived at about two in the afternoon. It was a sunny day. She was sitting on the sofa facing the big window, a stunningly beautiful woman. She smiled and stood up; I immediately noticed that I had grown taller than her. At least that would make me less insignificant, I thought. She came towards me; we kissed on the cheeks and I could smell the sweetness of her and felt her breasts against my chest. She looked very elegant too, in a dark top and a short, dark, skirt.

While we talked people came in and out of the living room and exchanged conversation with 'Delfi', as everybody called her now. She was supposed to be my sister's friend. These interruptions were quite useful in fact, since it allowed us a glance at each other without embarrassment and to study each other, to try to read each other's minds.

'Hasn't she changed? Doesn't she look gorgeous?' they would comment, looking at me. I had no choice but to agree; I was stunned.

Nevertheless, I kept my distance. She is so beautiful, she must have a boyfriend, I thought. She won't be interested in me; they live in the city centre, in an expensive area. Her father, being a colonel now, must have introduced his daughter to the young cadets of the military academy. With their beautiful, Prussian-style uniforms, and their short swords hanging at their sides, they are irresistible to every teenage girl. There is no question about it; she will eventually marry a cadet.

Nevertheless, summer was approaching and Delfina started to visit us more often, spending a lot of time with my sister. I could not avoid finding her more and more attractive. One day Delfi announced that she had to attend the annual officer's party at the exclusive Officer's Club; my sister and I were invited. It was a formal occasion, a ball, with a band. Her parents were not attending, and as she was not allowed to go by herself, we had to go with her. When my sister told me, my heart sank.

'I am not going,' I declared.

'But, why not?' my sister complained.

'It is not our world. It is for rich, well-dressed people. Besides, military officers are arrogant. How are we going to come back from there anyway? It is too far.'

Although the reasons I gave my sister were all true, the main problem was that I knew I could not compete with the hundreds of handsomely dressed and well-groomed cadets, all wanting to dance with Delfi. After some hard persuasion from Delfi herself I agreed to go with my sister and our cousin, Elena, a girl the same age as my sister.

I realised that I had no clothes for this sort of occasion, or for any other kind for that matter. One of the boys in the neighbourhood came to my rescue, with a beautiful brown sport's jacket and trousers. It was not a formal outfit, I thought, but it was nice. To my horror, on arriving at the ball, I noticed that I was the only one wearing a sport's outfit; all the other men were in cadets' uniforms or wearing formal dark suits. I felt terrible; I wanted to disappear, to be invisible. What was I doing there? This was not only humiliating, it was insulting. The banquet, all that food, the luxury, the arrogance.

Of course, Delfi was too busy to give us much attention. She knew quite a few of the cadets and the other girls present; she was popular and offers to dance came one after the other. My only relief was that my sister, who was very pretty and looked even more so in her lovely dress, received a lot of attention from the cadets too, making me feel a bit less marginal. Of course my sister could not be infatuated with any of these conceited cadets, I thought. I did not move from my chair, not even when Elena asked me to dance with her.

After a couple of hours and a few drinks, everybody was more relaxed. Delfi came to sit at our table for a while and a few cadets approached us, mainly to flirt with my sister and cousin. Eventually, Delfi sat next to me asking me if everything was all right. I just smiled at her without answering. She persisted, so I said that it was OK, but that it just wasn't my style. The music had started again and she asked me if I would like to dance with her. I stood up in disbelief. I felt completely exposed, as though we were the only couple dancing on the floor. I decided to ignore the fact that I felt as if I was dancing naked and concentrated on her beautiful face and on how much she had meant to me since I was a little boy.

'It is so nice to dance with you,' she said.

'You have danced plenty with the cadets,' I replied rather churlishly.

'Yes, I know, but it is different with you,' she responded

I could not believe it. 'She has had too much to drink,' I thought. We left the place after midnight. One of the cadets, wanting to chat my sister up, offered us a lift home. The nightmare was over.

A few weeks later, Delfi was at our house one Saturday when I arrived back home from the coach company. She was reading in the lounge and there was nobody in the house apart from my father. While I had something to eat, she explained that she was killing time, that she did not want to go back home yet because there was nobody there. When I finished eating I asked her if she wanted to go for a walk. It was a beautiful, calm, late spring afternoon; our street was deserted. It was one of those afternoons I loved so much, with a gentle breeze blowing in the acacia trees, bright sunshine on the flower-filled gardens and the pretty houses with their large porches.

We sat on a wall talking about friends, about our lives and about what we were doing. She had just got a place at university to study French. I spoke briefly about what I had done in the past four years. It seemed like decades. She told me she had no real friends and suddenly asked me if I wanted to be her close friend.

'What about the cadets?' I asked her.

'They mean nothing to me; my mum and dad like them, but I do not; I do not trust them.'

I nearly exploded with joy.

'Yes, of course I would like to be your close friend.'

'Is that true?' she asked.

'I promise,' I said. Still, I was not absolutely certain what it meant to be her close friend and was a bit disappointed she did not say boyfriend. But then she held my hand and after a while came closer to me and we kissed. She seemed so happy and we laughed and hugged. In the evening she asked me to accompany her home – it was one of the happiest moments of my life.

But although I had been waiting for this moment since I was six, it had arrived too late. I was already spending a lot of time with Oscar and other work colleagues at our regular study meetings, where we would read and discuss Marx, Engels' *The Origin of the Family, Private Property and the State*, Gramci, Russell, dialectics, materialism and almost anything that came across our path.

There was not much time for my girlfriend, who was very 'conventional'. She was more interested in going to the cinema, spending long hours with my sister and my family. Soon she gave up her university studies for secretarial ones and our relationship became more intense and physical.

Her parents became worried that their only daughter could become pregnant out of wedlock. A year after we started our relationship, her parents invited me to a meeting to 'discuss the future'. But our relationship was already on the rocks, and was full of contradictions. While my politics became more and more radical, it became more and more difficult for Delfi to understand my weekend absences and my desire for a socialist revolution in Chile. Poor Delfi, her face became sombre. She loved me, she said, and that was the most important thing in her life for her, and that I love her in return. The rest of the people came second.

Delfi's mother and father did not like me at all, the main reason for their dislike being that our family had fallen into financial catastrophe. I was a worker when I should have been a student. I was the only financial support for my big family, so what would be left for their daughter and an eventual baby? Did I not understand that I was 'less' than their dearest daughter? Was I not the cause of their daughter's rejection of wonderful and promising military cadets as suitors? Consequently, I was never invited into their house except on one occasion when Delfi had contracted typhus and, after long telephone negotiations, I was allowed a few minutes visit. Every time we went out I had to bring her back her by eleven o'clock. I then had a two hour journey back home.

Delfina was not present at our meeting, though she was in the house. 'We came to the conclusion that she really loves you and that you love her. We want the best for her, but you have to understand that she is our only child and we would not like to lose her. We also realise that your relationship is a serious one; it has been going on for a long time now. We think that you should get married and live here in a part of the house. We would not interfere in your affairs; we would only like her close to us.'

I felt insulted and was determined to speak my mind.

'I love your daughter dearly, have no doubt. But I believe we are too young for marriage. We are just beginning our lives. Besides, I still have financial responsibilities towards my family. We don't have much experience of relationships anyway; anything can still happen you know: she could meet somebody else, more to your liking.'

They were clearly taken aback. This was not what they were expecting. Their beautiful precious daughter surely deserved somebody better, a more mature, financially solvent man, a secure man, a military man. This young pauper! I could see them thinking. Any other man would be honoured to have been chosen by our daughter and be grateful for our offer. On the other hand, they were delighted. They were visibly embarrassed, not knowing how to continue with the meeting, feeling that they shouldn't have interfered in the first place. They did not know what to do with me, or what to do with their daughter, who was surely going to be hurt.

I realised that the meeting must have been discussed with Delfi beforehand. She must have told them of her feelings towards me and the direction she wished the relationship to take. But she had decided not to tell me, preferring her parents to do the job, as it were, of sealing the destiny of our relationship.

There was a sad goodbye from Delfi at the door. We did not talk about the meeting, but I felt confused. Here was a beautiful, ordinary young woman in pursuit of happiness in the most conventional and normal way, and there was nothing wrong with that. There was also the external pressure: my family just adored her, especially my sister, to whom I was very close. They thought that she was marvellous, that we were so well suited, it being quite obvious that we had loved each other since childhood; and so on. They could not imagine us apart. But my grandmothers' influence, the years of hunger, hard work, injustice and illness, added to my strong political beliefs and the influence of the Cuban revolution to seal my fate and that of my relationship with Delfi.

I would not have a conventional relationship, nor a conventional marriage, nor a conventional life. My relationships would be revolutionary ones, I had promised myself. I cannot bring my children into this unjust world without trying first to make it a better place to live in. I will not be like my parents, carelessly having seven children and then falling victims to the system. My children and my happiness will have to wait until, and if, I come back alive from the long and hard revolutionary struggle for justice. I definitely could not settle, and if that was Delfi's main objective, I would have to let her go. Painful as that might be.

The next time I met Delfi we went for tea and then had a long walk in the park. Summer was approaching, the weather was already warm and the park by the river looked marvellous. It was a sad occasion though, Delfi asking me why I had said what I had said to her parents. Had I stopped loving her? Weren't our wishes the same? And so on. No, they weren't. No, I have not stopped loving you. No, we did not talk about this before the meeting; we did not talk about our wishes and intentions. We do not have the same views towards the state of the country, poverty, injustice and the need for radical change.

'I want to have a baby,' she answered with gravitas in her voice and the conviction of an ancient desire. 'I do not mind if you do not stay with me, I want to have your baby, I will take care of it,' she said with tears in her eyes.

'I cannot, my love; it would still be my child and I would not be able to do what I have to do,' I answered with a degree of irritation. She did not understand, and she seemed selfish, thinking only about her own happiness. We were worlds apart and I felt sure that she would never change.

In the following months, two unrelated incidents would precipitate my decision to end my relationship with the girl who was the cause of my childhood heartbreak, my teenage suffering and longing, and then for a time my prospective companion for life. As my best friend and confidant, I decided to tell her what I thought about Che Guevara in Bolivia and the need for Latin American revolutionaries to join him in his struggle. I frightened her; she told my sister about my ideas and my sister panicked, having visions of me lying dead in the Bolivian jungle. My sister told our father, who threatened to denounce me and my friends to the police and Interpol. This in turn scared me, since a group of about five of us from work had already bought, on credit of course, 'basic equipment' consisting of no more than a rucksack and a pair of boots each, so that we could join Che in Bolivia. Of course, I cruelly used the incident to prove that Delfi was not a trustworthy person and that she had betrayed me in the most horrible way.

The other incident, occurring a month or so later, had, I was told, a chance in a million of happening. It was midday on a Saturday and I was in the office. Delfi and I usually met on Saturday afternoons and spent the rest of the weekend together, although this had become rather a rare event, since I often had meetings or training. It was about one o'clock when I decided to phone her at home. I picked up the receiver and asked the telephonist to give me a free line, which she did. I dialled the number and, after a short ring, her mother answered. I said hello, but my voice was quieter than a young woman's voice that said hello at the same time; I had a crossed line. Confused, I stayed silent. The woman asked for Delfi and identified herself; she was an old friend of Delfi's who I had heard of but never met. Delfi's mother replied that her daughter was unavailable; she was still asleep because she had been to a party with a man from work and they had come back at five in the morning.

'He is a very nice man, you know. An executive in a company. No, he is not married. He picked her up in a lovely car in the afternoon and brought her back at five, like the last time. The only problem is that he is from Ecuador. Can you believe it? Isn't it great! Why don't you ring her later.'

They hung up and I looked at the receiver in disbelief. I rang the operator who was a very nice woman and I told her about the two calls being accepted at the same time. She said to me that it was almost impossible for this to happen, but that Delfi's friend and I must have dialled the number in absolute synchronicity.

I had mixed feelings. I had an unsolicited golden opportunity to end the relationship without feeling guilty, but I also felt betrayed. Why hadn't she told me about this man? Why was she allowed to return home in the early hours with this man, while when she went out with me she had to be back by eleven? Was it because I did not have a car? Was it because I was poor? Was she tired of me, tired of waiting? Had her love for me run out? Most probably all these reasons together. I felt hurt and sad but I was also determined.

I decided not to pursue the matter and waited for Delfi to contact me instead. It wasn't until the Monday that she telephoned me at work. She was angry because I hadn't phoned her on Saturday or Sunday when she had been waiting for my call to arrange to be together for the weekend. I listened patiently in silence while resentment started to build up inside me. When she demanded an answer, I calmly unleashed what I had developed by then as my speciality: the use of words and voice to inflict the most damage possible when necessary.

'I did not phone you because I realised that, without a car, I could not possibly collect you early in the evening, take you to a nice place to "dance" all night and take you back home at five in the morning.'

A long silence and then, 'What are you talking about, Luis?'

'You heard me,' was my answer.

Silence . . .

'Who told you?'

'Did you have a nice time?'

Silence . . .

'Who told you?'

'It couldn't have been your mother. She hates me and she likes your new guy.'

'There isn't a new guy, Luis. I love you; you are the only one and you must know it.'

'Explain then.'

'There is nothing to explain, Luis.'

'We have got nothing to talk about then, Delfi.'

'Who told you, Luis? It is not true; let's meet and talk.'

'How I found out is beside the point, isn't it? The point is that it is the truth. I haven't been told. How long has it been going on without me knowing? The other point is that you don't have to explain yourself if you do not want to; I am a bit tired myself.' She was crying when I put the phone down.

She was waiting for me outside the office in the evening, with her eyes red from crying. We walked and walked holding hands, most of the time in silence. The man was an executive in the company she had been temping in. It was an office party. He was an economist; yes he was from Ecuador; yes he had a beautiful car; yes he really liked her; yes her mother was mad about him, except for the fact that he was from Ecuador. She believed that Ecuador was a jungle.

'But, tell me,' she said. 'Who told you? How did you find out?'

Poor Delfi: I was to keep my secret forever. She probably grilled her mother on her death bed to find out if she had told me. Being so unhappy about her daughter's relationship with me, she could have very well told me in order to break us up. Since I had no loyalty towards her mother, I would have, eventually, revealed my source. If Delfi is still alive, she probably sometimes wonders. Or maybe not.

She did ask me to forgive her. It was just an innocent office party. The man was very keen on her, but she was not on him. I told her that we were worlds apart, that I could not offer her the life she wanted. I did not have the means and, besides, I was going to pursue my ideals and dreams for Chilean society.

My father, mother, sisters, brothers, everyone in my family, if they were not angry at me, looked as though they could not comprehend. My sister just cried. In spite of all the pressure, I held my ground and refused to give explanations for my actions. I left home a few months later.

Delfi and the man from Ecuador married a few months after I left home. One sunny afternoon, almost a year later, I was walking down my childhood street to visit my brother and sister. I noticed a young woman on a bicycle approaching me in the middle of the road. I was shocked to see that it was Delfi and that the bicycle was my bicycle. She stopped and in her beautiful, soft voice said:

'I remember that you taught me to ride a bicycle when I was little.'

It took me off guard. She looked so young, so calm and serene. I could see her, when we were seven, and I was holding the bicycle for her. I felt a strong desire to embrace her, but I kept my pride, looked away and started towards the house.

'I have had a baby,' said the familiar soft voice behind me, hitting me like a brick.

'That's nice,' I said with a half-smile. I went straight for a cold drink in the kitchen and heard my sister shouting.

'Come and see Delfi's baby!' I had a look at the baby but I could not take in what was happening. We only exchanged few words before I left. I never saw Delfi again.

★ ★ ★

My sister did not last long in her job as a clinical assistant. She broke a medical instrument by accident, was told off, treated rudely and asked to pay for the replacement of the expensive instrument. I found her crying at home one day. I could not stand the sight. I told her to give up her job and go to university. I would support her. She went to study sociology.

In her desperate attempts to keep me 'safe' in Chile, my sister inadvertently introduced me to the most radical students in her faculty who, in turn, introduced me to members of the Movimiento de Izquierda Revolocionario [Movement of the Revolutionary Left] (MIR), which I joined together with a handful of friends from work in 1967. One of these students was a girl called Evelyn. She was the opposite of Delfi, sharing the same ideals and politics as I did, which was a revelation to me. Almost at the same time, I had started to see a young woman from work, Anita. These two women were attractive to me for different reasons.

Anita, a telephonist at work, was a very beautiful girl who enjoyed the attention of most of the male staff, especially since there were only two women workers out of about two hundred men. She was very formal and proud, always looking dignified in her blue uniform. She had light brown long hair that she kept in a pony tail. Her eyes were a striking shade of green. She had fair skin and was slender and tall.

There was never anything between us, apart from the usual formal greetings exchanged between colleagues, until the day when a group of us had to travel to a meeting. On the coach, everyone wanted to share a seat with her and I noticed that she felt a bit harassed. As I was probably the only one who did not ask, she declared to the rather large male audience: 'I would like to sit with this little boy.' And she placed her arm in mine as she said it. So, we shared the coach seat both ways, under a barrage of suggestive comments from the others.

I liked her courage and show of self-confidence, although I did not like her rather maternal way of addressing me as 'this little boy' and the attention it generated. Soon after this encounter, I learned through the other telephonist that Anita was going through a bad patch. Her relationship with her boyfriend, a married man, had gone from bad to worse. Her mother and younger sister were ill in hospital; they had apparently been involved in an accident.

After two or three days absence Anita came back to work a different woman. She looked pale, exhausted and seemed to have aged. I phoned her at the operator's room to see how she was and if she needed to talk. She thanked me and suggested we meet at lunchtime. This we did and went for a walk. She looked very serious, grave, unsmiling.

She asked me what I wanted to know, holding back her tears. I responded that I did not want anything in particular; I just wanted to know how she was and if I could be of any help. She put her arm through mine.

'I don't know how to say this,' she said. 'Or if I should talk to you about it.'

She looked deeply troubled inside. We carried on walking in silence for a long while. I did not dare to speak, allowing her to gather whatever strength she needed to. After a while, she said:

'I do not know exactly why, but I find you different from other men and I have decided to trust you. My father went berserk the other night and stabbed my mother and my younger sister. They are both alive, but my mother only just. He is in prison at the moment.' She burst into tears while I held her tight against my chest.

She composed herself, as if regretting what she had just done, glancing at me every now and then, assessing my reaction.

I did not know what to say, I just held her hand tightly.

'He has became quite strange lately, with terrible attacks of jealousy, like paranoia, and violent. But nobody thought he would do any thing like this.'

Her father had come back from work one evening and taken a small, sharp knife from the kitchen, gone in to the living room where Anita's mother and sister were, and attacked them. He had slashed the girl's face cutting through her upper cheek to the left ear. The mother had not been so lucky: she had been stabbed deep in her left eye, the forehead and one of her hands and arms while trying to protect herself. The youngest son, who was thirteen, was in another room. When he realised what was going on, the young boy ran into the street for help. He found his two older brothers who, while the neighbours called the ambulance and the police, gave chase to their, by then, fugitive father. They caught up with him soon after and handed him over to the police, unable to get an answer from him to their frantic 'whys?'

Anita's life was typical of a lower middle-class family who had fallen into bad fortune. There were five children, two girls and three boys. Anita was the eldest. She had been a nurse but had had to find a different job because of the miserable pay. Her sister and brothers were still at school.

This incident angered me immensely. Her situation and the circumstances leading to her father's violence were quite similar to what I and my family had been through. Unemployment and ensuing financial disaster had driven this man to desperation and eventually to madness. He felt a failure, devalued, with no respect from his family. We all know this happens from time to time, but it seems to be worse for families that have previously been comfortable, who have had a place in their communities that they can no longer hold.

The other girl, Evelyn, was from a middle-class family of four. She was full of the revolutionary ideas that were developing at the time, especially in the universities. She was reading Simone De Beauvoir and her ideas about women had taken a strong hold on her which, in turn, influenced me.

Evelyn was for me the ideal intellectual revolutionary companion. In contrast to Delfi, we never ran out of conversation, and it seemed that we never would. She was as interested in my life as a worker from the age of thirteen as I was in her idealism and her awareness of the complexities of life in our society. I was also fascinated by her family dynamics. Her parents, her father more than her mother, were more like friends than parents. They were supportive and understanding, participating in the discussions in a constructive way. They were up to date with what was going on in Chilean society at that time.

Among other things, what I appreciated most was that Evelyn introduced me to the university students' life and culture of the time, which included the renaissance of Chilean folklore and protest music, art and theatre. There was one problem: the prevalent 'revolutionary' notion among the emerging movement that in order to be able to 'make' the revolution, you had to break with the establishment. And this break included your family and your parents.

For me it sounded too much like a generational battle and I found it very difficult to sympathise with her, and others like her, in their efforts to antagonise their parents with almost everything, just for the sake of it. Because 'they were a produce of the bourgeois, capitalist system', they were therefore innate reactionaries incapable of seeing the situation for themselves. Many times I found myself in a difficult position, where my loyalties were tested. I could only see these loving parents, proud of their children, understanding, cooperative, and most of all willing to support and finance their ungrateful children. In my view, it was easy for these students to preach the 'unavoidable breaking and rejection of the family', knowing that at the end of the day they could go back home, have a hot shower, a hot meal and a comfortable bed to sleep in; in most cases all prepared by a house maid. It was not easy for them to understand a situation like mine, for example. A father permanently unemployed due to bankruptcy and depression, and me, having to support a family of nine on low wages. Or Anita's situation for that matter. There was a need for the students to come out of their comfortable homes in the suburbs and university campuses to visit the shantytowns and the factories surrounding Santiago, as well as their house maids' environments. 'We have to "create" the revolution with fathers, mothers, brothers and sisters who cannot leave their families; with workers who cannot leave their factories; because, if they did, there would be no proletariat to create the revolution with.'

At that point it seemed that I had hit the nail on the head (and I was not alone). The prevailing line of thought at the time was the notion that the revolution had to be 'created' by the revolutionaries, for the people. A small group of revolutionaries might achieve this, like in Cuba. The example of a small group challenging a mighty system had to be followed by the poor of both town and country until final victory was achieved. For, it appeared that a revolutionary was a different kind of human being, beyond the distinctions of social class. It did not matter, therefore, if he or she came from a bourgeois background or had never worked for a salary in his or her life. But this would prove disastrous for many young revolutionary organisations in South America, mainly composed of university students who generously gave their lives for their ideals.

*The Manual of the Urban Guerrilla*, written by the Brazilian revolutionary Maringhela, advocated that family life, including having children, was to be denied by revolutionaries, at least until victory was achieved. A clandestine life and the ever-present risk of capture and torture was incompatible with children and family life. As would prove to be true – sometimes fatally – children or other relatives of fugitives or the captured could be kept for ransom or used for extortion.

But the university students of Chile had the Popular Government of Allende as a proving ground. The mass movement generated by the hopes of the Allende programme would force the students to closer links with the working class and the poor of the country and the cities. In the most traditional and conservative faculties, workers made their way into the universities to hear lectures given by famous lawyers, economists and philosophers. So it would be true to say that the gap between the intellectuals and the workers was, to a great extent, breached in Chile during the Allende government. The proof of this was shown when, after the coup, university students were massacred in their thousands alongside their worker comrades.

Feeling idealistic, moralistic and with a good dose of omnipotence, I decided that I would be more useful, and was more needed, at Anita's side than at Evelyn's. It was not easy. It took me a week in the High Andes to decide, sleeping in caves with only Oscar and few political

sympathise with their tiredness – I was also working long hours doing masonry work, as well as studying and visiting factories. However, this made me devise ever more ingenious forms of delivery to keep my audience awake. I would take a portable record player and play folk songs of protest to the workers. I learned to effectively use a blackboard and different forms of participation. In short, I think I made the learning process a fun time for the tired workers. They stayed after working hours in increasing numbers.

The workers were taught about the process of production and their place in it, about the meaning of 'surplus value' and exploitation, about labour relations, about management, accountancy, economics, history, international relations, principles of philosophy, etc. All this was delivered in a way they could understand and relate to, using their own experience and real situations. Soon the workers, in their traditional sense of humour, would address each other as *Fuerza de trabajo* (work force), and the machinery as *medio de produccion* (means of production).

These were happy times for me. I enjoyed relating to the workers and developing friendships. I also learned enormously from them, their way of thinking, of relating to one another, their families, loved ones and the world at large, their simplicity and logic when facing and solving problems or coping with adversity. There was a factory making uniforms for the police force where the majority of the workers were women. Consequently there was a fair number of small children to be looked after during working hours. The building was totally inadequate in every sense and a health hazard. Nevertheless, the owner had accommodated a crèche and a rest room, where the boilers were, on the first floor of the old building. At lunchtime, when I used to go to help with feeding the children, their food had to be heated on a metal tray through which rusty metal pipes ran. The tray was filled with water, the food containers were placed on the tray, and then the valves were opened to let hot steam from the pipes heat the water to boiling point. It was a huge bain-marie where the mothers cooked their own food as well. The first time I was there I was shocked by the hazardous situation. Bare steam pipes running and leaking everywhere, the all-wooden construction perilously holding the huge boilers, among all the babies and toddlers. The heat and humidity were intense, which was probably OK in winter, but in summer it was unbearable, besides, everything got rusty and mouldy. Still, the workers put on a brave face and were happy to have the facilities and me helping, as this employer could not 'afford' everyday child care. Ironically, the demand for police uniforms was increasing, as more police were needed to beat up vociferous students and striking workers in the streets up and down the country. If there was ever a secure industry in the country, it was this one.

Teaching and helping women workers was strange for me. Due to my upbringing, with two grandmothers, an aunt, a mother and two sisters, I have always felt at ease in the company of women. At the police uniform factory I got used to their compliments and I learned to acknowledge most of them without going red in the face. I tried to create an atmosphere of 'the right of a woman to make a compliment to a man without the risk of being subjected to harassment'. I always felt in good company and I like to believe that in spite of their mistrust of the world of politics, they learned something from me as they came to trust me. I do not know what happened to them after the coup, or to the factory, for that matter, I have never seen any of the women workers of that factory. I don't believe that I will ever see any of them again. If some of them are still alive, it would be nice to meet again, to know about their lives after this chunk of history.

I also enjoyed visiting a small metal factory making parts for the automotive assembling industry. They also manufactured hardened metal alloys for the oil extracting industry. They were highly skilled workers, about seventy of them, but they were not well paid. During our work in the factory, I learned that the company was running out of contracts, was not making much profit and badly needed to work on health and safety issues. Some of the workers had to work in the process of protecting metals destined for drilling in rock. This process involves placing the piece inside a sealed small chamber, and bombarding it with silica sand at extremely high pressure. The makeshift chamber in the workshop had no door and the operatives worked with no protection apart from goggles. Some of the workers had already contracted pulmonary diseases from inhaling silica dust.

We approached the owner of the factory and arranged a meeting with all the workers, to discuss the health and safety issues as well as contracts for the factory and its future. At first the owner was reluctant, but when I mentioned that I could talk to people in high places to ensure that his company got more contracts from the state-owned oil extracting industry, he became more reasonable. After he became enthusiastic about the plans, I made the most daring proposition, already agreed to by the union: 'The workers want access to the account books, and a say in the decision-making process of the company'. In other words: co-management of the company. We were surprised when the owner agreed, but then the workers, after examining the accounts books, went a step further. 'In order to invest in safety and save the company from bankruptcy, it will be necessary to sell some of the company's assets'. These included two of the owner's private cars and a second house. The workers explained to him why he did not need two extra luxury cars and another property, all in the name of the company. Again, we were surprised: the owner stated that the proposals were reasonable, that he understood and that he would try his best for the future success of the company. In a fully attended general meeting, an overwhelming majority appointed the owner of the company manager director and he was assigned a salary that he was happy with, but he was no longer the sole beneficiary of the company's profit. I personally learned to like him and enjoyed a good relationship with him.

Affected by my time spent with the factory workers, I decided to leave the MIR. It was 1968 and the Party seemed to be ignoring the trade unions and other workers' organisations. Where was the democracy? Where were the debates? The Manuel Rodriguez Movimento Revolucionaria (MR$^2$) offered a credible alternative, and seemed to be more in tune with the workers' organisations. I and many other ex-MIR members joined them immediately.

★ ★ ★

By the end of 1968 I had reluctantly come to the conclusion that political solutions were no longer enough and because of increasing violence we had to be able to defend ourselves. The turning point came on March 9, 1969, when the Minister for the Interior, Perez Zujovic, ordered 250 police to surround a shantytown on the outskirts of the southern town of Puerto Montt. They tried to remove more than a hundred poor and homeless villagers. The villagers tried to defend themselves with simple weapons but the police responded with tear gas and brutal force. They finally burned the villagers' small huts and left fifteen of them dead. I realised then there was no turning back.

# Arming the resistance

4

Ever since I had started my office work at the age of seventeen, I had been fascinated by Armeria Italiana, a large gun shop on Calle Arturo Pratt in the centre of Santiago. I believed it was *the* arms store in Santiago, with a highly regarded workshop. Any revolutionary worth their name needs arms, and, if we were going to join Guevara in Bolivia, we would surely be more welcome if we arrived with our own supplies.

I had mentioned this to Oscar and asked him what he thought of the idea of 'expropriating' some arms from Armeria Italiana. Oscar had thought that it might be a possibility and late one night as we walked past the store, looking attentively around us, we imagined ourselves forcing an entry in the dark and escaping with a few guns with which to fight our revolution. But we did not act then as the situation had not yet become that desperate.

However, now, four years later, towards the end of the Christian Democrat government of Eduardo Frei, the MIR and other minor organisations had carried out a series of bank robberies or 'expropriations' as we used to call them. Although the main purpose was to support the activities of the full-time members of the organisation the proceedings of many of these operations ended up being distributed among the poor of the shantytowns. These activities were new in Chile and they were viewed by the populist press with sympathy, as if they were the actions of latter-day Robin Hoods. One of the characteristics of the raids was that nobody ever got hurt and staff were treated with dignity.

Thus when the MR$^2$ ordered that 'expropriations' were a 'revolutionary duty' and that every member should participate in the preparation and execution of such actions, I put forward my old idea of 'expropriating' guns from Armeria Italiana. The idea was well received and the Party gave me its support and a cell of two comrades to carry out the first phase of the work.

We worked hard for months, during the spring of 1969, observing the activities of the store and the area around it twenty-four hours a day. We climbed the tallest building in the neighbourhood to observe the rear of the shop through binoculars, entertaining the idea of entering through the back door. However, I also learned that other comrades preferred a forced entry through the main entrance. I was trying to think of a plan that would be the least conspicuous, the least provable, and the least obvious. Some comrades were used to carrying out bank robberies in broad daylight, with balaclavas and pistols in their hands, shouting 'everybody down!' But this was not like a bank where, at most, there would be one armed guard. Here there were hundreds of firearms and trained staff ready to use them. It had to be done with stealth during the night.

By now we had managed to find out the personal details of all the ten or so staff of the store just by following them home after work. We would then call pretending to be door-to-door salesmen and get the full family history. The manager proved to be a bit more difficult. He was a married man with three young children and a mistress with whom he would spend long hours after work in night clubs or cheap hotels. We had the idea of using this information to blackmail him into opening the doors and the safe for us; however, the idea was eventually rejected as being too unpredictable: we could easily end up with an overweight man having a heart attack and us leaving empty-handed.

I began to think about the buildings. Since the buildings in the block where the store was situated were quite old, I assumed that the partitions must have suffered many alterations over the years and that these might not have been properly constructed. Certainly nobody would have ever built them thinking a robbery was likely.

Next to the Armeria, on the right-hand side, there was the front door to a house and a sign hanging from the wall announcing 'Chiropodist. No appointments necessary'. I asked one of the students, a woman, to accompany me one day to the chiropodist, since my right toenail was in-growing and causing me a lot of pain in the process. There were a few people waiting in a small room behind the consultancy room. The corridor went deep into the house, ending in an internal courtyard. It was a typical house of Spanish design, the other rooms being arranged around this courtyard. I asked my friend to wait for me while I looked for a toilet. I ventured down the long corridor with its wooden floor, paying special attention to the wall adjacent to the Armeria. My heart jumped when I discovered an old wooden door that had been boarded up.

'Excuse me,' said a voice suddenly, 'the waiting room is over there.'

'I was looking for a toilet.'

'There is no toilet here.'

I apologised and took my place in the waiting room. The chiropodist was not a friendly or pleasant woman. After examining my toe she said I needed a small operation. I said that I was only passing and hadn't much time. Could I make an appointment later? And that was that.

I was overjoyed by my discovery: that door was certainly the weakest point in the Armeria's armour. I mentioned this to the comrades, but kept my next movements to myself. I had already decided that we would gain access to the store through that door. There was nothing else in front of it in the corridor, just an empty space under the stairs, and in the middle of the night, hidden from the street, breaking in and emptying the Armeria from there would be easy! Brilliant! I thought. So the next few days I spent planning the whole operation.

My next assumption was that, because the house had so many rooms and it was within walking distance from the city centre, rooms must be rented out, perhaps including meals, like in a *pension*. I got hold of what was called a 'reverse telephone book' where, instead of subscriber's names, addresses were listed in alphabetical order with the name of the subscriber and the telephone number. The circulation of this telephone book was restricted for obvious reasons. I found out the name of the person living next door to the Armeria; it was a woman called Alicia Alegria, her last name meaning 'happiness'. My next task was to observe the movement of people in and out of the house, day and night. But, as I did not want to show myself in the vicinity, I asked my superior in the Party to instruct a cell to do the job. After a few days and nights of observation we had a lot of information. It was a very busy road with lots of traffic but there were good points of observation because the buildings across the road had been demolished for development and the space was being used as a car park before construction started. Eight adults (four women and four men) and two small children were reported to be living in the house. There was one large, middle-aged woman who dressed in black; the other three women were young, in their twenties. One of them was tall and good looking, usually seen with one of the small children, a toddler, by her side. Another was short and thin, and usually looked after the other toddler. The third one was usually on her own, sometimes in the company of a middle-aged man. The middle-aged man was tall and thin. He did not look like a typical 'Chilean', but looked more European, with fair skin and hair. The other three men were young, in their late twenties. In the morning, all the men and one of the young women left the house as if for work. The busiest time was around lunchtime. One of the young men usually came back just for lunch but often did not return in the evening. There was usually no movement during the night.

I took the report and read it many times. It was thorough. My conclusions were, first, that the middle-aged woman was the owner of the house. She was a widow, the telephone subscriber and ran the house on her own. Second, two of the young women were her daughters or daughters-in-law, or both. Third, the young men were her sons or sons-in-law, and fathers of the children. Fourth, the middle-aged man and the remaining young woman were a couple. So there were a lot of people who would, somehow, have to be controlled in the event of having to occupy the house, which would be necessary for the operation to succeed.

When I presented the plan to my comrades, they were concerned about the amount of people in the house and the small children. The operation would require a large number of us: at least one for every household member plus the operatives needed to deal with arriving at the house, breaking into the shop, transportation of the arms, outside surveillance and escape. 'We are talking about eighteen people plus five or six cars; the answer is going to be no.'

I proposed that I would study the situation further in the next few days. I telephoned the house and asked to speak with Mrs Alegria. I asked her if she had a room to rent available. She hesitated a bit, saying: 'I do not rent rooms', probably not wanting to admit undeclared income. I pressed her.

'Look, a friend of mine used to rent a room across the road from you and he gave me your number. Of course the houses have been demolished now but he advised me to try, you know, maybe you have something . . . I don't know.'

'Look. I haven't got a room available at the moment.'

'Perhaps I can ring you another time, Mrs Alegria, if that is OK with you?'

'Yes, yes, certainly.'

This was all off the top of my head; I would need to plan my next move more carefully. I was determined to get lodging in the house. I had to go in and familiarise myself with the building as well as with the people living there. If I could live next door to the gun shop for a while it would allow me time to prepare a plan. I asked the Party for a false identity card making me three years younger, which was not difficult since I always looked younger than my true age. After a little while I received my ID and some money for a deposit and rent.

It was nearly March, when students return to classes after the long summer holidays. I needed to act quickly. I phoned the woman again and asked if she remembered me phoning her in the summer about a room. She seemed to vaguely remember, stating that there was no room to let.

I repeated my previous story but this time much more drama. I was an eighteen-year-old student from the south with a place at university but nowhere to stay. It was my first time in the capital and I was pretty much lost. I was trusting that the lady who used to rent rooms across the road would accommodate me as she did my friend. I had the name and telephone number of this woman but her house had been demolished, what good was that to me now? I had looked everywhere, but so far without luck. Everywhere seemed to be full. If only I knew the city better! My father was going to be very worried. I would be most grateful if she could put me up, even if only temporarily. My father, who was a bank manager in Chillan (a city in the south), would be most grateful.

The woman agreed to meet me. 'Give me a day or two to prepare the room,' she said, 'It is a very small one, and probably not very comfortable, but will probably do if you have nowhere else to go.' A few days later I borrowed a black suit, black shoes and glasses. I combed my short hair straight back with cream and faked a slight limp in my right leg.

Although it was very hot outside, inside the house was dark and cool. I had seen the woman before, from a distance, but she seemed more pleasant and affable in person. I could tell that she liked me; I was very timid, soft spoken, with an air of provincial innocence. She wrote down my personal details from my ID card without really studying them.

The room was very small and really gloomy; it was quite dark, with a window to the central patio. The toilet next door had no window and smelled mouldy. There was a sort of shower with no hot water, a small Formica table next to the bed and a small wardrobe at the other end. I pretended to be most grateful. I gave her the deposit. I would move in that evening.

I had married Anita by this time. We had decided to live together over a year before, but nobody wanted to rent property to unmarried couples. It lacked respectability; other residents would protest. I had left my job at the transport company since it was made very clear to me that they knew I belonged to an illegal political organisation. My presence was not welcomed and there was talk of informing the authorities. Although Anita understood why I had to do what I did, she was visibly distressed when I told her I had to be away for sometime. I told her that we would be able to see each other only about once a week. I told her that I had to undergo some training. Those eyes, her face at that moment, almost killed me.

There was great excitement at Mrs Alegria's house the evening I moved in. I met the two young women, one, Maria, was her daughter, the other, Olga, was her daughter-in-law. The toddlers were children of each. Her son, Juan, was unmarried, a man in his late twenties who was working in a government department involved in the distribution of cheap food to the 'disadvantaged'. There was another young man who was also her son, but who did not look like the other siblings. He was also in his twenties and married to Olga. He was not present in the household all the time for a reason I would find out later.

Soon after I arrived and was shown my room it was supper time. We all sat at a large table and food was served. I found it difficult to eat but I knew I had to have something. Although I made it clear that I had eaten something at college, the pressure to eat was overwhelming. As soon as I sat down, the questioning started. Where did I come from? How large was my family? What was I studying? Where was my home city and what was it like? I regretted not having learned more about my home city, to which I had been only once, a few years before. I was tormented. And this was before the young women started to interrogate me about girlfriends. I had no choice but to overact my role as a provincial young boy from a very traditional background, underdeveloped in all matters of sex and all that was supposed to be 'going on'. I showed politeness and good manners, showing surprise and amusement at the use of slang words. The young women decided that I looked very much like an Argentinean singer, very popular at the time, called Piero.

There were three people, apart from me, renting rooms in the house: the middle-aged man, a young woman, and another young man. They were not related to each other and they occupied the first floor rooms at the front of the house. I could not sleep that night, everything was so strange and I could not help revisiting, time and again, the conversation at supper time, the questioning and whether I had made any serious mistakes in my answers that could reveal my deceit.

The next morning I had breakfast with the other people at the large table. Mrs Alegria asked me what time I would be home for lunch but I had decided that I definitely did not like her cooking! I left the house after Mrs Alegria handed me a key for the front door. She told me I should be at home by ten thirty at the latest, after which she locked the door with an iron bar from inside. I walked towards Santiago's main avenue, La Alameda, to get a bus in the direction of the university where I was supposed to be studying maths. I had chosen maths because I assumed that very few people would be interested in talking to me about my course. After a few routine procedures to find out if anyone had been following me, I tousled my hair, swapped my glasses for dark ones, put my jacket in a plastic bag and proceeded to the usual business of attending Party cell meetings.

I was in charge of some three cells of five people, mainly students. We would discuss Marxist literature, Party policy and politics, and the country's political and economic situation. Other themes would be security – we were a banned organisation – new recruits, resources and logistics. Although the students were generally two or three years younger than me, I noticed that they saw me as a veteran revolutionary.

Once I felt more settled in my new life, I started to use a series of excuses to stay in the house after lunch, the quietest time in the house, and ventured up and down the corridor at the entrance. It was an empty space with no reason for anyone to be standing there. I would walk with a maths text book in my hand. One of my first tasks was to accurately measure the place, without a measuring tape. I counted my steps hundreds of times; the distance from the entrance door to my target door, the door leading to the Armeria; from the entrance to the different rooms, bathrooms, kitchen, etc. All was carefully recorded, and the records destroyed usually the same day. I drew various plans and maps of the place too. Sometimes I would wait, having made an excuse, in the hope that at some time everyone would be out of the house. The two young women and Mrs Alegria did not go out much. They looked after the house, did the cooking and shopping and took care of the toddlers. However, I did have a few opportunities in the three months I spent there.

I could confirm that the arms store was the size of four large rooms. I also discovered that behind my target door was a working bench, used by two of the men (we knew their names already) doing the repairs; there was also a big safe at the front of that room. Apart from the bench, the door appeared not to be blocked off, but it must have been locked and bolted. That was no problem, I thought. The worst scenario would have been a solid wall in front of the door. I did not think that it was even alarmed. In the days and weeks that followed I would always look through the keyhole, as well as listening to the noises that came from the workshop.

I became the centre of attention for the young women in the house and the subject of all sorts of fantasies. When Mrs Alegria was not around, they would come to my room, which was dark and hot – almost unbearable with the door shut during the day. Sometimes Maria, sometimes Maria and Olga, would sit on my bed and ask me about my love life. No, I did not have a girlfriend; yes I had had one back home, but not now. No, I did not have sex with her. I did not answer the question about whether I had ever had sex yet. I looked embarrassed, trying to show them that their question was inappropriate; they laughed.

I certainly did not like these visits to my room, which had become more regular while I was 'studying'. I was not so concerned about their gossiping and questions, which were almost invariably about love, girlfriends, boyfriends and sex. As long as the conversations remained around those topics, although embarrassing, I was pretty safe since they saw me as an innocent and were convinced they were 'opening my eyes' to these subjects. The worry for me was their accumulation of knowledge about me and the subsequent police photo fit after the robbery. To make matters worse, Maria was artistic, always drawing me while talking and sitting on my bed, which she did very often as she showed herself to be increasingly attracted to me.

A few weeks later I invented a girlfriend. She was my tutor's sister. My tutor was a young man who, taking pity on my provinciality and loneliness in the capital, had asked his younger sister to show me around and we had become close. This was a story that I hoped would slow down Maria's advances and would give me an excuse to spend certain nights elsewhere, when it was necessary for me to do so.

I would often leave half-written letters to my parents and siblings lying about my room. I would talk about the wonderful Alegria family, my tutor and his adorable sister and the big city. There was 'great pressure' from my girlfriend's family for me to stay with them, but I was not sure if accepting the offer was the right thing to do in the circumstances.

All this was necessary as my activities intensified. It was already the beginning of April and the comrades wanted the operation to take place on the 21 May, the day celebrated as 'the Glories of the Navy'. Increasingly I had to meet small groups of comrades in different locations to give talks about the 'objective' and the operative situation. I was taken to these meetings in great secrecy, blindfolded, without knowing where the meeting took place.

A problem had arisen as to the safe in the workshop. I had noticed that the small boxes containing ammunition disappeared from the store shelves just before closing time; I guessed that the only other possible place they could go was the huge safe at the back. When I informed my superiors of this, the 'experts' on safes replied that a 'controlled' explosion had to be applied to the safe's door to gain access. I immediately panicked, imagining that the 'controlled explosion' would transform the safe into a huge bomb once all the ammunition inside was ignited.

I took a gamble: talking as if I was an expert in the matter I managed to convince the comrades, through my contact, that the ammunition was kept in the enormous safe at night due to fire regulations. In the event of a store fire, the ammunition would not explode in the intense heat. If it did explode, it would be inside the safe, at a far lesser risk. Now, I continued, if this was a fire precaution, the safe's key *must* be on the premises for the fire brigade to be able to empty it in the event of a fire, if they had the time.

There were still concerns from 'above' that there were too many people in the house, requiring a large number of participants in the operation, and making logistics and security difficult. I counter-argued that, provided the participants were well segregated, my plan for the operation was safe for both the public and us.

There were eight adults and two small children in the house to control at night. Mrs Alegria's son shared a room with her. The two young women slept in a room each with their respective children and Olga sometimes shared her bed with her husband. The other three non-family members slept in the rooms upstairs, at the front of the house.

I decided that during the robbery the residents should be assembled in the living room, which was spacious and had plenty of seats. I would take charge of the children, giving them warm bottled milk and putting them together in one bed. The children had become very fond of me and often came to my room to talk or play, calling me 'Piero' all the time. Nobody in the house called me anything else.

On the chosen day I would tell Mrs Algeria that I needed to revise and study until late for an important exam the next day. My 'tutor' (the officer in charge of the operation) would return to the house with me 'after college', already in disguise wearing a false moustache. I would tell Mrs Alegria that he would be leaving late, as I had just realised that there was a lot more to study than I originally thought. This would be at about one in the morning. The operatives would begin to arrive then, three of four at a time, at intervals of one minute. There would be twelve of them, making fourteen in total.

In absolute silence everyone would gather in the living room after walking the ten or so metres from the front door over a carpet made from my bedding. If everything was quiet, the leader would give the signal for everyone to carry out what they had been training and practising for.

The plan was this: comrades would be posing as plain-clothes policeman under the command of an inspector who had orders to carry out a court search of the premises of Mr Juan Alegria. 'There has been a complaint about fraud being committed by the so-called Mr Alegria at the government offices of goods distribution where quantities of consumer goods have disappeared.' I, the 'student' of the household, would be placed with the residents in the living room to avoid suspicion at this stage. After everything was under control, I would be called to another room for 'individual questioning'. 'Students are always up to something bad.' After making sure the children were settled and getting Mrs Alegria medicine for her heart condition, I would clean the house with a special cloth and fluid to remove any fingerprints. By this time the people in charge of breaking into the Armeria would have finished drilling a big hole in the target door. My plan was approved in its entirety, with only a few changes.

Still, there was a long way to go in terms of training and information gathering. I had to draw different sketch plans for members of the group and get more accurate measurements, particularly of the 'target' door. I had to prepare a list of the names of all the residents, including the children, attaching a brief description of each, including their appearance, personality traits and likely reactions and behaviour to an unpredictable and surprising situation.

It had been reported in the press in the past that consumer goods often went missing from the National Distribution Centre and every now and then a member of their staff was found to have been diverting and selling goods such as flour, milk powder, grain, sugar, oil and other essentials to shops. Nothing on a big scale though. I had seen such products in Mrs Alegria's house due to the fact that her son Juan worked at the centre. I really did not know whether he had been stealing or not, but I thought that in the present climate, even legally acquired products in a member of staff's house would be suspicious.

Juan was a big but quiet man, so I did not expect him to resist. I also suspected he would feel guilty and would cooperate with the 'police' in this matter, as he would not like to upset his mother, in a bed only a few yards from his. I would expect the women to make a fuss about their children, but as long as the children were taken care of and remained calm, they would not put up a fight. The only person I wasn't sure would remain calm was Olga's husband, Mrs Alegria's younger son. He had a quick temper, I had seen him shouting at his wife, and Maria had told me he also beat her up every now and then. But he was quite short and skinny, easy enough to control by a couple of men bigger than him. As for the lodgers, I did not expect any sort of conflict with them.

It was already well known that the police patrolled the area at set times twice during the night in a police van. At these times it was crucial that there should not be the slightest unusual movement outside the house. I was told, that as the Armeria was only two blocks away from the Ministry of Defence, the precaution of placing patrols in adjacent streets in walkie-talkie communication with the operatives inside the house should be taken. Other comrades would also be in charge of the getaway vehicles.

In this respect I had a bit of luck. I recognised the man that ran the car park opposite the Armeria as a former driver in the coach company where I worked less than a year before. I remembered that he had given up coach driving to be the personal chauffer of one of the two sons of the owner of the company. I guessed that the land and the car park must belong to the company.

In any case, the good thing for me was that I knew his name and the name of his boss. With this information I invented a plausible story by which my comrades could gain access to the car park when it was closed, in the middle of the night, without force. This would allow them to oversee the operation while waiting in their vehicles without raising any suspicion. Comrades, after calling the man to the gate, would identify themselves as friends of his boss (name provided). They would tell him that they were involved in a business transaction of a quantity of German bus engines from Argentina, which were supposed to arrive earlier that day but which had been delayed in one of the frontier passes that was blocked by snow. They needed to leave their cars in the car park for the night. The comrades could, if necessary, also help themselves to some of the few cars left overnight there.

Mrs Alegria was very cross with me. I had told her that I was going away for the weekend, how come that it was now Tuesday night and I did not have the decency of telling her that I would be late? She had been worrying about me, that something could have happened to me and she had nobody to contact, no address, and no telephone number. This was not acceptable; I could at least telephone her. She did not know the name or the address of the university I was studying at. Soon her daughter joined in haranguing me, a sarcastic look on her face. Where and with whom had I been? She implied that I had been away for a dirty weekend with my new girlfriend. The 'provincial' quiet boy was spreading his wings very quickly.

In fact I had been on one of those training weekends which had run into trouble. We were delayed by bad planning and miscalculations. The place chosen for the training, though beautiful and isolated, was too far away. It took us the whole of Saturday to reach it, changing buses twice. The place was so isolated that when we arrived we had to walk for more than an hour. Then I realised that the organisers had not taken into account the fact that I had to be back in Santiago by Sunday night. There were no buses until Monday evening.

Of course, the people I was with had no idea of who I was or that I was living in a house next to the Armeria Italiana with the purpose of breaking into it and robbing it. They could not understand my urge to be in Santiago by Monday evening at the latest. All I could say was that it was of paramount importance. I was furious because I feared that this could seriously compromise the whole operation.

In my unexpected and prolonged absence, the people in the house would surely go through my scant possessions in the room: one almost empty suitcase, some underwear and a shirt that seemed to wash themselves, two books on maths, one novel and two or three notebooks. Mrs Alegria might even contact the police about my disappearance, which she was determined to do the next day had I not turned up.

I decided to appease their anger rather than add to their curiosity, particularly Maria's, and not leave the door wide open for whatever sexual fantasies she might develop from my prolonged absence. I lowered my head like a little boy, allowing myself to be told off at length until Mrs Alegria had nothing else to say. When she had finished, I said that I was terrible sorry, that I had got carried away by my girlfriend and her family and that it would not happen again. After that I excused myself giving the impression that I needed to reflect on the situation. I was happy that I did not have to answer their questions about a contact telephone number for 'my parents' or details of my 'college', and I hoped that they would not ask again. Excrutiatingly, I had to behave like a good boy for a week, joining the family for all possible meal times and enduring frequent visits by Maria and Olga to my room: for there would be more absences required as the day of the operation approached.

I phoned Anita almost every day at her workplace; I also managed to stay overnight at our home a couple of times, but it was heartbreaking to say goodbye the following day. She looked at me as if for the last time, guessing that I was going to do something big. She did not ask, and I did not tell her; I do not think she wanted to know.

One day I travelled to one of the last meetings with a few comrades from a shantytown who were going to participate in the operation. I arrived there by public transport with another comrade I had met on the way. It had been raining the day before, and as there were no roads it was just like a river of mud. There were three men in their thirties plus a couple of young male students. I only recognised one person. I had met him before at a student gathering at the university; his nickname was 'Guajiro'. I knew the police were looking for him as a suspect of a failed operation two years before to rob a bank. We discussed the personalities in the house and how we would handle them. After this we were due to attend a further meeting that evening with another cell to discuss the operation with more emphasis on technical details.

We were driving from west to east along a wide avenue in a Mini Cooper, talking about the most appropriate date for the operation, when the driver slowed down, not due to the traffic, but because there was a police barrier ahead.

'What should we do?' he asked calmly; there were no side roads to speak of in this part of the avenue. There must have been six policemen with machine guns, plus two police cars.

Quickly, Guajiro, who was sitting at the back with me, opened a holdall and took out two paper bags. He passed me one of the bags; inside there was a pistol.

'Hide it under your jacket. You will use it against the policemen when I say so. Is that clear? In the meantime stay calm.'

'We are going to stop,' he instructed the driver. 'Drive very slow, stay calm and answer their questions. We are not getting out of the car. Do not switch off the engine; find an excuse. If they ask us to get out, you drive off fast in the direction you know and let us get out if they are not too close.'

He opened the other paper bag and took out a beautiful mahogany case and a hammer. He opened the case and quickly started to assemble a small machine gun, his eyes fixed in the distance to where the police barrier was. The closed case formed the butt of the machine gun. He signalled me to lodge a bullet in the barrel of my gun; the other man did the same. As we were closing in to the barrier, Guajiro told me that if he gave the order to shoot, I should aim at the two policemen to my near left, the other man should aim to the policemen on his near right side. As the back windows of the Mini Cooper did not open, we would use the hammer to smash them before shooting.

Later I found it incredible how concentrated my mind was on what was going on. My eyes fixed on the movements ahead; my brain busy calculating speed, distances and registering every move. It was clear that the situation depended very much on the driver, his nerves and the speed with which he could drive the tiny but powerful machine.

We came to a halt on the hard shoulder of the road in front of the wooden barrier. Two policemen, one on each side of the car, came towards us. The one on the left bent down to talk to our driver. He asked him to switch off the engine. The driver said that there was something wrong with the carburettor; it would take us hours to start it again. My right hand was holding the already unlocked pistol, my index finger on the trigger. Guajiro had his paper bag on his knees.

It may have been just a survival thing, but all I could imagine was our car speeding off, having caught the police by surprise, through various roads and streets and neighbourhoods until the chase was over. Suddenly the vision came to me of these deceivingly morose policemen firing their machine guns non-stop into our disfigured bodies. And that would be all; that would be it, the end of everything.

The policeman asked our driver the usual questions: 'Is this your car? Can I see your licence? Where are you going? Are these your friends?' The other policeman was looking straight into the car, at our tense faces, the paper bags; looking calmly for a sign. There was still the possibility of being caught alive, followed by interrogation and imprisonment. 'I am sorry Mrs Alegria, it's just that I met the wrong people.' How long is this going to last? They are moving in slow motion, I thought. 'It's all right, you may continue,' the policeman said.

We sped off. With the corner of my eye I was trying to look inconspicuously through the back window of the car. I could almost see the policemen getting into their cars and chasing after us. After a while we relaxed our muscles and could look at each other in disbelief.

'Beautiful piece,' I said to Guajiro, looking at the paper bag on his lap. 'Yeah,' he said, still with dryness in his mouth. 'It's a Luger. We call her "Lulu".' He explained that this kind of machine gun was given to German Nazi officers as a reward for good service. 'Do not ask how it got here,' Guajiro said, and then he asked everyone how we were. I was impressed by the craftsmanship displayed on the Luger; it was almost a work of art. Were the victims of its bullets meant to admire it and feel grateful for being shot and killed by such a beautiful thing?

The date of the operation was set for 19 May. The leaders had wanted it to be 21 May, to coincide with the day of 'the Glories of the Navy', but developments in the house made it more difficult then. It was a telephone call that brought great excitement to the Alegria household. The telephone call was from the United States. Unknown to me, Mrs Alegria had another son living in the States. He was married and had two children. He was coming for a visit with his family, and they were going to stay in the house, arriving on the 20 May.

'We can still do it, even with all those people in the house,' declared the comrades.

'I suppose so,' I said, but thought it would be a lot more risky. The other son, the one who worked in a department store, but who did not normally live at the house, was also likely to be there too, probably with his family, and he would be staying, since there was going to be a surprise party for the son from the USA. So there would be about three, possibly four or more adults and two, possibly four more children. And if there was a party, people would be drunk, and there would be a lot more unpredictability and noise. I was very concerned. My reasons against 21 May won the day; we would do it on the 19th.

In Mrs Alegria's house the preparations were under way. It was necessary to clean and paint. The 'girls' were going to paint the lower parts of the walls, leaving the upper parts and the ceilings to a painter and decorator. There was not much time. I suggested to Mrs Alegria that, since she was going to be short of room, I could arrange to stay at my girlfriend's house. I was sure her parents would agree, as long as we did not sleep in the same room, of course. She was delighted, although I could always stay and join them at the party; I was 'one of the family', she said.

'The only problem,' I told Mrs Alegria, 'is that I have a lot of studying to do. I hope you do not mind me staying up late in the house, possibly with my tutor, my girlfriend's brother. He is very helpful and I am finding it a bit difficult.'

'Oh no! That is not a problem, please ask for anything you need, food or use of the living room, as there is more space there than in your room,' she replied.

'Thank you, Mrs Alegria,' I said.

I started my own cleaning up operation. Slowly I emptied my suitcase and removed my books, leaving only the bare essentials. My aftershave was replaced by Colodion, a kind of transparent glue used by actors to create false scars. This would be used profusely by my 'friend' and me to cover our fingerprints. A complete first aid kit was introduced. Apart from my 'natural' disguise, I would be the only one not wearing make-up.

On the day of the operation there was hardly anything in my room. It was just as well, since I had offered it to Mrs Alegria for her extra guest. The time of the operation was set to start at exactly one o'clock the next morning. I left the house as usual in the morning and later on I phoned Anita at her workplace. We asked about each other and said 'I miss you.'

I walked the streets feeling as if I had everything written on my face and people had just to look at me to know what I was going to do that night. At times I wanted to hide. Time passed very slowly, and I looked back to the beginning, thinking about how long it had taken us to prepare everything, how the idea came about, me living next door, occupying 'enemy' territory as it were, deceiving people. I had grown fond of Maria, sitting on my bed with pad and pencil drawing my face while talking about her aspirations, her dreams. Telling me how privileged I was to have the parents I had and being able to study at university. The imaginary parents of my pretend life. She wanted to be an artist. That reminded me of my mother's dreams of being an artist. 'You can be one if you want to,' I said. 'You just draw; don't stop drawing.' 'But please do not draw my face', I wanted to say. There was a world between us; she was a simple, young woman with a small child, dreaming of a rescuer, a prince charming who would solve all her problems, and she could then be an artist and a mother. She believed that men like me would have a comfortable life ahead assured: I would fall in love with another young university student, with a respectable career at the end of their paid-for studies, getting married, a nice house with a swimming pool in a pleasant neighbourhood and a maid to look after the children and to do the housework.

At the prearranged time and place I met with 'my tutor'; in reality the comrade from the executive committee in charge of the whole operation. He was in his early thirties, very handsome, wearing a sports jacket and a shirt. His black hair was long and wavy; his moustache made him look mature and respectable. We had met briefly only once before.

His show of confidence and enthusiasm surprised me. We walked towards the house talking about things inside. I told him that it was a bit of a mess. They were still painting and I did not believe they were going to finish today. I rapidly went through his role in my adopted life; he laughed enthusiastically and told me that he actually loved maths.

We arrived at the house at about four in the afternoon; I introduced him to Mrs Alegria, Maria, Olga and the children. The women were over the moon. They could not believe that such a handsome young man was in their house at arm's length from them. They did not hide their feelings. They behaved like the members of a fan club in front of their idol. They took turns in coming into the room every five minutes with offerings of fruit juices, tea, coffee, sandwiches and whatever they could think of while we were trying to pretend we were studying, doing complex equations and logarithms, which made me hate maths even more.

Towards the evening, Rafael, for that was his name, told me that in his opinion everything was all right, that I had done a good job, that all the information seemed pretty accurate and so on. He was satisfied, but he thought that it was not a good idea to wait for so long in that little room and, like in a zoo, be scrutinized and harassed by the girls, who at this point were painting the outside walls of my room, on a ladder, trying to have a look at my friend through the window above the door.

'Let's go out,' he said. 'Let's go to the cinema.'

'To the cinema?' I asked in disbelief.

'Yes,' he repeated, 'let's go to the cinema.'

There was an old cinema nearby that was showing a Chilean musical based on a romanticised view of life in the countryside and a young peasant girl who wanted to live in the big city. It was a very bad film, far from the reality of life in the country, but the cinema was packed with working-class people that cheered and sang along with the popular songs. The film irritated me, and I found the experience of being seated in the middle of an enthusiastic working-class crowd a bit overwhelming in the circumstances.

It was already dark when we came out. During the walk back home I harshly criticised the film and its ideology. When I finished, Rafael calmly explained to me that whether the film was good or bad was not important, what was important was that the people in the cinema, the poor people, liked it; they connected with it and that had to be respected. We should ask ourselves why people liked it and what was in it that they liked: the lyrics, the music and the feelings these inspired in them. These were our people, the people we were supposed to lead and whose support we were seeking.

I carried on arguing that, nonetheless, we should criticise its content as a distortion of reality, because that was what people were applauding and connecting with, an illusion, a degrading portrayal of them.

'You have to accept the fact that the people like it, for whatever reason, and if you look at their faces at their moment of jubilation, full of joy and feeling, you cannot avoid the desire to join them. That has to be respected and one has to work with it.'

Rafael was right. How many times during my most miserable days had I felt like these people? It was not surprising that people turned to a different reality in songs and films. But that day I could not take my mind off what was about to happen in a few hours time and my stomach was suffering from cramps.

The girls were delighted when we got back. They were still painting and the painter was also there, up on his ladder. It was seven o'clock in the evening. We went into my room and sat down at the small table, pretending to study. Suddenly, without preamble, Maria and Olga appeared at the doorway with two trays of food and drink. Rafael seemed to be in heaven while I, at the sight and smell of the food, nearly vomited. He smiled and thanked them profusely, saying that we hadn't eaten, while openly flirting with them as well. I wanted to kill him. We were going to frighten them and tie them up in few hours and here he was laughing and flirting as though it was the most natural thing in the world to do.

I could not eat, but Rafael insisted that I had to or they would become suspicious. I looked at him for a long moment trying to figure out whether he was serious or just teasing me while devouring his egg and ham omelette. Time seemed to pass very slowly. Juan and Julio, Mrs Alegria's sons, arrived, going through their routine and then to bed. Maria and Olga stayed up painting and cleaning. Their brother and his family were arriving from the States the following day at midday. I was becoming anxious about the painter, who was still working at eleven o'clock at night. If he carried on until the time we had to let the operatives in we would have to tackle him first, because he was working in view of the front door. He would see that we had opened the door and let the others in and he could alert the family.

When I told Rafael my concerns, he was dismissive, saying that the painter would not be a problem, only that he would have to be controlled first. We were 'studying' furiously and there were quite a few exercises we had to complete before we could call it a day, I explained to Mrs Alegria. I told her that she shouldn't worry as I would put the security bar across the door when I saw my friend out. It was quarter to twelve when the painter finally left and it was too late to be 'studying'; we started to make the noises of winding up and getting ready to leave. We covered the tips of our fingers with the super glue-like fluid to hide our fingerprints.

The time had arrived. We left the room and started the rehearsed and measured walk through the internal patio, into the corridor towards the door, twenty paces. We looked at our watches, it was twelve thirty; we counted: one, two, three, four, five. I opened the door and there they were, like a portrait, three faces with half-smiles and bright eyes full of excitement. They were calm, silent and polite, well dressed in suits and ties.

We shut the door, counted to five again and opened it. Like magic, more faces appeared as though they had been hiding inside a magician's box. We repeated the operation a few times to let all the operatives in and when we finished I turned around to discover that they had already rounded up the lodgers from upstairs and put them in the living room. I could hear the comrades counting their steps and whispering 'door to the left' or 'door to the right, Miss Maria's room, Mrs Olga's room.' And so on.

I was suddenly called to Mrs Alegria's and her son's room; I was needed for the 'act'. 'Ready?' Then the whispering: 'One, two, three.' I discovered that Guajiro was Chief Police Detective Inspector Henriquez with 'Lulu', his Luger machine gun, hanging from his shoulder.

'So, you are a student!' he shouted out loud, for everyone to hear. 'Show me where Juan Alegria's room is,' giving me a firm push in my back.

'It's here,' I said, sounding a bit frightened.

'What is going on?' cried Mrs Alegria from her bed.

Two or three comrades stormed into the room shouting Juan Alegria's name and ordering him to come forward with his hands up. He asked if he could put some clothes on while he was being firmly handed. He put up no resistance while the 'inspector', in a loud voice, exclaimed that a misappropriation of goods belonging to the State had been reported; the suspect was Mr Juan Alegria of this address. The premises had to be searched, by order. Would everybody please cooperate, stay calm and assemble in the living room. Everyone's hands would have to be tied. In the meantime I tried to explain to Mrs Alegria that when I was saying goodbye to my friend at the door, the detectives had arrived in two or three big cars, and they just pushed me in, asking for Juan Alegria; my friend was taken to one of the cars. I looked across the patio and I could see that Julio, the other son, was protesting, and saying that he would not allow himself to be handcuffed. He became argumentative and insolent, so that some comrades had to restrain him on the floor.

I was taken to the living room together with the others. A couple of 'detectives' were there keeping an eye on us. Once everything seemed under control, one of the 'detectives', who was the second-in-command to 'Chief Inspector Henriquez', very calmly, in a low voice began to explain the 'operation' while pacing around offering people chewing gum.

'Don't you worry, this is a routine operation, and nothing is going to happen to anyone. You should not be frightened by Inspector Henriquez's rough manners and ill temper. He is always under stress, but deep down he is a very reasonable man.'

About twenty minutes after the start of the operation, a couple of 'detectives' entered the living room asking in a loud voice for the 'student'.

'Where is the student? Bring the student,' another loud voice shouted from outside.

The 'inspectors' caught me by the arm to take me outside when Mrs Alegria said:

'Leave him alone, he hasn't done anything.'

'You never know what students are up to, madam, there has been a lot of disturbances caused by students in the streets,' the 'Inspector' replied.

As soon as I was outside, the comrades removed the handcuffs telling me that the children were awake, asking what was going on and where their parents were. I asked how everything was and they said that everything was fine and going according to plan. They were already finishing the drilling on the door.

The entire floor of the long corridor was covered in bed sheets and blankets taken from the house's beds. I went to the bedroom where the two kids were sitting on the same bed. They recognised me immediately, asking where their mothers were. I sat on the bed, calming them down. I told them that some friends had arrived and they were all in the living room talking. I told them that I would bring them warm milk in their bottles.

The comrades, who had taken charge of tending the children, could not find the bottles. I went to the kitchen and prepared the children's mixture of milk and baby food and put it to warm in a bain-marie. When I went back to the room a comrade was sitting on the children's bed telling them a story. I gave them their bottles; they were soon back to sleep.

I went out to the patio, past the living room to the corridor where all the activity was taking place. The comrades were entering the store; one of them was deactivating the alarm. There was a lot of excitement. I was informed that the car park across the road had been successfully taken without incident. Rafael was all smiles; he asked me if I thought the time was right to tell the people of the house what we were doing. I looked at the time; it had been just over an hour since we started. Let's wait until the problem of the safe has been solved and we start loading, I said.

My hands were tied again and the 'inspectors' took me back into the living room. The atmosphere was much more relaxed. Mrs Alegria was untied; the medicine for her heart condition had been brought to her. The 'good' detective was chatting and distributing cigarettes to whoever wanted to smoke. To the people who asked too many questions he warned them that it would be in everybody's interest to be quiet and not to know too much.

Time passed slowly; more so when our 'hostages' kept asking for the time. The 'inspectors' kept telling them the wrong time, an hour or so earlier than the real time.

I panicked when I saw one of the inspector's false moustaches falling off without him noticing. Maria and Olga had become more restless and were demanding to go to the toilet and to see their children. I demanded to go to the toilet too.

I was allowed out first. As soon as I was out of the room I hurriedly pointed out my comrades loose moustache. He was truly embarrassed by it and we hoped that nobody else had noticed. I was of the opinion that the situation in the living room could change into a volatile one. Although everyone had their hands tied, apart from Mrs Alegria, the hostages were not terrorised since there was no need to do so. But the way we proceeded was not that of a typical house search by police detectives. The suspect had not been separated from the rest or interrogated, for example. Not everyone would have had their hands tied, certainly not with wire. Mothers would have not been separated from their children. On reflection, it was clear that these were my concerns. I was beginning to feel sorry for the four women and four men of the household. If truth be told, they had been deceived, both by me, whom they trusted and treated as one of the family, and by the operation itself, being falsely accused of theft.

Soon the two mothers' hands were released and they were allowed to go to the toilet and see their children, who were still asleep. People were brought cups of coffee and water. The atmosphere was much more relaxed. Four hours into the operation I went for an assessment tour.

There was good news all round. There was a large quantity of arms of all shapes and sizes that were already being taken out of the store. They were removed in huge sacks through the big hole in the door and then on to cars that were arriving one at a time at the house door. I had been right about the safe: the keys were found in a drawer. There were large quantities of ammunition inside the safe. There were also some documents, licences and a small amount of cash. We decided to reveal ourselves to the people of the house.

Rafael thought I should be the one to address the people of the house with a prepared speech, explaining our motives. This caught me by surprise, as I had always assumed that he would be the person to do that; he was, after all, the leader. It gave me the impression that he was nervous or shy, but then he said that I was the brain of the operation. I had started it and I should finish it.

Rafael and I went together to the living room flanked by 'Inspector Hernandez' and the other 'detectives'. The people had not seen Rafael throughout the operation and now he was standing there next to me.

'Ladies and gentlemen,' I started. 'We belong to the Manuel Rodriguez Revolutionary Movement. We have just entered into the Armeria Italiana next door to expropriate arms necessary for the people's struggle for justice and their rights as human beings. We are Marxists and believe the only way to achieve justice for the poor in today's Chile is by revolutionary action. After considering various alternatives to expropriate the Armeria, we were left with no other alternative than the way it has been done tonight. I would like to apologise to you all and in particular to you Mrs Alegria. I would also like to thank you, Maria and Olga, for your hospitality.'

Maria looked at me as if she wanted to kill me, tears running down her cheeks.

'Now,' I continued, 'I would like to introduce comrade Rafael, who would like to say a few words.'

Rafael expanded a bit more on the reasons behind our action. Then he proceeded to inform them that their telephone line had been cut off as a preventive measure. Money would be left for the repair and reconnection fee. A number of bed sheets and blankets had been used on the floor; money for their replacement would also be left. Two packets of cigarettes found elsewhere in the house had been used; replacement money would be left, together with that to replace the coffee consumed.

The party could afford to do this through its funding by members, sympathisers and the occasional bank 'expropriation'.

The following instructions were to be rigorously followed to avoid casualties. They were not to raise the alarm before seven in the morning. The car park across the road had been taken and our people were watching the front door. Anyone attempting to leave the house before then would be severely punished.

Maria was the first to speak, saying that if we had told them beforehand about what we were trying to do, they would have helped us; we should have trusted them. Rafael told them that it was safer for them this way. Then, as if she could no longer wait, looking directly at me, she asked: 'So, everything you told us about you is untrue?' Sadness enveloped me and, for a brief moment, I wished my pretend life was true. I did not answer; I just shrugged.

Julio, Maria's younger brother pointed out that he was suspicious from the start. The machine gun was a very peculiar one, he said. He had completed military service and had never seen anything like it. It had been agreed that I should be the first person to leave the scene for various security reasons. First, too many people knew me and I knew too much. Second, if anything happened, I should not be linked to the arms or to anybody else involved in the operation. Third, to avoid any connection, it was necessary for me to leave the scene on foot and alone. I would be looked after, from a distance, by comrades covering the area.

Directions to a safe house were given to me there and then by Rafael himself. He told me I should remain in hiding at that place for at least three weeks. An armed comrade would be there in case of an emergency. Should I need to leave the safe house for any particular reason, the armed comrade would accompany me, like a bodyguard, everywhere.

Before leaving the house, I went over every imaginable surface with a cloth and fluid cleaning up possible finger prints. I emptied the room of my last remaining things and placed them in one of the bags to be taken away. Then I went to the children's room, where Maria and Olga had by then been allowed, since the children were now awake. I kissed them goodbye, then I kissed Maria on her forehead and left.

The comrade in charge of the door checked the outside before allowing me out. I stepped on to the street; it was still dark and cold. I walked to the next street where the traffic was one-way, towards the south. A small taxi approached and I signalled it to stop. I got in the back seat and gave the driver directions, but not the full address. Just in case, I thought. After a while, when the taxi driver asked me for further directions I had a shock. I realised that we knew each other. Worse still, we had been colleagues in the transport company that I had worked for a few years before and like me he knew the man in charge of the car park across the road from the Armeria. He also knew Anita, my wife.

A few minutes later, after a thorough inspection in his rear mirror, he switched on the car's internal light and exclaimed:

'Good Lord, is that you, Luis? I almost didn't recognise you. You've changed. What are you doing at this time of the night? It is almost morning.'

I did not know what to say. The picture in my mind was that of him listening to the news on the radio later on or reading a paper and making connections. He knew I was a 'lefty'. I just shrugged, and felt relieved when he said:

'It is not long since you married Anita and you are already cheating on her. You are coming home from screwing another woman!' He laughed. Because he was a womaniser, he assumed that every man was up to something similar.

'You just keep it quiet,' I said. 'You understand.'

'Don't you worry, you can count on me.'

Although I was more than half way from my destination, I asked him to stop, and when he asked if we had already arrived, I said that I did not want to get out in front of my house. He understood immediately. I waved him goodbye, crossed the road and walked for a while. When he was out of sight I hailed another taxi for the rest of my journey. I felt disappointed at this stroke of bad luck when everything else had gone so smoothly.

I arrived in the neighbourhood of the safe house and got out of the taxi two or three blocks before the house itself. The streets were deserted at this time of the night; even the dogs had become tired of barking at the shadows and noises of the night. I paid my fare and started to walk slowly to allow the taxi to disappear before I reached the address I had memorised.

I knocked gently on the door. A good looking middle-aged woman in a dressing gown opened the door. She signalled for me to sit at a small table. A man of about my age entered the room from another door struggling with his trousers. 'We could not sleep for waiting,' said the woman. 'I will not ask what you did or where you came from,' she said. 'Whatever it was you can relax now.' Then she showed me to a small bedroom. The man asked me if I was all right. He would have to leave for work in a couple of hours, he said. He showed me the bathroom and then disappeared. I guessed they were mother and son.

The next day I woke up after midday. For a while I did not know where I was. There was silence in the house, though from outside I could hear dogs barking and children's voices. I ventured out of the room and into the bathroom. I got dressed from a bag I had prepared and had given to comrades a few days before, then went to the living room. There was a man I recognised sitting at the table reading a paper. I did not remember his name but I did know him from somewhere. He stood up and extended his hand to me saying, 'Good afternoon, comrade, how are you? I heard it was an excellent job last night. My name is Antonio and my job is to be your bodyguard for the time being. There is nothing in the morning papers, of course, but here is the afternoon paper; it is on the front page.'

I now recalled Antonio. We had been sent on a propaganda mission together a couple of years before. I had been put in charge of a small cell for an operation which involved the throwing of a noisy device attached to leaflets protesting against a sharp increase in the price of bread, the poor Chilean's main food. He was very impulsive at the time and I had had to restrain him, since he was putting the operation at risk.

A few minutes later, the woman of the house arrived; she had been shopping. She greeted me with a smile. 'It seems that you slept for a long time. I hope you had a restful sleep.' She looked more attractive than the night before. She must have been in her early forties. We sat, and after the woman had left the room Antonio asked me a few details of the operation, and then he explained to me what his instructions were. First, I should stay in this house until we received instructions to the contrary. Second, I could only go out after dark, for a walk, if I so desired, but in his company. Third, I should not use the telephone in the house. Fourth, although the household was safe, and the owners would surely guess my involvement, we should not talk about the operation to them. I said that I agreed with the instructions. Soon after the woman brought some food to the table and we ate.

After the light meal I asked Antonio to do something for me. I instructed him to go out and locate a public telephone that worked in the neighbourhood and that was not too exposed. I needed to make a telephone call before office hours ended that evening. I also needed him to locate a safe place nearby where I could meet someone the next evening but he could still see me. He was intrigued, but agreed to my demands. That evening we went to a phone box a couple of blocks away.

Anita, who was working for a communications company as a telephone and telex operator answered the phone. 'Hello', I said. I could hear her silent cry at the other end.

'It was you! It was you! That's what you have been doing all this time. I heard this morning.' She could hardly speak.

'Listen,' I said, 'I can't stay too long on the phone. I am all right, don't believe the papers. If you want we could meet tomorrow after work.'

'All right,' she said, 'are you coming home?'

'No, Anita, but you can get a bus to this place. Get off the bus and wait at the bus stop. Follow instructions from there. Trust me.'

That evening, the whole family plus Antonio and I ate together. It was then that I met the beautiful eighteen-year-old daughter of the woman and learnt that her father had died. Antonio was behaving like a teenager to impress the girl. Before going to our rooms I asked Antonio if we were contributing our expenses to the household.

'Yes we are. This is a hard-working, modest family.'

'I noticed that,' I said, 'and that is precisely why you should behave with more decorum and restraint towards their daughter.'

It was a weird feeling to read in the papers about what had happened the day before. It was clear that the Alegria family did not raise the alarm until about eight o'clock in the morning, giving us a clearance of over three hours. However, we did keep them in the dark about the time and I remembered putting their clocks and watches back by an hour.

Mrs Alegria's younger son, Julio, gave a fantastic account of the events, in which he was a hero, having 'resisted arrest' fighting his assailants. To their embarrassment, they did not remember my name, or the name I gave them. They only knew me as 'Piero', because I looked 'almost identical to him'. Later they appeared to have remembered my name but gave one completely different to the one I booked in with.

The tabloids, particularly the paper supporting the opposition, called the operation 'Operation Baby's Dummy' on its front page; placing all the emphasis on the fact that we had acted like gentlemen, had fed the babies, provided medicine and had paid for any damage we had caused.

The fact that we had gotten away with hundreds of weapons and large quantities of ammunition seemed not to have impressed the editor.

In contrast, *El Mercurio*, the conservative broadsheet considered 'the authority' of the press, reported the news with 'alarm'. 'But the police are confident that they are following good leads, with information and forensic evidence collected at the scene, including a photofit. All this is contributing to the police confidence that the so-called "Piero", the main culprit, will be arrested within days.'

My instant reaction was to laugh, thinking that they hadn't got a clue, but then my blood froze: what if they did have a good lead? What if they had my fingerprints? What if Maria, who used to draw my face almost every week, had now drawn a masterpiece for the police? What if the taxi driver and ex-colleague of mine made the connection and went to the police? After all, he knew the car park attendant as well as me. It has been reported in the press that 'the subversives' called the attendant by his name suggesting inside information.' I had left the company only a year before. I had boarded his taxi only a few yards from the car park. What if one of the participants in the operation is an informant? What if . . . ? What if . . . ? I decided to leave all those questions suspended in mid-air and allow events to take their own course.

That evening Antonio took me to a very beautiful small square full of trees, bushes and flowers in the middle of a quiet suburb. We sat at a bench in the deserted garden. I gave him Anita's physical description: very light brown hair, taller than the average woman, pale skin, big clear-coloured eyes, one being visibly lighter than the other, a nice, slender figure, oval-shaped face, formally dressed, handbag, medium high-heeled shoes, twenty-five years of age.

Antonio asked me to wait there. I would be safe, since he was sure we had not been followed and he had studied the surroundings earlier on. It was the middle of autumn, but there were still plenty of leaves in the trees and flowers in the gardens. The air was still, the temperature perfect. The houses surrounding the square were all white with nice front gardens and set back a few yards away from the square.

I heard steps from one corner of the square and as I stood up I could see Anita starting to run towards me. She looked beautiful. I hadn't seen her in more than three weeks. We had a long embrace. I held her in the air as she sobbed uncontrollably. While Antonio kept his distance, pacing around the square with a smile on his face, satisfied with his job, Anita and I sat on a bench looking at each other unable to articulate what we had been through. She told me that as soon as she heard the news on the radio before going to work, she knew that it was me who had done it.

'Only you would have thought about the welfare of the children and taken care that their food was warmed up on a bain-marie!' she laughed with tears in her eyes. 'When you rang yesterday I had to run to the toilet, I could not hold my pee. I sobbed in the toilet until my colleagues knocked on the door asking what the matter was. I told them I did not feel well. Let's go home now,' she added. 'I want to be with you now. I miss you so much.'

I explained to her that I really needed to be in hiding for a few more days and that we did not have much time that day either. I do not think she fully understood why we had to be apart. She looked sad when she left, looking back every few paces. My heart ached.

On the fourth or fifth day after the operation Guajiro turned up at the house. There were two other men with him. He looked excited. In front of Antonio and the other two he addressed me formally, which I found a bit embarrassing and out of place.

As if it was a prepared speech he told me: 'Companero, in the name of our organisation and the poor of the country and the cities of our country I came here today to congratulate you for your ingenuity, determination and courage and the successful operation carried out on the 19 May. The executive committee,' he continued, 'has instructed me to salute you and present you with one of the pistols we captured.'

Opening a briefcase, he asked me to choose between three pistols: a nine millimetre Luger that I found too big, an Italian Beretta 7.62, and a Spanish Astra of the same calibre that was too shiny, in my opinion. I chose the Beretta, totally unconvinced of the need for me to have a pistol at all! I explained this to Guajiro who seemed a bit offended by my response and I realised that perhaps this was the only way the organisation could express gratitude and reward its members. The member was supposed to feel proud and thankful, but not me. Nonetheless, I accepted the offer and Guajiro also gave me a little money for transport and other small expenses, promising that the organisation would try to get more support for me in the near future, given my new circumstances.

# Desert 5

My brother Eduardo, who had finished his studies at university, was working on a restoration project in the north of the country, financed by the university. He had graduated in 'public ornament and restoration', which involved sculpture, the history of art, architectural design and basic engineering. The building to be restored was a Spanish church built by conquistadores in the sixteenth century. It was made of a mixture of mud and chalk; the roof was made of a wooden frame covered by a thick mixture of mud and straw.

My brother said that they needed a photographer for their next trip and offered me the post. There was very little money available, so they could not pay me a wage, just something for the photographic materials. They were leaving in few weeks' time, he and two other students travelling separately. As it was convenient for me to 'disappear' for a while, I accepted. There was no way we could pay for our fares so we started to make contact with friends who might know of somebody driving that way. After a week we made contact with a driver who was taking a cargo to Iquique, the second northernmost city in the country, about 1,500 kilometres north of Santiago, on the coast in the Tarapaca Desert. The church was situated in an oasis to the north-east of Iquique, nearly 3,000 metres above sea level and about 150 kilometres inland.

The driver agreed to take us both, my brother and me. The truck was fully loaded, so he did not know how long it would take to get to Iquique. It could be one or two days, maybe more. My brother had already been to Matilla, the oasis, and Pica, which was the name of the next, bigger oasis a couple of kilometres higher up in the mountains. He had been there several times, so he was known to the local community who held him in high regard for having already restored the altar and the bell tower of the Matilla church and the foundations of the larger, all-wood church in Pica.

I was very excited. I had heard a lot about the desert, one of the driest in the world, as well as read a lot about its recent history in the hands of the Chileans. Before the so-called 'Pacific War', Chile was a much shorter piece of land. The northern frontier was with Bolivia not Peru, as it is today. It was wider in the south as it had been in possession of a large chunk of Patagonia. The southern territories, though, were not under the complete control of the central government, since these were occupied by the indigenous population, save for a few fortresses along the coastline.

With the exploitation of vast quantities of nitrate deposits on the surface of most of the desert, mainly by British companies but also by two or three German ones, quite a few ports along the desert's coast were built to ship the nitrate to Europe. Thus the city of Iquique was built almost as a small replica of an English city. There still stands in the middle of the city a huge Big Ben clock tower made of wood. The Victorian houses are also made entirely of wood. There is, obviously, no wood in the desert, but the ships brought plenty of it as ballast to negotiate the strong Humboldt Current. It was Oregon pine. The pavement and even the roads were covered in pinewood.

Various economic interests played a part in the events of 1879, when Chile decided to invade the northern territories belonging to Bolivia and Peru. It seemed that Chile offered better conditions for exploiting the nitrate than Bolivia and Peru, apart from the fact that, for the companies, it was easier to deal with one country rather than two. Also, the Chilean aristocracy was eager to get their hands on the relatively easy money-making business of extracting and exporting nitrates to Europe. Encouraged and armed by the British, the Chilean army embarked on a colossal campaign towards the north. Soldiers were forcibly recruited from the furthest corners of the country, knowing that casualties would be heavy in the dry desert sands.

Not long after the war started, Chile gained several successes and the Bolivian resistance was soon broken. Due to the geography of the area, Bolivia was unable to efficiently govern their Pacific coastal territory. Being mostly desert, miles away from any central kind of government and supply centre, it could not be populated, save for a few isolated villages.

Bolivia sought to ally itself with Peru, claiming that the Chileans would not be content just with the capture of Bolivian territory, but would continue their advance towards Peru. So persuaded, as Chile refused to give any guarantees, Peru joined Bolivia in their war effort against the aggressor. They soon realised that the Chileans were unstoppable, so they tried desperately to persuade Argentina, the big Chilean neighbour over the Andes, that if the Chileans succeeded it would be next.

An ambitious and cunning (in Chilean eyes) Argentinean minister and diplomat called Sarmiento negotiated a non-aggression pact with Chile. Argentina would not ally itself with Peru and Bolivia against Chile, which would have surely sealed Chile's fate. However, Chile would hand over Patagonia to Argentina. Thus, Chile, faced with the worst possible scenario, conceded Patagonia, or a big chunk of it, to Argentina. After all, who wanted that cold wasteland, inaccessible except by sea, especially since the *Mapuches* (Chilean natives) occupied the land from just five hundred kilometres south of Santiago for about one thousand kilometres? Patagonia was indefensible in any case. Nitrate! Nitrate! Nitrate! seemed to be the only objective in the mind of the Chileans at the time.

The Chilean army defeated Bolivia and Peru, its triumphal impulse allowing them to occupy the Peruvian capital Lima for over three years. It is said that the Chilean generals in Lima, drunk in their triumph, had to be persuaded against embarking on an occupying march further north to Ecuador.

Many years ago a Chilean exile found, in the library of a small town in the south of France, a book about the biology of the Pacific coast of South America. He bought the book and was astonished at what he found. The book had been written by a French officer on board a French warship at the time of the Chilean occupation of Lima. The officer was a biologist. Although the Peruvian army had surrendered, and the 'civil' authorities were 'cooperating' with the occupying forces, there was one general who did not surrender and who led a guerrilla war against the occupying forces. The French officer writes that the Chilean generals decided to put an end to the 'rebel's' attacks. Were the rebel general not to surrender his arms, the precious jewel, the pride of Peru, their beloved Cathedral of Lima would be burnt.

The French officer, who had seen the cathedral since his ship was anchored only a few yards from the coast, could not tolerate such barbarity. He persuaded his battleship commanders to point the ship's huge guns towards the Chilean troops camping on the city's main square, sending them a clear message: 'leave the cathedral alone or face our guns.'

Unfortunately, threatening to burn down the cathedral was not the only thing the occupying troops did in Lima. Like any other occupying oppressor, they looted, abused, and raped. Obviously, these facts do not form part of any curricula of the Chilean education system. Only the 'official' version of the events is permitted, whereby Bolivia and Peru decided to conspire together against the less numerous but courageous Chileans. With incredible sacrifices they were able to defeat the desert, Peru and Bolivia.

In fact, so courageous were these generals and their troops that after three years of occupation of Lima and after the signing of the armistice, the 'victorious' armies, instead of going back to their barracks, decided to go straight to the south to massacre the prosperous *Mapuches*, occupy their territory and distribute it among already rich landowners and newly imported European colonisers, mainly from Yugoslavia and Germany. The *Mapuches*, who were the main exporters of wheat and dried meat, were forced deeper into the Andes, towards the most inhospitable areas. They are still being imprisoned and killed today for attempting to recover a fraction of their stolen territory.

It took us four days to reach our destination. Soon after we left Santiago, it became apparent that the lorry was overloaded. It was a fairly new vehicle, no more than two years old, but designed only to carry a six-ton load, it found it difficult to cope with eight. The journey became painfully slow. But the driver was not in a hurry. He was a young man, full of himself, with the fantasies of a mid-western cowboy. Apart from a few other goods, the cargo consisted of big sacks of peanuts. As I was not in a hurry either, I set out to enjoy the journey as much as I could.

It was like a journey to another planet and sometimes we were left wondering how people could exist in such places with so little to live on in such a barren environment. The desert and its mountains were a powerful sight, the vastness of space. When one reaches the desert proper, the Atacama Desert, there is nothing, not a plant, not an insect, not a bird, not a breeze, not a cloud, not a living thing. This deadness is both frightening and fascinating at the same time. It attracts you like light attracts a moth.

One mid-afternoon, while we were rolling along on the worn tarmac in the middle of nowhere, I looked out of the window unable to believe my eyes. Very far away, travelling parallel to us was what looked like a toy steam engine cut out from the horizon. At first it did not seem to be moving but after a while I detected some motion. I told my brother and the driver, who were engaged in animated conversation, to make sure I was not seeing things.

They both agreed that it had to be a small English steam engine, of narrow track, serving some of the several mines hidden behind the high plateau; they carried on their conversation. I interrupted to tell them I had the impression that the train was getting nearer to us. Again, they looked, but it failed to make enough of an impression on them to deserve a comment.

I was fascinated by the little train on top of the Atacama Desert. With my head resting on my arms on the cabin's window sill, the warm breeze rustling my hair, I watched it. Sometimes it came a little closer to us only to distance itself again, making itself smaller still. But then, after probably forty-five minutes of keeping pace with us, the train started to suddenly grow in size. It was definitely coming closer to us. I could not see any rail track. In the shimmering heat the train seemed to be moving over water at times and floating in the air at others.

It was impossible to predict where the train was going in the vast, flat emptiness. It could go anywhere it wanted to go, floating above the sand, but it decided to come closer to us until I could see the outline of the driver in the cabin. The engine was a rusty colour and covered in dust. It looked like a ghost train. The small trucks it was pulling were all flat platforms on wheels. When the train was about three hundred metres from the lorry it managed to attract my brother and the driver's attention. The train and the lorry where travelling at the same speed, parallel to each other like two friends walking together, seemingly purposelessly since there was nowhere to go in the lunar landscape.

Suddenly the train whistled; I waved to the driver who had awakened me from my ghostly dream. My brother and the driver seemed to have awakened too, shouting greetings to the train driver. The train continued whistling. Poor train driver, we thought, maybe he doesn't see a soul in these parts for days. We waved. But then the engine made a slow turn to the left, towards us. It was then that it occured to me that the train track crossed the road at some point ahead of us. 'No,' said our driver. 'If that was the case, there would be a sign or something.' That was true, there were no signs anywhere, but the train, in its big loop, was definitely going to cross our path. After ten minutes or so, the train was in a diagonal position, the nose of the engine pointing towards a point in front of us that looked frightenly like our path. We were on a collision course. The train whistled again, and now we realised that, all along, the train driver had been trying to warn us rather than greet us.

Our driver was now desperately trying to calculate distance and speed to assess who was going to pass over the junction first: us or the train. He turned his head in rapid movements, first right, then ahead of him. The train tracks were now visible as was a sign reading 'BEWARE OF THE TRAIN!' in the middle of the road. There was no time to stop the lorry. Due to the length of the train, we would hit the trucks. The train was not stopping either; the train driver must have calculated too that he had no time to stop. Our driver decided to accelerate, only to change his mind seconds later, then accelerate again; he was worried, looking frantic, changing gears, without really being able to change the whole situation; a drastic avoiding manoeuvre would certainly overturn the lorry.

My brother and I looked at each other in disbelief. Here we were, in the middle of this huge emptiness, the only humans for hundred of miles around, with nothing between us and the horizon but still locked on a seemingly unavoidable collision course. We three in the cabin of a modern machine set to collide with a ghost locomotive from nearly a hundred years before. The stuff of nightmares had come to get us in the end. He, the ghost driver, fastened onto an objective that appeared to have been chosen by an evil mind. There was no reason for this happening; everybody could see everybody else; there was nowhere to hide. We knew of each other's presence nearly an hour before. The only certainty was the rails of the train, the rest was all vague, relative, an illusion even, a mirage. Anything can be a road: courses and speeds could have been altered.

But it was clear now; we all trusted the desert, the nothingness. If there is nothing, nothing can happen. Of course we were wrong and our ignorance brought us to this deadly point. There are no referents in the Atacama Desert, therefore, time and distances are difficult values to estimate unless you have lived in it.

My instincts were now making me consider opening the door and jumping from the truck in the hope that my brother would follow me; the driver I hoped would do the same. His foot was flat on the accelerator, the engine struggling. At least now our equation speed–distance seemed to be right: the lorry's cabin would pass but whether the rest of the truck would survive was less than certain. The lorry kept slowly gathering speed; only the tail would be hit. Then silence, not a sound, the engine of the lorry seemed to have stopped; we were moving forward, but it was as though we were floating.

We missed, possibly by an inch or two. We looked at each other in silence and remained so for a long time. Mysterious things might happen in these places; we had better be alert. A few kilometres away from our encounter with the ghost train we stopped to relax. Switching off the engine stopped the source of noise, giving us the sensation of having lost our hearing. We stepped off the lorry to find that we could not hear anything apart from the strong beat of our hearts, the air going in and out of our lungs, the clicking of our bones when we moved and the rustling of our clothes. The lorry was a different phenomenon altogether: it gave the impression of dismantling itself. One could hear, very loudly, the clicks and clacks of the metals readjusting themselves to the new situation of stillness and temperature change. There were no other noises whatsoever.

I walked about two hundred metres away from the deserted road where the full impact of the immensity of nothingness hit me. The absence of noise brought me immediately inside myself; it was just me and the infinite space with the sun above as a silent powerful witness, and a reminder that there, with nothing between him and me, I did not stand a chance. I turned a rock and under it there was a rust-coloured powder.

'Do you realise that you are the first thing that has turned that rock over in probably millions of years?' my brother said. 'You see, all this used to be the seabed of an ancient ocean, you can still find seashells here and there; there has been nobody and no reason for anything to move that rock.'

These words my brother spoke in a very quiet voice. Even 50 metres away from me I could hear him as if he was whispering in my ear. There was nothing to interfere with the sound waves leaving his lips and again I felt overawed by the sheer magnitude of the place, of being a guest on the planet who had no right to disturb the million-year-old processes. Grand Uncle Juan 'the Old' came to my mind. He was one of grandma's brothers who came to see us every summer. He would arrive unannounced one sunny day; nobody knew how he arrived, loaded with bags and square baskets full of lovely things from the country. In the bags there would be walnuts, almonds, dried fruits, big lumps of raw sugar, roasted flour, an assortment of cheeses and dried meat. In the square basket there would be live chicks he would set free, like a bright yellow spillage of fluff in the garden for us to chase and take care of.

Uncle Juan would then lie on the sofa with a glass of lemonade and start to tell the stories of his travels in the north searching for gold. He had been everywhere in the desert's mountains and caves, digging for gold. He had seen the nothingness and had lived in it. His face told you, with the skin cured by the sun. Uncle Juan 'the Old' had no age; he could have been in his thirties, forties, fifties or even seventies. He had lost his age walking up and down the long and narrow strip of land squeezed between the Andes and the sea, looking, I believe, looking for something more than just gold.

He never married, had no children, and he was very lean and not very tall, always wearing a sombrero, dark trousers, a white shirt and a black jacket. There was always a white silk scarf around his neck. Although he was an affable man, his face would remain serious most of the time and gave me the impression of being in another world, of never actually arriving and desperate to leave after two or three days. Where to? According to grandma he had no home and no family apart from some cousins in the south, from where he brought the full bags.

He did make a living from the few grains of gold he managed to extract from the mountains, which contained more significant amounts of copper, iron and silver than gold. He was looking for the big mine of gold, said grandma, because he had been following a rumour since he was a young man: miners' stories, full of fantasies and secret mythology. He could read the secrets of the desert's mountains, or sometimes the mountains would tell him their secrets. It was all a matter of knowing how to listen, silent and patient. 'I believe the sun has got into his head,' grandma said. After two or three days spent in our house talking almost solely with his two sisters, drinking maté and eating very little, Uncle Juan, 'the Old', would leave as quietly as he arrived, reminding us to look after the chicks.

One day Uncle Juan 'the Old' never returned. Nobody knows what happened to him. No letter announced his death. No official came to knock to give anyone the bad news. He simply vanished. Slowly the years went by until he was no longer missed by anyone. Only now, standing in the middle of the driest, most lonely desert in the world, I wished Uncle Juan 'the Old' had told me his dream and his secrets, because I was beginning to understand his fascination, his bewitchment with the place.

Standing there in the middle of that vast empty immensity something strange seems to happen to you. It is like being back in the womb. All you hear are body sounds and nothing else. It is just you and the intense, blue, limitless sky; you, the barren landscape, and the heat, without a shadow, with nowhere to hide. You need a good sombrero here, like the one Uncle Juan 'the Old' used to wear. Where is his soul now? I asked myself. And his bones? Somewhere out there, inside the mountains, murmuring their secrets in indefinable words that would be carried not by the wind, but by the ones who knew how to listen and decipher the mountains' language. Like the singing of the sirens, the mountains luring the miners to succumb to their depths. The ones like Uncle Juan 'the Old' don't lose their lives in this desert; they give their lives to it.

Our lorry driver was a stubborn man. He said that in a previous journey similar to this he had not enough fuel to reach the port of Antofagasta from the last fuel station. It was, therefore, necessary to drive about 20 kilometres inland from the main road to a remote mining post, one of the few still extracting and processing nitrates, to ask for gasoline. This he did one evening despite our advice, based on careful calculations, that the journey to and back from the mine would use all the extra fuel he would get. In fact he used slightly *more* fuel in the process. Towards sunset the driver announced that there was not enough fuel to reach Antofagasta anyway. But he knew a trick: the last 150 kilometres or so before Antofagasta were all downhill.

'We will switch the engine off and "glide" down to the port. We will need no petrol for the last 150 kilometres.'

I looked at my brother as if to say, 'This guy has lost his senses'. The desert really drives people mad. It was already dark when we reached the highest point at El Paso de el Agua (not that there was any water there). The driver put the lorry in neutral and switched off the engine. The relative silence that surrounded us made the situation more frightening while the overloaded truck started to gather speed.

We started to speculate on the curvature of the earth and other reasons to explain the fact that we were dropping like a stone in the middle of the desert night into what appeared to be a huge black hole.

It wasn't long before the lorry started to vibrate furiously with the driver clearly struggling to keep control of the steering and the road being extremely difficult to make out in the gloom. Also, the truck was one of those typical American ones with the engine in front of the cabin and since it was about two tons overloaded it was a lot lighter at the front. This imbalance made it unstable at high speeds and it gathered a worrying sideways wobble. I was not worried about the vehicle coming off the road, we probably would not notice anyway since we were travelling through a vast plain; it looked as if the road could be anywhere. During the day I had noticed wheel marks leaving the road every now and then so this was not an uncommon occurrence.

A luminous dot appeared somewhere on the pitch-black windscreen. A vehicle was travelling in the opposite direction no doubt on a collision course with us. This was more like being in space. We were surrounded by stars under one of the clearest skies in the world. They spread like a dome over us, with nothing in the way, the stars everywhere. The road was hardly visible, jet black in contrast to the sparkling sky. The luminous dot in front of us got bigger and bigger, the driver's eyes fixed on it, his brain desperately making calculations. Suddenly it became apparent that we were going too fast to pass safely. At that moment it was impossible to ascertain which side of the road the dot was on but it looked to be directly in front us. A few minutes later two headlights were clearly distinguishable. There was no doubt now that it was necessary to reduce the lorry's speed to bring the wobble and the zigzag under control, if we were not to collide with the oncoming vehicle.

It was then, when the driver tried to apply the brakes and get into gear, that he realised he could not do either with the engine switched off. He tried to switch it back on but his attempts resulted only in a terrible noise and panic ensued, with the driver swearing, his hands glued to the steering wheel making continuous short movements to left and right to give the sense that he was in control. It seemed that whatever he did made no difference.

Again, a feeling of absurdity overtook me. With such an empty space, no trees, no buildings, no lampposts, no plants, no large rocks, no people, no nothing, still we seemed to be unable to depart from our course, attracted like magnets to each other on a destructive path. As if trapped in an invisible tunnel our fates were already decided.

In a second we understood everything: the light was another lorry, it was on the other side of the road but we were too close and too fast. There was just time for a little adjustment, a little pull to the right of the steering wheel and the hope that that would be enough. Too little and we would collide; too much and we would veer off the road and surely turn over. We skimmed past, the sound of our tyres on the edge of the road impossibly loud. I caught a glimpse of the white, frightened face of the other driver, a mirror of my own. Then we were alone again, with nothing in sight but the stars.

After this second narrow escape we arrived in Antofagasta at midnight, parked on the beach and settled to sleep once more on the sacks of peanuts. It was 1969. Two Americans had just landed on the moon. I was wondering what kind of view of the stars they might have from there and thinking that their journey seemed to have been less hazardous than ours on earth.

After four weeks with my brother and the two other students in the Oasis of Matilla and Pica, I went back to Santiago on my own in another lorry. All I'll say about that nightmarish journey is that the driver said he could not afford to stop for a break, so during the night myself and another woman passenger looked at each other with horror each time he fell asleep at the wheel. On discovering this a few seconds after, he would slap his face hard to wake himself up. Well into the night we persuaded him to stop and he slept for about half an hour. And so to Santiago.

# Stalking the CIA

6

I went back to work with my cell of students: two girls from sociology, two from dentistry and a boy studying medicine. Another cell was composed of workers liaising with the unions in the factories. There was another cell I was working with whose members were a university lecturer, a girl studying economics and two factory workers in a shanty-town of homeless families.

I kept my fellow Party members guessing about my involvement in the Armeria Italiana affair although it was not difficult to deduce that I had played a significant role in it. I was genuinely surprised, though, to find that they looked at me with admiration and a degree of envy. At the time I honestly believed that what I had done was nothing to be proud of.

The Party was divided as to whether we should participate in the electoral process. In the end I think we were taken over by events, particularly the enthusiasm of the people and their decision to fully participate in the process and their determination to elect Allende as president. A few days before polling day the Party therefore decided to take part and gave the order to its members to vote for Allende. A group of us were going to vote anyway.

It was the first time I had exercised my right to vote. It was an emotional moment, especially since we were very pessimistic about whether Allende would be allowed to take office even if he won the election. The night of 4 September 1970 was a night of carnival in the streets of Santiago, a carnival of the people – the modest workers, forever exploited, at last had something to celebrate.

Soon after the election, our leaders decided to hold the first congress, which also turned out to be the last. There were two main arguments presented to the assembly. On the one hand, there was the official proposal to continue with the current organisation while negotiating its alignment with the Socialist Party. The opposing argument proposed the integration of the Party with the organisation it had split from two years earlier, the MIR. Although I had been supporting the second proposal I was surprised by the high standard of argument and discussion. The most sophisticated speakers were graduates from the school of economics whose comprehensive analysis concluded that the revolutionary movements should work alongside the Popular Government without joining it, as proposed by President Allende. They should remain independent, playing the role of its critical conscience. This was the same policy as the one adopted by the MIR, so it became obvious to some of us that we should rejoin them. There was no sense in remaining an independent organisation in the present circumstances.

However, Rafael, the comrade in charge of the Armeria Italiana operation, and by now the General Secretary of the Party, was vigorously opposed to this idea. A philosophy graduate, he made a passionate speech about the revolutionary tradition of the Socialist Party and its roots in the miners' movement at the beginning of the century. Our proposal, he stated, was, in effect, advocating the annihilation of our glorious organisation. His discourse was, of course, more passionate than political, but achieved quite an effect. The majority of the assembly shouted 'Treason!' and demanded that we openly admit that what we were proposing was the 'disappearance' of our organisation and an amalgamation with the MIR without condition. It was left to me, on behalf of my camp, to answer their questions. I rounded up our argument, stating that in the end it was the people, the working class, the peasants and the poor of the country and cities who were deciding our destiny. That required modesty on our part and we should put ourselves at their service. Furthermore, I declared, our stand was making it difficult for us to even discuss whether or not to join the forces of the process created by the ballot vote. I ended up by proposing that the assembly approve the closure of the congress and the dissolution of the organisation that was no longer serving the purpose for which it was created. To the cries of 'Traitors!' we left the room, followed by a considerable number of comrades.

Rafael came after me. 'We could negotiate better conditions in joining the MIR,' he suggested.

'I have no other ambition than to serve my people the best I can and according to my beliefs; I have got nothing else to negotiate,' I told him. And therefore we rejoined the MIR.

We would meet some of those who had advocated the minority position seven years later, in Paris, at a conference of the MIR; again, even without having had contact for so many years, we found ourselves agreeing the same position and, again, we were in a minority.

They had had the time and the resources, having been in exile for many years and with three of them studying at the Sorbonne, to prepare their argument. This time, though, they were only allowed to put their political analysis and position in writing. Party policy withdrew the right to speak and vote at the conference from all of those who had sought asylum and 'abandoned the people to their fate in their most desperate moments'.

Although that was true, and I did not agree with running away from the battle, I did not condemn them for having done so; after all I was glad they were alive. One of them, Carlos, later became finance minister in the first democratic government after Pinochet. He now holds a seat in the Senate. As it turned out, I therefore became their voice at the conference. Most of the changes that we envisaged at that time would become reality years later.

Against my wishes, Anita became pregnant. She probably thought it was safe to bring a child into this new world that had been blessed with the popular movement. Our daughter Dalia was born on the 13 July 1971 and I was besotted with her. Sadly, though, Anita and I quickly grew apart. The last straw was when she found a box of TNT that I had hidden under the bed sometime before. Eventually we initiated legal proceedings to separate (divorce did not exist in Chile until 2004). I later learned, however, that our marriage had never been annulled as our lawyer had been murdered by the military during the coup.

Soon after re-joining the MIR I was asked to give up the work I had been doing and pass on my contacts with the unions, factory workers, homeless, small landowners and peasants fighting for their rights and better living conditions. It was sad to say goodbye to the old way of working which was, in my case, quite personal, with the people involved becoming like a part of my family. The 'new' way was more impersonal,

Me and my daughter Dalia by Anita, aged three, photographed by Diana.

as the people in charge were constantly changing. This was due to the fact that the organisation was growing at an unprecedented rate and members with some experience in working with the people were very few.

When my background became known to the leaders of the Party, they thought it would be advantageous for me to be a member of the newly created intelligence and counter-intelligence section. The training we received was very basic, relying mainly on old CIA and Cuban G2 training manuals. The rest of our information was gleaned from classic novels based on first-hand Second World War experiences. I already knew the basic rules and techniques of surveillance and how to avoid being tailed.

In the Chilean case, the main targets would be the natural enemies of the new Popular Government who had already revealed their intentions even before Allende took office. Internally they were the Chilean extreme right and their paramilitary wings, the conservative party and the armed forces. Externally they were the American CIA and the armed forces of other South American countries, particularly Argentina and Brazil. The CIA could make use of all of the above, so this was just for starters.

We knew that the CIA would adopt one of its classical tactics in these cases. Chile was classified as enemy territory; therefore their base would not be established there but in a neighbouring 'friendly' territory. At the time, Argentina was the ideal place, with its long border with Chile. In case of an emergency, the base could be easily moved to Uruguay or Paraguay. Peru and Bolivia were not considered suitable due to the long distances separating their main urban centres from Santiago and their lack of infrastructure.

Once the base was established, the work on the ground would be allocated to a 'commander'. This was basically a secret agent, with multiple skills, unlimited resources as his disposal, and a 'licence to kill'. He would not do all the work himself, like in the films, but would create networks of people and infiltrate organisations, institutions and enterprises that would do the work for him. He (it is almost invariably a man) would coordinate operatives, train them and allocate resources. Once established, he would be able to carry out any job required of him.

It was not long before our Party managed to infiltrate the most prominent of the Chilean extreme right organisations, Patria y Libertad (Motherland and Freedom) and its associated Frente Nacional (National Front). It was thanks to this infiltration, which reached their highest ranks, that we managed to obtain the scant details that would lead us to the American agent in Chile, who we called 'Mr X'.

Although Mr X was trying to control all the anti-Allende activity in Chile, there were groups and sections that acted on their own, nationally and internationally. Thus it was necessary to monitor the extreme right in their overseas activities, which revealed the extent of the cooperation they were getting from extreme right and associated economic interests the world over, from South Africa to Israel, the British government at the time, the Italian Logia, the Freemasons, and the German extreme right. The Americans, of course, with Kissinger at their head, deserve a complete chapter.

As can be imagined, our task was enormous. Our resources, on the other hand, were Lilliputian and artisan. Our first 'missions' were to track the movements of certain individuals (invariably members of the upper class, living in beautiful villas in rich neighbourhoods) who were coordinating the smuggling of large quantities of arms from Argentina, especially machine guns, grenades and explosives. These 'missions' were followed by monitoring conspirators within the armed forces, whose generals had already revealed their ambition to be the rulers of the country, but had no popular support. We knew of their movements thanks to information gathered by more democratic members of the armed forces, who sympathised with Allende.

All the information about Mr X that our informants could manage was 'look for a red Camaro on the Costanera Road'. The Costanera is a wide, six-lane avenue travelling west–east through the capital, bringing the heavy morning traffic from the rich neighbourhoods of the east to the city centre and further west following the Mapocho river. In the evening rush hour the traffic direction changes to west–east as people make their way home. 'Be extremely careful, we were told, the driver is a very clever and dangerous person.' We were asked to find out everything about him.

Maria Cristina, a beautiful, young and extremely intelligent university student and I were assigned responsibility for the job. We could count on four other comrades but we had no cars in which to follow the Camaro. So our plan of action had to be very primitive: we would have to play 'spot the car'. This, we thought, might not be difficult since there must have been no more than a handful of Camaros in Santiago at the time. Probably all of them were red. The problem was the speed and density of the traffic in the rush hours.

We decided to start with the eastbound evening traffic, travelling back home, assuming that any driver would be too tired at that time of day to pay much attention to his surroundings. We chose a spot in a park beside the avenue, sitting inconspicuously on the grass among the trees, almost at the beginning of the avenue's west end. We thought that a couple of hours would be long enough.

In the first four days no cars of that description were spotted. We found it very difficult to distinguish makes and models, besides which nobody had seen a Camaro before. I had some idea of the car's shape which I tried to communicate to the other comrades. On the fifth day, we struck lucky. I spotted the car. I was able to see that the number plate was an ordinary one, not an American or diplomatic one, though due to the speed of the car I could not actually get the registration number. I was full of excitement and duly recorded the time.

The next day, we placed ourselves further up the avenue. The car was spotted again and this time the number plate was recorded and a vague description taken of the man inside. The driver was blond, with short hair, in his late twenties or early thirties. We continued our surveillance in this manner, using other comrades two or three at a time further along the avenue, until the Camaro was seen turning right one day. I went with Maria Cristina one midday to the point where, we were told, the car had turned right. We studied the likely next route of the car and possible safe points of observation. The road was a short one leading to the main Providencia Avenue. It was easy to conclude that this road was not his destination, as there was too much traffic and it was too exposed. Providencia itself was too busy, too crowded and too exposed as well, for he would have had to have a couple of aerials for CB and FM radio communication; no, not Providencia. Where then? It was anyone's guess. We chose a nearby bus stop as a point of observation just to confirm which direction the Camaro took at Providencia. Different people would observe from there, just in case.

It took three days and four more stakeouts to find Mr X's house in a leafy street of large detached mansions. Maria and I found the car one late evening, parked in the front garden of one of the houses. This time I had managed to borrow a car; the street was deserted as we drove slowly down it, trying to remember as much as we could of the scene. It felt sinister to us. The car, the house, the street, the whole thing gave off a feeling of arrogance, a completely different country to the one we were used to.

Our next task was to find out where he went in the morning. Perhaps he ran some bogus company that provided cover for his centre of operations. We would wait at the point where we had started the week before. From there it was possible to see, this time looking west, the vehicles taking lanes to different parts of the city.

With Maria Cristina's arm in mine, we pretended to be a young couple on their way to work as we watched the morning traffic. Sure enough, the Camaro took the left lane, to the near part of the city. On an impulse

Maria pulled my hand in hers as she ran; the car had got stuck, first at a traffic light and then in a jam. Our circle around Mr X was closing.

In the meantime, two female comrades had been finding out about Mr X's family. A few days later the report came back. The two comrades had dressed up as nuns and visited the neighbourhood, knocking on doors asking for charitable contributions for a children's home.

'Mr X's wife is very helpful. She is in her twenties, blonde hair, slim, about five foot, nine inches tall. They have two small children and come from Washington. Their names are . . . The husband appears to be a businessman; he works in the city centre. Further observations: they live on their own and have no maid – as is the usual custom for a family of their status. There is no visible equipment in the house, or antennae on the roof or garden. The wife tries to meet with other Americans, mainly from the embassy. She doesn't go out very much, apart from doing the shopping. The house is privately rented. Nothing interesting came from a visit to one of the toilets upstairs. We believe we were very convincing and the visit will not cause any suspicion.'

Eventually, after discreetly following him, Mr X led us to a central building where the Peruvian embassy was situated. We needed to find out whether he was using the Peruvian embassy as his base or another office in the same building. His home was definitely not being used for his work. The Peruvian embassy building turned out to be a very difficult place to observe without being seen. Maria Cristina and I eventually stopped our direct involvement with the surveillance of Mr X in his 'red bird', as the Camaro had become known to us.

Surveillance was often difficult and a great deal had to be learned. One time I was delegated to follow another suspected undercover agent but I wasn't careful enough. He ended up chasing me through the streets of Santiago: me in my 2CV and he firing his revolver at me through the window of his Ford Mustang. Only my local knowledge of the streets and sheer adrenalin enabled me to lose him in the chase. That and stopping briefly to let my comrades out to give my 2CV more speed!

Eventually, we discovered that, in just under a year, Mr X had developed an extensive network. He had a group of saboteurs who could become active in a few months, bombing bridges and electricity pylons. He had also been advising the right-wing agricultural society, big landowners and producers who had already begun their sabotage of production, creating shortages of produce and an atmosphere of chaos in the country. He gave advice and provided financial support. The government responded by accelerating and extending the land reform to maintain minimum levels of production; the landowners responded with paramilitary activity and the burning of crops. A group of well-known right-wing journalists were also added to Mr X's payroll and their articles became more arrogant, more daring and more vicious in their attacks on the government.

However, the Chilean army generals were in no need of further encouragement. They had been 'educated' and fully trained in American institutions, and were just waiting for their 'master's command'. But seeing no sense in so much 'education', training and preparation, and not being able to test it for so long, a few became restless before time and made a shambolic and ultimately unsuccessful attempt to seize power. Some of them were undoubtedly on the CIA's payroll.

An interesting fact concerning Allende's Popular Government, and of which not much is known about, is the magnitude of the international collaboration gathered together to destroy it. It is almost incredible that such a small country, lost at the bottom of the world, far away from everybody else, with no significance for the world's economy, became the target of a concerted effort by so many powerful nations to prevent a socialist revolution from succeeding. Such a concerted effort to assassinate a dream. The pressure on the Popular Government was intense and inevitably led to a political and military crisis.

# Chaos

7

2.30 p.m., September 11, 1973

After making my way through the city, I arrived at the safe house in the western suburbs; the curfew was going to be imposed from three o'clock. There were four other comrades there: Lautaro, who smoked a pipe with an air of an English gentleman, along with James, Jote and Claudio, who, years before, had accidentally been shot with a short calibre bullet in the head. Although he fully recovered, the bullet could not be removed and he lost quite a bit of inhibition. We were confused, feeling frustrated and powerless. I had heard nothing from Diana. We sat down to drink coffee, smoke and watch television. Between the programmes, the new official communiqués were read by a faceless voice.

'The glorious Chilean Armed Forces, in an attempt to save the country from chaos, have today taken control of the country. Salvador Allende refused to surrender, put up resistance in the presidential palace and died. Citizens should show restraint and go back to their homes to await further communiqués. Workers of essential services and utilities should remain in their posts until further notice. Anyone found to be committing acts of sabotage or resisting the armed forces will be executed.'

We could not sleep that night. There were helicopters hovering overhead and shooting throughout the night. Road patrol vehicles and armoured personnel carriers were shooting people indiscriminately. On the second day the telephone, which had been out of order, rang. Claudio answered the phone. In a few moments his face had turned grey. 'It was a man. He said that he is an air force officer and that he knows we are hiding here. He lives across the road and has been watching us. He will give us four hours to leave the house or he will report us to the military.' We were astonished. We felt even more defeated. We had to abandon the house. It was still early in the morning when, one by one, we left the house.

There were bodies lying in the streets. There were open municipal lorries collecting the corpses and piling them up on the back of the trucks for everyone to see. It was unbelievable. It was macabre. A few days before, everything had looked so normal. There were children playing in the streets, but they were now deserted apart from the armoured personnel carriers, the municipal trucks and a few furtive pedestrians. And it felt cold, very cold.

I had to move fast. There was not much time. Although the curfew was at three in the afternoon the streets were not the safest place to be. I made a couple of phone calls and I secured a place in another safe house posing as the boyfriend of a comrade, who was the eldest daughter of the family; but you never knew who the neighbours were. There was nothing to do but wait. Wait for instructions. Wait until the killings stopped. Wait until you knew that this time it was not the neighbour's house they were knocking on, helicopter hovering above, but the one you were in, and the uncertainty, for you, would stop.

It was the fourth day since the coup and there was still no news from Diana. Where was she? How was she? Was she alive or in prison? What was she doing? Nobody was going to work. The junta's instruction to the population was to stay at home. Businesses were all closed unless related to the distribution and acquisition of food supplies. Only workers of the essential services were allowed to return to their workplaces. The junta had also broadcast a long list of names of people who were requested by the authorities to present themselves to the Ministry of Defence buildings in central Santiago. They were all public figures. Allende's government ministers, heads of departments, Party leaders, union leaders, media people, prominent public figures, journalists, academics, etc. The revenge had started. Unbelievably, many people did give themselves up; their fates would shock the international community a few months later.

The situation at the safe house started to turn sour. Too many days and nights in constant tension started to take its toll on everybody. There were two searches in nearby houses. In one of them the military shot a man dead. My host family were giving me the unspoken message that my staying there posed a risk for them. Tension started to build up and the neighbours grew increasingly suspicious of my presence there. Time to move. I decided to go back to my own house since it was not far away.

I arrived mid-morning. Everything was as we had left it. I was apprehensive because the landlord, who lived with his family in the front part of the house, was right wing and his son belonged to the Frente Nacional. I lay down on the bed and fell asleep, reflecting on the episodes of the last few days and how they had changed my life completely, and what the prospects for the future were.

Steps outside woke me up. It was Diana. We embraced and wept for a long time. We looked at each other in disbelief, hardly believing that we were both still alive. We talked very fast, trying to catch up with each others' lives since we had separated days before. She had been in the shantytowns of the east of Santiago, talking with the people, gathering information, giving some comfort. The repression had been ferocious in that poor area of the city and there were some pockets of resistance that had been quickly and viciously dealt with by the army. People had been executed on the spot.

It was too dangerous for us to stay in our house. Arrangements had to be made for us to move elsewhere. This we did a few weeks later, moving to a small flat in a building in the old part of Santiago. I liked the old fashioned building, which had a small square in front of it that must have been part of the Cousino Palace. The Cousino Palace was a huge, old, colonial manor house in the centre of Santiago. It was built of mud by the Cousino family, one of the most powerful landowners at the time. Towards the Andes lay the other, bigger palace where I had collected figs and blackberries as a child. It was still surrounded by beautiful gardens and vineyards and produced and exported good wine.

The road was very short, and the neighbours kept to themselves. The flat had no external windows, but opened onto an internal courtyard, with an enclosed corridor with red tiles. This is typical of colonial Spanish architecture. I often felt a bit uneasy and pursued my habit of trying to find a possible escape route from everywhere I went. In this case, the only way to escape other than through the main door would have been by climbing one of the tall internal walls on to the roof. So I decided to make a ladder disguised as a few discarded household objects. An advantage of the location of this was that it was within walking distance of the centre of the city. We lived there until the landlord was detained in April 1974. Hastily we moved to another rented house in a middle-class neighbourhood called la Reina. Happy in our anonymity we stayed there until the autumn. In October Diana told me she was pregnant but in November events beyond our control changed our lives for ever.

# Maria Cristina

8

Somebody once told me that Maria Cristina was the most beautiful woman in the Party. I knew it was an exaggeration. Yes she was pretty, but that wasn't what impressed me most about her and, to tell the truth, the first time we met, she did not impress me at all. It was soon after Allende had been elected president in September 1970, we were at a workshop for Party members. There were about twenty people, of whom only five were women, and among them was Maria Cristina. Of course she attracted most of the attention of the men in the workshop and she was enjoying it, giggling like a little girl. I have to admit that I did not like this. We were supposed to be serious revolutionaries and I thought that we should behave accordingly and not get distracted by childish behaviour; or was I jealous that she didn't smile at me or give me any attention? It was possible, although at the time I was a bit of a 'purist', not inclined to mix revolutionary work with pleasure.

I met Maria Cristina again about two months later at another training session, but this time there were only four men and five women. Still we did not acknowledge each other; our eyes seldom met and we certainly did not smile at each other. When we left the place, the group walking together down the street, she made a comment about me walking too slowly for the others and they all laughed. I noticed this, and I made a comment about the way she giggled and, again, everybody laughed. But she did not laugh; instead she looked at me with hate in her eyes and complained that the comment was unfair. I was surprised to see that she was so furious, and she repeated that I had been unfair and vicious in my comment. I pointed out that I could see that the comrade liked to have

Maria Cristina: comrade and friend.

fun at other people's expense, but if anyone attempted to reciprocate, then that person was unfair and vicious.

I was already working in the intelligence and counter-intelligence section of the MIR when I received an order to find a vehicle for the day and meet a comrade who would have further instructions for me. I adopted the pre-arranged signal, carrying a bag of oranges under the left arm, and was astonished when that comrade turned out to be none other than Maria Cristina. We greeted each other very formally without smiling, walked to the car, got in and sat there while she gave me the instructions for the job ahead. It was about eleven in the morning; we had to drive to a wealthy neighbourhood and observe the movements of people in and out of a big mansion. We had to remain there until the evening. We sat there in silence, for hours, taking notes every now and then. The atmosphere was unbearable, but I began to feel a certain tenderness for this serious young woman sitting in almost complete silence next to me. She also looked prettier when serious.

But it was not me who would break the silence. Suddenly, she said,

'Comrade, I would like to apologise for my behaviour a few weeks ago. I realise now that you were right, I should learn to tolerate teasing as well as I tease others.'

I replied that in fact it was I who was the one who should apologise because I had gone a bit over the top in my reaction and I was very sorry I had upset her. We carried on for a while taking turns to apologise to each other and after that we could not stop talking, in the usual Party member relationship style (i.e. talking about millions of general issues without touching on the personal). We left in the early evening and I was happy because I thought I had made a friend. We would meet again in many similar jobs when there was just the two of us. I began to like her more and more, finding her ever more attractive and extraordinarily intelligent. Although I was on my own at the time, I was convinced that she could not possibly be interested in me; besides, she had told me that she had a boyfriend.

It turned out that we would be spending a lot of time together because we were working in the same section of the Party and because we seemed to be the most dedicated members. As a result, an incredible friendship and camaraderie developed. There was a point when our work took us apart and we stopped seeing each other; nevertheless, every now and then I would get a message through the normal Party channels to meet somebody with a certain coded signal. More often than not it would be Maria, with her lovely smile and her way of walking, swaying a little sideways, making her long, light brown hair sway in the opposite direction.

'We need to think, Luis; that is why I have arranged this meeting. Let's go somewhere quiet where we can sit down and think.'

We got used to these 'thinking sessions', where we would come up with the most incredible answers to problems we needed to solve in our work at the section. We made real progress and as a result the Party benefited from first-hand information from within those institutions that we managed to penetrate.

After a period of not seeing each other for about two months, we met by accident at a political meeting. Afterwards we talked for a while. She looked a bit down and I asked her what the matter was. She said that she had just broken up with her boyfriend. I asked if it was a definite decision and she answered that it was. I had an almost irresistible desire to hug her and comfort her as her eyes filled with tears. But although I was not in a relationship at that time, I resisted the temptation. I did not wish to appear an opportunist and I felt that she needed to be alone for a while. So, despite my feelings, I took my leave of her.

Not long after this encounter, the Party decided that our hand-written reports were not always up to standard and that we were in need of typing skills. Maria and I were given the name and address of a typing academy where we were to go and enrol. We went together one day and when we were enrolling we realised that this was not a Party friendly academy, this was a normal commercial typing school. Thus we were asked, at the same time, for our personal particulars, including names, addresses and ID cards. It took us completely by surprise and we hesitated, went red in the face, and then gave our real names and produced our ID cards. When we left the place, we looked at each other like furtive accomplices; by accident we had broken one of the fundamental rules of a Party that always had to be prepared absolutely for operating clandestinely: 'A comrade must not know the real name and other personal particulars of another comrade, unless this is absolutely necessary.'

'Your name is beautiful,' I commented when we were outside.

'So is yours,' she replied. 'My mother is half-English and my father is Spanish; that is why my name is Lopez-Steward.'

'That is funny,' I said, 'my mother is half-French.'

We left it there and we never touched on the subject again. We did not need to. From then on we committed further, voluntary infidelity to Party rules, and started to talk about each others lives. She was twenty, I was twenty-four. She had attended the Italian School for girls where she had been a brilliant student and a student leader. When I asked what it was like to be the top of the class and a leader, her answer was that it wasn't the case that she was more intelligent but that the other girls were a bit stupid. I thought that hers was a very modest, intelligent answer. 'You had better sing me a song,' she said to change the subject, and I gladly sang a song for her as we walked through the park. She was then studying history at university.

One summery day we were on a mission to take photographs of some place and we must have been near her parents' house, where she still lived. She said that sadly she had left the film for the camera at her parents', so we went there at about midday. It was a beautiful bungalow in a very quiet street in the Apoquindo district. She asked me in. I vaguely remember her mother in the house going about her chores without paying much attention to us. There was also a small boy about 16 months old, just learning to walk. To my amazement, this was the focus of her attention. The little boy was the son of the young home-helper and Maria Cristina was really fond of him. She treated him as if he was her own son. I was amazed to see such tenderness in her, the care, the sweetness with which she was treating that child, the way she talked to him. This was a completely different person to the Maria Cristina I had known until then. It was a transformation from the extremely clever, tough, sometimes cold, Party member, to this soft, motherly, tender and sweet woman, who had revealed herself in front of me.

It is quite painful for me now when I remember the time just a month or two before she was captured. I was taking her to a safe house on the outskirts of Santiago in my car. She looked tired and sad. Suddenly, as if she had awoken from a dream, she said, 'I want to have a baby.'

As had happened so many times with Maria Cristina in the past, it took me completely by surprise. She had that ability to shock with her frankness. I did not know what to say; I was speechless. But before I said a word she answered herself by saying, 'But it is too late now, they may kill us at any time.' The reality dawned on me, on both of us; it was true that we were going to be killed; they were killing us; they had killed us already. The day I saw her with that child came back to me. She would be a lovely mother, I thought to myself.

There were no more secrets between us. It was not long before I would take her to meet my father and brothers and then she would accompany me on my Sunday trips to collect my two-year-old daughter Dalia. Still, working for the party was all-consuming and we stopped seeing each other for quite some time. It was during that time that I met and fell in love with Diana. Maria Cristina, I learned later, had started an affair with a comrade who was my superior in the Party.

★ ★ ★

It was after the coup, just before Christmas 1973, when I was taking Maria Cristina to another safe house outside Santiago, on the then almost deserted road to La Florida, that she, in her usual way without preamble, said: 'You know, Luis, I think we have made a mistake, a big mistake.'

'What is that?' I asked.

'We should have lived together, you know, you and me. It must be beautiful to live with you. There have been only two men I have wanted, really wanted to live with. One was Jorge [somebody I did not know] and the other one is you.'

Once more she had left me speechless and it would not be the last time. I was choked, numbed. Here she was, this woman who I had learned to love and admire. The woman I once wanted so much to have a relationship with. The woman who, by then, had become my closest comrade and my best friend. The woman I thought would never want me as her lover, telling me that she not only wanted to have a close relationship with me, but had wanted, for a long time, to live with me as a partner! She did not wait for an answer, instead she carried on talking as if in a trance.

'You know that time, at that political gathering when we met by accident and I told you that the relationship with my boyfriend had ended? Well, I thought that you were going to declare your love to me then, but you did not. I really liked you then. And you know why you didn't propose? Because I was your choice. Then you started the relationship with Diana. She wasn't your choice, I know. Other people decided for you.'

I told her what happened at that time, why I did not declare my love to her and that I was hoping for a clearer signal from her. I also told her that I really loved her, that I had learned to love her over time, that I admired her and that I genuinely believed that she was not interested in me as her partner. But the sad truth and the tragedy, I realise, was that on the whole, she was right. I felt terrible, stupid. Why did I never ask her to be my girlfriend? Probably because of my strong belief in letting people, particularly in a close relationship, decide for themselves, as freely as possible, the kind of relationship they want to have. For me, if there is no clear indication from the other party of an interest in a closer relationship, then it is paramount to keep a healthy distance. In this case I thought the relationship, as it was, had reached its maximum in closeness and that it was just a matter of keeping it that way, with plenty of room for growth in intellectual and professional areas. We were also sharing our life experiences, even in the most intimate aspects – all this without the constraints and the sense of appropriation invested in a sexual relationship.

All very neat and tidy, but deep down there was in me the fear of being rejected by her, of losing what we had achieved, of losing the privilege of being so close to her, to such a wonderful person, a woman so admired by so many men and women alike. This woman who in many other ways was just a girl and whose picture had been printed on the front page of one of the tabloids as the most wanted female 'terrorist' in the country.

'I know how much you love Diana now. But we have been through so many things together and we have been able to solve so many complicated problems and situations together. We will find a way to solve this,' she added.

*Maria Cristina*

'Maria Cristina,' I said, 'there is something I want to ask you. Why didn't you make a clear pass at me, if you were so interested?'

'Because when I realised that I really wanted you, you were already with Diana and I could not take you away from her or attempt to do so. I couldn't do that to her. It was too late for me; it is always too late for me,' she said, her eyes filling up with tears.

'How were you so sure I would have left Diana for you, had you made a pass at me?'

'I wasn't and that is why I couldn't risk it.'

'Why are you telling me all this now then?' I asked.

'Because we are going to die. We are going to be killed, Luis; it is only a matter of time and I cannot go with these feeling inside me,' she said, crying.

After that we spent the rest of the journey in silence; it was a screaming silence so loud you could hear your heart pounding in your ears and feel a heavy pressure on your chest.

On the way back, after I had left her, I stopped the car and cried for some time. 'We are going to be killed' kept ringing in my ears, and every time I repeated the words, it sounded more and more real. This is unbelievable, I thought, she is so young, we are so young, and she is so precious. 'I love you, Maria Cristina!' I shouted into the emptiness of the night.

Just before Christmas, Diana said to me that we should buy Maria Cristina a present and, as she was indoors most of the time, it would be sensible to get her a nice piece of material so she could make herself a dress. We bought a beautiful piece. The only free time available for me to take the present to her was Christmas Eve in the afternoon. Later on in the evening Diana and I were due to go to her sister's for a family Christmas. Diana's mum and dad had come to Chile from Israel for the festivities. We had arranged that if one of us had not arrived by eight o'clock that evening the other would leave the house on the assumption that the other had been captured and might be forced to give the home address away. In those days telephones were not so common and, apart from business telephones, residential ones were very rare. Communications were, therefore, very difficult, relying mainly on badly maintained public telephones.

I arrived at Maria Cristina's house at about three that afternoon. The house belonged to a couple of friends of mine who were university lecturers; he taught physics and she taught maths and they had two small children. It was a sunny, warm summer's day. Maria Cristina was dressed in a white dress and looked extraordinarily beautiful. We had cold drinks and sat in the living room for a chat. I noticed that there was something wrong with Maria Cristina. She wasn't her usual self and she looked more vulnerable than usual. Although she smiled when required, it was clear that she would have rather cried.

Time was passing fast and I was desperate for a moment on our own, so that I could ask Maria Cristina if she was all right, or whether there was something wrong, but there was no opportunity. It was getting late, and it was a long drive back to my house. I stood up and told them I had to go. Maria Cristina stood up as well and said that she would see me off at the front garden gate. When we were outside Maria Cristina held my hand and with her usual directness said:

'Luis, I know I shouldn't say this, but I want you to understand that I have to, I cannot hold it inside me; it will kill me. I want you to stay with me, to stay with me tonight.'

She paused and looked at me with those eyes and that expression on her face that after twenty-seven years is still imprinted in my mind as if it was yesterday, and it will be until the day I die.

'I need you so much,' she added.

'Oh my love!' I cried, 'You know I can't. I cannot do this to Diana. She wouldn't know what had happened to me and you know she will assume I have been captured.'

'I know,' she said, 'but I had to say it.'

We embraced and she cried in my arms. I told her that she did not know how much I wanted to stay. I left with my heart completely torn apart. How much I loved her and how much I wanted to stay with her! But I knew I would have been unable to live with it. I loved Diana too much, and was looking forward to seeing her that evening and driving together to meet her parents for the first time. But nothing would be the same again. Maria Cristina would be sunk in my heart like a knife, aching with every breath, with every movement.

When I arrived home it was just past eight. Diana was lying on the bed fully dressed and crying. When she saw me she got very angry. I apologised for being late and gave her the present I had bought for her. She took it and threw it at me, missing my head by a millimetre.

'What were you doing with that whore?' she shouted. 'Why do you do this to me? Don't you know it is hard enough as it is?'

'You knew I was going to take the present to her,' I said.

'Yes,' she said, 'but what kept you for so long? Did you sleep with her?'

'No, Diana,' I responded with a sadness that dried my mouth and throat, my words barely audible. 'You do not know what has happened,' I said to her with no intention of telling her because it was something incomprehensible to anybody else, something unbelievable.

'I do not want to know,' she said. I felt the loneliest person in the universe, about to explode from the feelings and the memory of what had happened about an hour before. I wanted to be on my own and cry to the heavens.

Eventually we reached Diana's sister's house a few minutes before the curfew. There were a lot of people there in a festive mood. I was introduced to Diana's parents and other family members I had never seen before. It was hard to smile; it was harder still to talk. For these people it was as if nothing had happened. They were all business people, they had money, they supported the coup. The future was promising for them, they were confident that nothing bad would happen to them. I went out to the balcony and looked at the lights of the city below, a city under curfew, a city in a state of emergency. A city we, as Maria Cristina said, 'may never see the lights of again.'

★   ★   ★

We were in the car. Nano was driving and he had just asked me to join his team. He did not tell me what the job was but I guessed it had to do with the Party's executive committee. I was absorbed in my thoughts, trying to imagine what we would be doing and that whatever it was it must be very high risk. All the dictatorship's repressive apparatus was desperately hunting the Party's executive committee. Suddenly Nano looked at me and with a sarcastic smile on his face he said: 'You know, your friend has been captured and I hear she is giving you away.'

I was shocked. When I first heard the news I did not want to believe it. When Diana told me that Maria Cristina had been captured I had hoped that it was a mistake. The Party information was transmitted by word of mouth and mistakes about the identity of the captured were often made. But now, coming from Nano, it had to be true. He told me that Maria Cristina had broken under torture and that she had talked, talked about me. It had been confirmed by prisoners who had seen her at the torture centre and who had then been taken to detention centres. She had given my real name to her tormentors and also my father's home address.

The fact that Maria Cristina had been captured was a tremendous shock. I had come to love her in a way I had not known before and would never know again. But that wasn't what really upset me when Nano gave me the news, it was the way he said it, as if he was saying your friend is betraying you, don't trust your friend. The other thing that took me by surprise was that Nano knew that we were close, that we loved each other. Somebody must have told him and that somebody could have only been Maria Cristina. This discovery confirmed the feelings Maria Cristina had towards me and increased my emotional turmoil, emphasising the strangeness of it all.

I turned to him and told him: 'Do not talk that way; she is one of the best members of the Party. She is my friend and I love her and she loves me. You do not know what they are doing to people, how they are torturing them, and even if you knew, it is impossible for you to imagine what it is like until you have lived through the experience yourself. I respect her; she must know what she is doing and is doing it for a reason. That reason is, to me, paramount and I respect it. That it could be detrimental to the Party and that it could even cost me my life, then so be it. I still regard her highly and I still love her. And don't you ever forget, she is not the one who is committing the crimes and all these atrocities, it is the military. You have no right to speak like that.'

I asked Nano to stop the car because I needed to get out. He apologised and said,

'You know, if I ever get caught, I am going to use what I am carrying here,' and he pointed to the space in between his legs on the car seat. There was a hand grenade and an automatic pistol there. 'Because I cannot stand the slightest form of pain inflicted on me.'

'And you think that is very courageous, don't you?' I said. 'But, I think you are a coward. Why don't you just kill yourself now? Why don't we all commit mass suicide? You see, what takes courage, real courage is to try to avoid more comrades getting caught. And if you really are a responsible human being, fight for life. If you get caught, face them, accept the consequences of what you have been preaching.'

My captors would show me the blood-soaked inside of his car five months later.

'This is what is left of your friend and his wife. We machine-gunned them both inside the car the other day.'

I got out of Nano's car and walked and cried for a long time. I was surprised at my reaction and my feelings. This was close, I thought, this is how you feel when a loved one has fallen into their hands. What next?

One of my brothers, who still lived with my father, would tell me later that the secret police arrived one night at the family house with Maria Cristina, looking for me. My brother, who had met Maria Cristina before, told me that she looked very ill. They searched the house and took whatever of value they found, including some money from my dad. When they were leaving they told my dad that if he did not tell them where I was they would take my brother. My dad followed them to the front gate and, at this point, Maria managed to take hold of my dad's hand and, referring to my brother, told him, 'Do not say anything, he will be all right.' They took my brother, but fortunately he was released a few days later, abandoned at dawn in the outskirts of the city.

I have asked my brother many times over the years to tell me what happened that night when they came with her. I have always wanted to see through my brother's eyes that image of Maria Cristina sitting on the sofa in the living room; always wanted to snatch that image from my brother's brain and keep it in mine; always tried to read in my brother's face a message that Maria Cristina could have left encoded, some kind of signal. But all I can see is fear. My brother's eyes look down, his face turns dull, his words disappear like those of the disappeared prisoners. He does not want to talk about it. 'It's OK,' I say and give him a hug, and in that hug I embrace Maria Cristina, as she was then, sitting on the sofa in despair, in fear, captured, a defenceless prey to the butchers, but still resisting. My dad's hand. Oh dad! What did she tell you through her hand? She held your hand to give you courage, to ask you to be strong, to tell you that if you knew, not to tell them where I was. She, captured, tortured, abused, humiliated, wounded at their mercy; she asked you to resist, dad, as she was resisting.

Maria Cristina, lost forever. The world deprived of your smile, your tenderness, your intelligence, your love.

# Captured

# 9

They are torturing people you know,' somebody told me, 'and they say it is terrible.'

'Yeah,' I would say, 'but what do they really do to you?'

I was trying hard to imagine what could be done to an individual that it would make it so difficult or impossible to bear. I would think of the time I broke my elbow playing roller skate hockey when I was thirteen and the bone came out of the socket. When they took me to Casualty, two men tried to put the bone back, without anaesthetics or painkillers, by pulling, the two of them at the same time, and each placing a foot on my chest. That was painful enough, but that had been a long time ago and the memory of the unbearable pain had faded. So I believed that I could stand the pain caused by any method of torture. What else can they do to you? The same elbow pain for a longer period of time perhaps?

Or the dentist at the primary school who used to save on anaesthetics and perform fillings without it; me in the waiting room hearing the screams of the other kids begging for an injection. Then it would be my turn and I would open my mouth as wide as I could, waiting stoically for the drill. After a while I would feel nothing, so I always believed that if I could get over the initial fear I could bear any physical pain. Younger still, I must have been two or three, we were on holiday in the country. I remember it was in the evening and a charcoal fire was being prepared in the garden in a container to be taken inside later on. I must have felt fascinated by the flames and the embers glowing in the dark; the fact is that I felt this irresistible impulse to touch the fire, which I did with my left wrist. My older sister, who was next to me, screamed in horror, prompting the adults to come out of the house. The result of my experimentation was a severe, large burn on my left wrist and part of the arm where a big bubble of burnt tissue had rapidly formed. We were miles away from any town; the only means of transport was a horse-pulled cart and it was pitch dark.

Everybody was crying: my mother, my aunts and my sister. The strange thing that everybody remembered for years to come was that I, the one that should have been crying the loudest, was absolutely silent. They could not understand what was going on; my arm was stretched out, my mother was holding it with one hand while someone else was holding a pair of scissors ready to cut the burnt tissue, but she could not stop crying. I was standing there, very straight, my arm rigid and my head held high, as if saying, 'Come on, stop crying and get on with it.' I do not know what happened because, although the burn was quite severe, I do not remember feeling more than a tingling sensation, as if a sharp needle had been inserted in my arm. Being in the country, the story went around with divine and magical properties attached to it. I would wear, without pride, the big scar for the rest of my life.

These events had invested me with a certain feeling of omnipotence: pain, or at least physical pain, appeared to be something that was perfectly bearable to me. Of course, nothing of what I had experienced before would have prepared me, or anyone else for that matter, for what was going to happen to so many people in Chile. In my mental deliberations about pain I even entertained the idea that because the military were also human, then they must know when a person had had enough, and they surely would stop. But then Pinochet's secret police did something so that the whole country got the message, a message of horror designed to terrorise the population and in particular to terrorise us, the ones that were trying to organise some kind of resistance. The macerated and tortured body of Lumi Videla, a woman comrade well known to me, who had been captured alive about a month before, was thrown during the night into the gardens of the Italian embassy, which at the time was full of asylum seekers. It was not that until then they hadn't committed similar or worse barbarities, it was just that this time they made sure that the news reached every corner of the country. This was their signature, their seal, the rubber stamp of their modus operandi.

Although I realised that the situation was bad I was still convinced that I would be able to bear the pain. With all the horror stories that were emerging though, my imaginary threshold was getting lower and lower as I tried to practise withstanding the varieties of torture being inflicted in my imaginary torture chamber, while other parts of my brain became numb with fear. I was under no illusion that I was going to pass through these terrible times in the history of our country unscathed. I was here to stay, I would not seek asylum in one of the embassies in Santiago, which were overflowing. During my political life, and probably before that, I had acquired an indelible sense of duty; I would suffer the consequences alongside the people of Chile, my people, and if I had to die, so be it.

My pain; my death. But contemplating Diana's pain, Diana's death, my unborn child's pain, my unborn child's death, that was harder to bear. Diana had disappeared on 18 November. Nobody knew where she was or what had happened to her and my heart would leap in hope at the sound of high heels clicking along the street outside our front door.

★   ★   ★

They surrounded me in the street. One of them hit me in the head and then another one punched me in my nose and mouth once we were inside the car. I had a glimpse of his eyes and I knew that something very sinister was going on. These were not the eyes I was used to; these were not the eyes of normal people in hate or anger; these were evil eyes. These were the eyes of absolute madness; eyes that had gone beyond the point of no return and all they could do was to continue in an ever more sinister spiral of feeding themselves with the blood, the pain and the fear of their victims.

Blindfolded, handcuffed and with chains around my ankles they started to shout and scream, hitting me and behaving like a frenzied pack of wolves. No time for thinking here, no time to reflect; you are only allowed to react, to defend yourself the best you can, internally, using very primitive reactions.

They felt all-powerful and safe, in control. Nothing could impede the abuse. On the contrary, to abuse the victim is rewarded; it was seen as a courageous thing, a sign of loyalty towards the pack, contributing to the cohesion of their group, uniting them in the committing of the crime. Ultimately it unleashes the darkest aspects of their personalities. The little traumas of their sorry lives become a murderous, sadistic pathology, and one is in their hands, at their mercy.

Still, I refused to believe what I was experiencing and when they asked me where my car was, where the money was, where my comrades were, their names and addresses, I, in a Quixote-like attitude, replied that I could not tell them. Not just that I did not know; they should understand that I had my principles, my morals, my dignity, my integrity and therefore, I could not tell them, even if I wanted to. All this baggage of ancestral learning passed on from generation to generation over the centuries, and perhaps over the millennia, did not allow me to tell them anything. They should understand that all this was imprinted in every single cell of my being and that, as far as I was concerned, was the end of the matter. In a way they did understand, but only in terms of their own language. One of them declared: 'this is a tough bastard; he won't talk.' And so I was taken to Villa Grimaldi. It was one of the most important interrogation centres for the DINA (Dirrecion de Inteligienca Nacional) and, as I was about to discover, it contained all the sickening apparatus needed for extracting information. I would remain blindfolded, handcuffed, with legs chained together the entire time I was there.

There is, of course, a division of labour in torture, but not that much since most of them enjoy their roles immensely and often compete for a share of the victim: for the opportunity to practise their particular perversity. There are the men who, after you have been stripped of all your clothes, tie you up to the metal bed, known as the *parrilla* ('grill'), and attach electrodes to the most sensitive parts of the body. They do not miss any part: the toes, the penis, the anus, the nipples, the mouth and the ears. Then they proceed to apply the high wattage electrical current, but they do not ask questions. The questions are shouted, rather than asked, by the most senior members of the team. In my case the man in charge was the infamous Captain Miguel Krassnoff. The others just shouted and screamed as if in a frenzy and made obscene remarks. The pain is unbearable; anyone who has not experienced this kind of torture is unable to imagine anything close to this amount of pain. Furthermore, the body suffers violent convulsions, which in turn help to cut open the flesh at the wrists and the ankles tied with wire to the metal bed, and sometimes even dislocate them. The frenzy of the torturers increased as my screams filtered through the thick piece of cloth placed inside my mouth.

The screams. Oh, those screams. They are sounds you never imagined you would be able to produce. You never imagined that a human could make such sounds. They are the sounds of very primitive creatures, the sounds of creatures long ago extinct. But the bestial torturers do not know, do not realise, what they are opening up. In their brutality they are awakening the ancestral memory store in us. The memory before language, the memory of walking on all fours, of crawling perhaps, when the cells we are made of could only use one language: screams. Screams to portray anything from the joy of living to mortal pain. But although we still carry the same cells and some of the memories of the awakening of time, we are too far removed from the beginning, and the awakening of these memories, via horrendous pain, will surely have disastrous consequences.

It has taken us millions of years of evolution to be here today, and every piece of the marvellous system that makes us what we are needs to function perfectly for us to be called humans. It takes just a few minutes of torture to wipe out everything. They have given themselves the right to violate evolution. Because by suffering torture one is forced to regress to the primitive state, and the primitive state has no reasoning to understand what is going on, has no language to express what is being experienced, so our bodies' system cannot comprehend. There is only horror and disbelief, there is no explanation; the learned world of words disappears, there is only alternation between cries and silence. There are no answers for the 'Whys?' and then only the eyes are left, eyes that keep widening as if by widening they will be able to grasp some understanding. But in vain, the answers do not come from the horrible faces and the voices of the tormentors.

This is one of the reasons why they keep you blindfolded or with a hood over your head, because they cannot stand those wide open eyes fixed on them requesting an explanation; the eyes of tortured women, men and children. Not uncommon is the practice of dislodging people's eyes from their sockets. If one survives the torture chamber and your sight is safe, one is still left with wide-open eyes for the rest of one's life. Because one is forever trying to find – via staring – some explanation for this horror, perhaps in a cloud, a tree or another person's eyes. Needless to say, there are no answers.

This is, in my view, the only way to explain what somebody close to me once described as my long, unbearable silences. There are others that do not talk anymore. There are those that build a wall around themselves called madness. And those that embark on industrious activity and become very successful. But there are also those who, like Primo Levi, will not be able to cope with the pain, with the sadness, with the immeasurable sadness, with the vastness of the darkness: no explanation, no answer, not ever, until the sleep, the heavy sleep, the forever sleep takes hold, still with eyes wide open.

The interrogation and the torture go on forever. They do not stop, they will not stop, they never stop; they do not know when to stop; stop before it is too late, before everything goes, before love, trust, beauty, dreams; before my flesh goes. They did stop, though, for a while. After a few hours of electric shocks they feared that my heart had stopped.

'This bastard is dying,' they declared.

And I probably *was* dying too. I felt as if I had decided to die. As if they would not have what they wanted because in a few minutes I would be dead and the bastards could carry on torturing my body in vain because I would not be there, I would have abandoned them in the middle of their frenzy. I would have gone forever with my dreams, with my memories. It was as if I was spitting in their faces in defiance, saying, 'look how futile what you are doing is, you bastards, I am dying and you will not get to my sacred secrets.'

They stopped and revived me, but it was already too late, the damage had already been done and nothing would be the same again: not flowers, not the sun, not the moon, not the stars. Nothing, not the crying child, the faces of loved ones, laughter and happiness, love, words, kisses, caresses, smells, not even food would taste the same again. Everything had changed forever; even my feelings would betray me more often than not. You have killed something inside me, I can feel it. I went there, to where the dead ones are and now I am back and I feel very sad. It is just so sad, an enormous sadness. If I could only contain this sea of sadness. How will I navigate it, forever lost and in anguish?

'You can't sleep now,' the young guard said. 'I suffer from insomnia, and if I can't sleep, you won't sleep either.'

He started to kick the wooden box where I had been imprisoned for about two weeks since my capture, and where I would remain for the next few weeks. The box, known as a 'Casas Chile', was like an upright wooden coffin and I could barely move. From the moment I was placed inside I started to figure out how I was going to survive. I could not stretch my body in any direction as the box was too small. I managed to dislodge the cloth they had used to blindfold me by rubbing my head against the wood, but there was nothing to see: the box was completely sealed except for a small hole above my head at the top of the door. I could not sit; the only possible positions to be in were standing or crouching. After long hours in those two positions you feel that you must find an alternative or your body will go mad.

A terrible internal battle started to unfold inside that wooden box: with feet chained together, handcuffed and blindfolded, there is no room to manoeuvre and the body knows it. The body wants to give up; the body is saying that life is no longer viable under those conditions. But the brain persists, the brain has been successful for so many thousands of years, repressing pain and carrying on; the mind is looking for something, for yet another alternative. So I ended up upside down inside the box to give my legs a rest, calculating, thinking, that if I could sustain this position for a while, then I could change to that other one, and then another one until a full day had passed and then a full night, and so on. You see, it is not that bad after all.

The system cannot tolerate this regime and is forced to split. The brain, the master, the king, is adamant that it will save itself at whatever cost, even at the cost of a limb or an organ.

Yes, I did survive, even when one day they placed another prisoner inside the box. This comrade had a bullet lodged inside one of his legs and he was in pain, so he was moaning all the time, calling the guards to give him this and that and the other, to the point of losing his dignity. His wound was not severe, although it seemed that the bullet had damaged a nerve. In any case, I started to fear that sharing the small box with this man could be a serious threat to my sanity, among other things. We were there glued to each other and he had no will, no dignity, no integrity left. He would cry and humiliate himself all the time.

Yes, I survived, but the price I have had to pay has been phenomenal: complete detachment from my body; a sequence of illnesses beyond comprehension; panic attacks with a force that seems to generate itself from the stomach, and so much more misery that makes life not seem worth living.

It must have been on the second day of interrogation when I was taken to a room where they sat me on a chair and somebody ordered my blindfold to be taken off. The young Captain Krassnoff said that it did not matter whether I saw his face because he knew me and I knew him. We had been at the same secondary school when we were twelve or thirteen. He started to recall the teachers' nicknames so I could be sure we knew each other. Because we were ex-schoolmates, he continued, he would offer me a deal.

'Diana, your woman, received a few bullets when she was arrested and is in intensive care at the military hospital. If you cooperate with us, the intensive care treatment for Diana will continue. If, on the other hand, you refuse to cooperate, the medical treatment will be suspended and Diana will die. It all depends on you. It is in your hands; it is your responsibility if she dies.'

I asked him why Diana had been shot. He said that when they asked her to stop in the street she started to run, so they shot her in the back. I could not believe what I was hearing. Diana shot? Running in the street? But she was wearing a tight skirt and high heels the day she never returned home, almost a month before my own arrest. How could you shoot a defenceless pregnant woman unable to run more than a few metres?

'We couldn't say, "Excuse me, miss, don't run; we want to detain you." So I shot her.'

I threw at him all the insults I could gather, called him a fascist, a coward, a murderous pig and more.

'I want the addresses of the members of the executive committee, I want you to tell me where the money is and the cars,' he said. I replied that there were two problems with his proposition. First, I had no reason to believe his story about Diana, and therefore, I would like to see her and talk to her first. Second, that even if I wanted to, I had no access to the information he was requesting. He told me that a visit to Diana could be arranged, that he did not want an answer to his request that day, and that I should think about the proposition overnight and answer him the next day.

The following day I was interrogated, and tortured, by a different team. I never heard about the deal again. But every time I was interrogated and they demanded answers from me, I would tell them that I wanted to see Diana first. Of course I never saw her, not then, not ever. Lost forever, 'missing', 'disappeared', euphemisms for calculated, premeditated murder: plain butchery.

The torture continued day after day and forever. Beatings with poles, with hammers, with sticks, with bare fists, with iron bars, with pistol handles, with machine guns; on the floor, sitting on a chair for a few seconds just to kick it over later, pick it up and then beat you with it. Beatings. Always beating and shouting and insulting. Blood ran from my nose and my mouth, my chest sounded like it was cracking, there was a pain in my back, my wrists and ankles burned with infection, as did the skin between my legs and my toes. But that was not, of course, enough. They would hang you from a bar, either by the wrists or by the wrists and ankles, so that the weight of your body would pull at the sockets, or they would plunge you upside down in a barrel of filthy water and hold you there almost to the point of asphyxiation.

★ ★ ★

Do not hit my ears, I won't be able to hear the birds singing anymore. Nor the lullaby that my grandmother used to sing to me while I fell asleep. Nor the words of wisdom she had spoken. The grandmothers; they came from the country, from the Indians and the first Spaniards, and then from great-grandparents who had rebelled against Spain and fought for freedom. What could I do? The fighting for freedom had been implanted there a long time ago, together with the pride, the dignity, the morals and the principles I held.

Grandmother's voice was sacred, she could heal and she could put you to sleep. She could make you dream, see in the dark and see from the sky, she could make you fly too. Do not hit me in the ears, you bastard! You don't know what you are doing!

My mother used to kiss my lips when I was little and my grandmother used to touch them with her fingers and moisten them with some kind of magic water for the fever. I have kissed my loved ones and my little girl; I have kissed the beautiful faces of Maria, Anita, Manuela and my sisters and my brothers, when saying hello and goodbye. Don't hit me on my lips; do not destroy my lips, they are sacred too. I can whisper my grandmother's lullaby in my little girl's ears and I tell of grandmother's wisdom in those little ears too. I have asked millions of questions with my lips when learning about things. Do not hit me on my lips, you bastard, because you don't know . . . But he has. He has just destroyed my lips, the bastard.

# Villa Grimaldi                                    10

It was Christmas Eve 1974 in Villa Grimaldi and there was an atmosphere of great excitement mixed with fear. Most of the prisoners were going to either be freed or transferred to open prisons or concentration camps. About one hundred, mostly men, were selected. Most of them, as far as we knew, were not hardcore activists, just people named by informers or neighbours. Most of them had not been detained for long, two to three weeks at the most. Many of them had been ill-treated, but not tortured as they tortured others. One or two had not even been interrogated.

Late that night two refrigerated vans arrived. The guards confirmed that the prisoners were going to be transported in the vans to their destination. Nobody showed great surprise about the use of this means of transport. It was most probably just a problem of logistics, some thought. Not for me, though, and a few others who kept repeating 'Refrigerated vans? To transport frozen fish, maybe, but not people.' The vans belonged to the Arauco Fisheries Company, which until September 1973 had been the state-owned fisheries company.

This is not a problem of logistics, I thought to myself. This is the murderer's solution: to conceal a human cargo to be transported in the middle of the night. History has seen it all before. The Nazis used to transport their victims in cattle wagons during the Eastern European winter and many would suffocate or freeze to death.

There were a couple of Diana's distant relatives who survived the Nazi concentration camps. There was Aunt Pola, who had a very long number tattooed on one of her arms. Like many other Eastern European refugees who arrived in Chile after the Second World War, she spoke a type of

Spanish almost impossible to understand and anyway she did not seem to care whether she was understood or not, as though being understood was no longer important. I would learn years later that once one has been through inexplicable horror, one is not keen on trying to make others understand.

How long will the Chilean prisoners' journey be? How long before they suffocate? How long will it take them to die if the freezer is switched on? This was the Chilean equivalent to the Nazi solution, with the added help of modern technology. A refrigerated lorry would do both: suffocate and freeze to death.

I began to think about when it would be my turn to get into one of the refrigerated lorries and tried to imagine the slow death awaiting me and the others. There will be no journey to freedom or to an open prison because this is not an accident, this is not a brilliant, last-minute idea. This has been carefully planned and rehearsed many times before. The contempt for human life, for human dignity, is present in every single action. The pleasure and delight shows in the guards faces, at the prospect of treating other fellow human beings like dead fish inside the refrigerated lorries. In lorries belonging to the company whose workers had fought so hard for it to be nationalised, to be a patrimony of the nation, to exploit the rich seas to feed its people. This is what the generals had planned. 'Destroy their dreams, shatter them.' The Popular Government had managed to nationalise or run in partnership so many industries and companies, from the copper mines, coal mines, steel producers, all the utility companies, maritime transport, and so on. All of them together, a huge infrastructure. That enormous infrastructure, previously used to serve the whole country and its people, was now in the hands of the military to serve their macabre goal of eliminating all opposition and spreading terror throughout the population. Thus, while some people were about to end their lives inside a sealed box, stinking of fish, others would end up being imprisoned, tortured or killed, thrown from the air into the sea or high up in the Andes, abandoned in the driest desert in the world by their tormentors, using the vast infrastructure at their disposal. The state-owned airlines, sea transport, the mines, the countless factories, their vehicles and resources were all used in the brutal torture and extermination of the people who had created them.

I did not have to board one of the refrigerated trucks. None of the people taken away on Christmas Eve 1974 was ever seen again.

★ ★ ★

The only journey I continued to make was to the toilet, where we were taken with our feet chained to each other. This was a very painful journey. It wasn't very far, only 50 metres or so, but it was a fun time for the guards. They would pull and push us until, chained, handcuffed and blindfolded, we would invariably fall to the ground, one after the other in a domino-like way, much to the guards' amusement. Then they would beat us for having fallen and wasted time and as a punishment they would allow each prisoner only one minute in the toilet. Obviously you couldn't do anything, even if you were desperate to go.

One day, when we were very near the toilet and the guards were unlocking the chains from people's feet to let two at a time inside the toilet cubicle, the voice of a woman spoke from behind me. Almost in a whisper she told me her name, which sounded familiar, and said: 'I saw Diana when they brought her here. She had about four bullets in her, three in her back and one in her leg. She was in a very bad way but she wouldn't talk. They applied electric shocks to her but she would not say anything. They didn't keep her here long because she was very ill from her wounds. She was taken away, in an ambulance, in the evening of the same day she arrived, to a clinic, they said.'

My heart sank. I wanted to believe that Captain Krassnoff was bluffing when he told me that Diana had been shot in the street and that her life depended on whether or not I would cooperate with them. It was true, then, that she had been shot. It was true, then, that she could be dying or was already dead. I felt crushed, as if an enormous weight had been heaped upon me. I felt like shrinking and falling to the ground. A huge hole seemed to open in my chest, the rest of my body being swallowed up into it, only my head remaining outside, naked, exposed, not knowing what it could possibly do.

I was taken back to the tiny, dark, windowless room that I now occupied, known as a 'Casas Corvi', and pushed to the ground. I managed to drag myself to the mat on the floor and I lay there, lifeless, on a dark journey to the edge of madness. How many more blows were needed to finish me off? Why wasn't there a switch to turn off the torment?

Although there is very little left of me, I can still say No! No, I will not eat like a dog on all fours on the floor. You can make the others eat like dogs, but not me. You see, stupid bastard, I have been there and back;

you helped to take me there, where all is silence. Having been there, where death is, the fear has been taken away, or any fear that might have remained in me. It could also be that my grandmother's hands were very strong hands and held me very straight and I felt secure and fearless. So I will remain standing and I will not bend to eat like a dog. Besides, my terrible hunger has just disappeared. Oh yes, you can beat me up, as my feet are in chains and my hands are handcuffed and I cannot see you. I will fall to the ground and you will kick my face and what is left of my ribs . . . You have just done it, little bastard, but I have not eaten like a dog, you understand? The next day all the others ate like dogs, but you did not have the guts to carry on beating me; I ate with my hands, standing.

But being in the room in front of the torture chamber was so much harder to bear. They were torturing men, women and children of all ages every day of the week, all day and all night. Husbands in front of their wives; wives in front of their husbands; parents in front of their children; children in front of their parents; children as young as two and people as old as eighty. The screams of the victims, their pleadings, their begging, the breaking of people's dignity, of their integrity, the torturing until death, the breaking of bones, the blood, the killings, the madness. Witnessing the frenzy of the torturers and interrogators, the perverse sadism of these psychopaths, their pleasure and enjoyment at inflicting pain on another human being.

This orgy of cruelty, brutality and sadism was sickening. The shock I had experienced before, when I felt I was being taken back millions of years to a primeval time, was then multiplied hundreds of times, with hundreds of people, women, men and children being subjected to such bestiality. I began to believe that I would not be able to make it. The real fear of going mad started to settle in. I started to think that I would reach a point where I would be unable to take decisions. Unable even to take the decision to kill myself. That was really frightening. It is incredible how one learns very quickly that death is all right, that there is nothing to fear about it, that, on the contrary, death is preferable to what one is experiencing. But madness is something else, madness is terribly frightening and totally unacceptable, at least that is what it felt like for me.

I was thinking about my daughter, who at the time was only three: what if they bring her here and do what they are doing to other people's children to put pressure on their parents to talk? A cold chill ran down my spine. Then everything fitted into place. That is why they placed me in this room in front of the torture chamber. They wanted me to know what they were doing to the children. Sure enough, they came one day early in the morning, about four of them; the other captain did the talking.

'You think we are stupid,' he started. 'I know you have been messing around with us and the truth is that you haven't given us anything. All you have done is tell us lies and give us false leads. You know what we are going to do? We are going to bring your daughter and then we shall see if you still want to mess about with us. What do you have to say?'

There was a long silence, then I raised my head, as though I was looking at them through the blindfold, and said 'It's OK, bring her.'

My voice came out defiant, deep, but defiant. Somebody pushed me to the floor and they left the room. Suddenly I felt very tired, immensely tired, as if a powerful drug had just hit my brain. I was on my own in that small room again where I hadn't been able to sleep for the previous four or five days.

I woke up to the screams and the other noises which had become so familiar to me by then: the dull thuds, the crackling of electricity, the shouting, the muffled groans, the wrestling noises of people being dragged along because they could not walk, some of them paralysed due to the torture, others because their feet were tied up. It was late in the evening and I was still on the floor. I must have slept the whole day. I was very thirsty and hungry. They have probably forgotten about me I thought. They have been too busy and now the meal time has gone and the toilet time has passed as well. Maybe I have been unconscious; maybe this is another day; maybe they had already interrogated me in my little daughter's presence; maybe I did say something; maybe they tortured her in my presence and I passed out; I may be going mad. It may be that I have been mad for some time and this is just a mental institution; maybe I have been imagining things. The fear: that fear was there, very clear, sharp, fierce.

It took me quite some time to realise what was going on, what had happened, where I was, what I was doing there, why I was handcuffed, blindfolded and there were chains around my feet. But as I was able to see through where the blindfold meets the nose bone by making my head almost touch the back of the neck, I hopped towards the door. At the top the door there was a small window and I was able to see a little. There was light coming from the torture chamber and there were people at the entrance. Maybe they are interrogating somebody there; maybe that person's screams woke me up and they are now silent. But I could still hear the noises of a body being tortured with electric shocks, the sound of convulsions on the metal bed. It went on and on but there were no screams. They would stop for a while and then continue with the same pattern. I began to think that they may have put too much cloth in the person's mouth or pushed it too far into the mouth and the screams could not be heard. There were no noises, no more convulsions, just the torturers shouting: 'The bastard is dead!'

'Are you sure he is dead? Call the doctor!'

'The doctor is not here,' answered another one . . .

No more noises, not ever. That comrade succeeded in dying before it was too late.

They never brought my daughter in and then I realised that they were probably doing the opposite of what I wanted, or at least the opposite of what they believed I wanted. Around this time they took me out in a car one afternoon to identify a comrade they were about to ambush in the street. And, as we were coming back to the torture centre empty handed, one of them drew his gun and placed the barrel on my temple and said that he was going to 'blow my brains out' because 'I was just a bastard that would never learn anything'.

I just looked through the windscreen, smiled to the Andean cordillera illuminated by the sunset and said: 'Go on, do me a favour and pull the bloody trigger.'

For a few seconds I could feel the cracking on my skull, the bullet penetrating it, shattering the bone and then easily working its way through my brain assassinating my dreams.

He hit me in the head with the gun instead, saying, 'I do no favours.'

There was another occasion when I was on my own in the 'Casas Corvi' when Captain Miguel Krassnoff came to the door to ask for some information and I just stayed there on the floor facing the wall and did not move.

'Look, you are not behaving like a soldier, lying there on the floor and not facing me and not answering my questions,' he taunted.

I turned around and looked at him through my infected eyes and told him: 'I am your prisoner, one of the victims of your perversity and you can rip my body apart bit by bit, you can kill me, and, I demand you kill me right now. But here,' I said, pointing to my head, 'you will not enter. The rest of my body has been all yours and you have violated it, abused it, humiliated it and tortured it. But this is mine, only mine, and when I am gone, after you kill me, it will go with me, with all my secrets and all the secrets before me; and now you can leave my room.' He left without a word. My room! I laughed. That rotten wooden box, my room. Leave my room! I could not believe what I had just said. But in a way, in a perverse way, it did make sense. He was trying to get into my space, my most intimate inner space, into my secret box, and that I would not allow. And, unexpectedly, it seemed that he had gotten the message. I was expecting a bullet in my head. He chose not to kill me.

Where did my defiance come from? I do not know. How could I have told them that it was OK to bring my daughter to be tortured? I do not know. Perhaps I was very angry; perhaps I was saying don't mess about with me: you either do it or not, but do not threaten me, and if you want to go all the way, go all the way, I'll be waiting here! I do not know. There is, one thing I do know though, and that is that I could never look at my daughter's beautiful, big green eyes again without being transported to that time, to that moment when, I will always feel, I betrayed her. I traded her little life for my pride, for my stubbornness. For a long moment in February 1975, her life was held in suspense because her father decided to throw her on to the gambling table of that battle of wills, to take a chance, to see what would happen.

Fear. Pure, raw fear from my hair to my toes, like a cold steel blade slowly passing through my head and down my spine. Big, beautiful, green, innocent eyes. Can you see the blade when you look at me, my little one? I hope you never discover what it is. It is betrayal. Yes, that is what it is. I did betray you. I gave you away. They were testing me to see if I loved myself more than I loved you. If I loved my ideas, my principles, my dreams, my people, my readiness to die for all of that, more than I loved you. And I gave you away. Do not get me wrong, my love. I love you immensely. It is just that I am going mad, you see. Everything is spinning around very fast and it is just that I want to hit back at them, my little one; I want to defy them. They shouldn't have done what they did, you see, because it corrupts everything. Just don't look at me too intensely, my love. It is a flashing light; perhaps a shining object that resembles a polished blade, perhaps a visual illusion; it is not important. I am very tired now, my love, I am just falling asleep and I do not want to wake up, but I will be there for you, in some other place, far away. You won't see that flash in my eyes and I won't see the blade because I'll be far away, in another land. Yes, my love, it is called exile.

★   ★   ★

During my time in the torture centre they took me out several more times to identify comrades, which I always refused to do. Once, they took me out to identify a comrade that was supposed to be on a street corner, waiting for somebody else who had already been detained. I did not say anything, so they blindfolded me and started to punch me and hit me with their pistols until they drew blood from my head and my nose. 'We are going to hang you now, bastard!' they said. 'You refused to recognise that other bastard friend of yours and now we are going to hang you and give you what you deserve, and as for this one, we are going to kill him one of these days anyway.' His name was Chico Olivares.

They did kill him, although not immediately, for I met him again one more time. It was in the winter of 1977 in London, when I was convinced that I wouldn't be able to survive the cold and that the Pinochet regime had driven me to exile in England in the knowledge that I would die of cold there. When the cold became unbearable, I would take shelter in the blowing heat of shop doorways, and travel on the warm underground, which, surely, would increase my chances of surviving the winter.

I used the Central Line quite often to travel from my cheap hotel lodgings in Shepherd's Bush to English classes in Oxford Street. Completely absorbed in my thoughts one evening on the tube, I saw a familiar face. I did not think it was possible, since I often had flashbacks, but Chico Olivares was sitting a few seats away from me. Almost in slow motion we looked at each other in disbelief. We spoke at the same moment, as if we had been rehearsing the encounter for a long time.

'What are you doing here, of all places?'

'I thought you were dead.'

'No, they told me that *you* had been killed.'

We touched each other to make sure we were not deluded. We had learned not to trust our senses; what had happened makes you doubt everything; anything could be both possible and impossible at the same time, as if a magician is playing tricks on you all the time.

'No, I have been in London for two years now,' said Chico. 'What about you?'

'Just a couple of months,' I answered.

I reflected for a bit and then, suddenly, I was no longer on an underground train in London, I was in Villa Grimaldi.

'No, no, no. I saw them kill a man in front of me because he wouldn't tell them your whereabouts. At one point, when he couldn't resist anymore, he gave them what was supposed to be your home address; they went there in force, at night and stormed the house. It turned out to be the house of a prominent chief of the police. When they came back later on, I saw the man lying on the floor and about five of those butchers jumping and stomping all over his body. I could hear his rib cage breaking and collapsing. Do you know what this man did? He laughed and laughed in their faces until he could not breathe any more, until blood poured out of his mouth.'

'I must have been in detention by then, about to be expelled from Chile', Chico replied. 'You see, I was captured by the Air Force secret services. They took me to a military court and I was sentenced to two years in prison, which was then changed to exile. It was very quick,' he added.

At that moment I could no longer contain my tears and my emotions and tried to dismiss what Chico was saying. 'It is not true Chico! Where were you in April two years ago?'

'I was probably in prison, waiting to be expelled from Chile,' Chico reiterated.

'It is impossible, Chico! Two years ago in April I was taken away from the concentration camp and brought to a secret place for re-interrogation. Most of the questioning was about you and your whereabouts and you are telling me that you were already in prison? It does not make sense!'

'But you must know, as well as I do, that the secret services of the different branches of the armed forces were fighting with each other over who had supremacy over the repressive process, so there was no coordination between them. It is therefore possible that the Air Force did not inform the DINA of the prisoners they had, and it was unlikely that the DINA agents would look for a suspect in a prison.'

Chico's explanation made some sense, I realised. But I was not totally convinced. I started to wonder how Chico was able to leave the country by plane, undetected by the DINA, when I had seen them bringing people from the airport to the torture centre. They had plenty of agents at airports and ports. Surely Chico would have been detected there.

'Did you leave with your own passport?' I asked him.

'Yes, of course,' he answered.

I couldn't accept this: so much pain, suffering and even death for a man who was already in prison, twenty minutes drive from Villa Grimaldi? All those killings because the secret services could not coordinate their actions? Because of a mistake? They tortured me ad infinitum and they killed that man in front of me because we didn't want to give any leads to Chico's whereabouts, or because we did not know. All for nothing? All because of a mistake? No, it was not possible.

On the one hand I felt glad because Chico had escaped the worst and on the other hand I felt resentment towards him. This is madness, I thought. I had better stop talking. I had better keep silent and open my eyes wide and look through Chico, at a point in space behind him, and beyond, because nothing makes sense and I need to keep my sanity. A sudden departure is required.

'I'll see you some other time then. I'm glad you are here. You've got the hotel number. Goodbye.'

'By the way,' Chico added, 'my wife will be glad to see you.'

Another shock for me. Had he got out of the country under the very noses of one of the most efficient killing machines in the world with his wife and child?

After he got off the train, another, sinister, thought crossed my mind: what did Chico do in order to get out of the country unscathed, with his family? With his wife, who was also wanted by the secret police? Anything could be both possible and impossible at the same time. I went back to the hotel and straight to bed to try to sleep.

A few weeks later Chico came to see me at the hotel and, as I was about to be re-housed somewhere in Birmingham or Coventry, he told me that the Party needed me in London and that I should stay with him. He was living in a squat in Vauxhall with his wife and child, plus two other comrades. As my face showed surprise, he rapidly explained to me what a squat was in the UK, that it wasn't illegal, that it was safe and nobody was going to do anything to us. I wasn't totally convinced: squatting is something that if you do it in Chile, the police turn up in riot gear to evict you, and there is tear gas, beatings and arrests. I accepted the offer, I think, because it is in our nature: never reject an offer to challenge the system, to be on the margin, on the other side, no matter how small. After all, we were marginal, discarded, rejected here.

It was a two-storey Victorian terraced house with a basement, designated for demolition. I was given the basement room at the back, which had a broken window that looked out on a frozen garden. It was quite a damp room. The next thing was to visit the skips of the neighbourhood to collect a bed, a mattress and a huge electric heater that looked to me as if it has been designed for industrial purposes. It ended up being a very efficient companion in such conditions, and I was very happy with it, that is, until the electricity bill arrived; the consumption was industrial as well. I was asked, by the other residents, to get rid of my lovely electric heater companion; but by then it was time to move home. Not, however, before a DSS officer came to assess whether I needed money to buy a bed, bedding and other essentials. She decided that the damp mattress, pillows and borrowed bedding I had collected from the skip were enough for a refugee and denied me the badly needed payment. What the hell, after all I was alive. I couldn't ask for more.

It wasn't easy to live with Chico. I found it too difficult to get used to the seemingly normal little quarrels of married life. His wife, whom I had briefly met during my hiding in Chile, was an attractive, vulnerable woman. Chico was a strong character who had been a manual worker and held old-fashioned ideas on the relationship between husband and wife.

I could not understand how he could treat his wife the way he did, trying to put her down all the time. I could not accept the situation any longer and decided to talk to him. I told him that I thought it was disrespectful of him to behave the way he did, particularly in front of me; that he should realise that I was just coming from a situation where a lot of abuse, humiliation, and death had taken place. Death was all around you. There you learn that life, respect for other humans – especially in personal relationships – is very precious. That one has to be considerate and delicate. I could no longer tolerate his outbursts of temper, and I had to go. He answered that I had to learn to live in the real world now, but accepted that it was better for me to leave.

A few years later Chico would be horrendously murdered by Pinochet's secret police after entering Chile illegally to join the resistance. His family did not believe the official version of events: that he had died when attacking the 'security forces'. The family opened the sealed coffin they were given. Inside was Chico's mutilated body. His right hand was missing, as were two fingers on the left; some toes had also been cut off. His body was riddled with bullet wounds, criss-crossed from head to toe.

★　★　★

They did not hang me. They took me back to the torture centre. I was taken into a room and they stripped me again and a group of about six people, among them a young woman, started to punch and kick me and beat me with poles and what felt like an iron bar while they shouted insults and abuse. Blindfolded and tied up I fell to the ground where they continued with their attack for a long time until I lost consciousness. When I woke up they were dragging me outside. They lifted me onto a wooden platform and then proceeded to tie my arms to a wooden bar. Once they had done this, they took the platform away and left me hanging from my arms. This was particularly painful as I had previously broken my left elbow, and this had left the arm slightly bent because the injury had never healed properly. Once hanging they attached electric wires to parts of my body again and restarted the electric shocks. This time there were no questions asked. There was just shouting and howling, and laughter from them. They laughed at the convulsions my body made. Perhaps my skinny, nude body made a funny shape hanging in the air. Perhaps they were drunk with cruelty and perversity. I did not last too long there. When I woke up I was on the ground all wet and shivering; it felt like night time.

★　★　★

'Yes, I know, my little one, anyone can climb the monkey bars at the playground.' We are in London in Alexandra Park. 'You want me to do it first and then you will follow. Yes, I am coming, I will do it, I will help you; I am getting ready, I won't be long. How long, I do not know. Yes, I can hear you. I am coming! Let's go home now my love, I am cold, it is getting very cold.'

'It is not cold daddy. It is a hot day, come on.'

'Let's go home. It is time to go and it is getting cold.'

'We just arrived, daddy.'

'You make me lose my patience, let's go.'

I am irritated with my daughter because she won't come back home. 'But there are things I cannot tell you, my darling. I cannot tell you why I do not like hanging from the monkey bars. I cannot help you to hang from them either because . . . because . . . because . . . because your little arms may not be able to support your little body. Yeah, I know that is crap. I do not know what to say. I can see from your inquisitive little face that you cannot understand. Daddy is a bit weird; he changes, sometimes very quickly, from smiling and playful to serious, silent, grumpy and sombre.

'If I could only shake it off me, my darling, I would climb all the monkey bars and all the tall trees under the sun and hang from them like monkeys do. And I would not feel this sudden coldness, and my muscles would not feel so weak, so tired. I would not feel this terrible pain on my right side either. Something is not right there, I know.

'Maybe I am getting old. I know, thirty-seven is not that old, but maybe I am not thirty-seven. Maybe something strange happened to time. I did not know what time it was back then, nor what day, nor whether it was day or night. Maybe I travelled back in time, to a very old time, millions of years ago. I think I did. It was a very long journey, a terrible journey to the beginning of existence. You see, that made me very old, a lot older than I appear to be, especially in my body. Sometimes my body does things on its own, as if it wants to remind me of something, and I do understand. But the problem is that, during the long, dark journey I lost contact with my body. You have to, you see, otherwise you do not survive. Now, disconnected from your body, you do survive the journey but the price is that you do not know what is going on anymore, because the body has its own memory and you have lost access to it. I think that is all I am prepared to tell you tonight.

I am glad you are asleep because you could not have understood, and the truth is I do not want you to understand any of this. What did you hear my sweetheart? I was only humming. I hope you went to sleep during the monkey bars bit because I can assure you we will climb together one day. Sleep, my little one. I'll be here awake for a long time, guarding your sleep so nobody comes to take you to the dark corners of life. It doesn't matter, it is always the same; it is difficult for me to sleep, especially at night because the night is a dark corner. So I usually fall asleep when I can sense that a new day is going to be born, when the birds get a bit restless and people begin to turn in their beds.

# Diana Aron and Anita Maria 11

It was October 1972, the time of the lorry drivers' strike. The strike that we now know, due to the declassification of its files on Chile, was financed by the American CIA to the tune of about US$4 million. What we always suspected is now public knowledge: that the CIA was completely involved.

The Party had ordered that information gathered from all the different regions and layers of the organisation be processed by the intelligence and counter-intelligence section. My unit was the one chosen to collect the information from the regional delegates and each member of my unit had a delegate assigned to them. We were to meet them once every two days until the crisis was over. For reasons of security we did not know who we were going to meet until we actually met them, and one day, due to the others' reluctance to get up early, it fell to me to meet one of the delegates at seven o'clock in the morning.

That was the first time I met Diana, though at the time I knew her as Ursula. She was the only delegate that brought a typed report in a folder. She dressed very formally but delicately too; her hair was long and black, tied in a ponytail. She wasn't the typical young Party member, usually casual, even scruffy in their appearance. She would arrive punctually at the meeting place, in a hurry, as if anxious to deliver her report, crossing the busy road trying to avoid the traffic, even jogging sometimes. She would address me very formally too: 'Here is the report, *compañero*. Any comments from the last report, *compañero*? Would you like to confirm the next meeting, *compañero*? She reminded me of a joyful bird, always fresh from an early morning dip in the pond.

When the lorry drivers' strike ended and the crisis was over we had a last, brief, morning meeting. I told her that it would probably not be necessary to meet again, that her reports had been most useful and that everyone in my section was impressed with them and would like to thank her. We fixed a meeting in three days' time but I told her about the possibility of me not turning up; she should not wait for more than five minutes.

As it happened, I could not attend the meeting. I was disappointed that I could not see her for one last time. On the other hand, this was probably the best outcome as it wasn't a good idea to get too fond of someone who I knew nothing about and who was supposed not to know more than was strictly necessary.

A few weeks later I was at a regular section meeting when, almost at the end of the session, a woman sitting opposite me slid a folded piece of paper across the table towards me. When we finished, I stood up and read the message. It said 'I wanted to say goodbye, *compañero*, Ursula.' I felt terrible. I remembered that I did not attend our last meeting but, I thought, I did say to her that I would probably not be able to go. Now it seems clear that she was expecting me to turn up. That, although it was not a certain arrangement, I would turn up just to see her once more. I ran after the woman who had given me the message and asked her if there was any possibility that she could send my deepest apologies to the *compañera*, that Party responsibilities beyond my control had prevented me from turning up that day. The woman told me that it would be difficult but that she would try to reach her. Then, very cautiously, I asked her if she could give me a telephone number. She said that she would see, giving me a reproachful look. A week later she came with the number. Again, she gave me the same look, as if to say 'I should not be doing this, you should not have requested this, be careful.' But she was also an accomplice in breaking the Party rules, which did not allow contact between members in case of capture and interrogation.

I phoned the next day and to my relief 'Ursula' answered. As Party security regulations had been broken, I apologised profusely and tried to keep the conversation on that level, but we both knew that we could not keep it that way, that it was silly to carry on with formalities.

'Can I see you?' I asked.

'Yes,' she said, 'I have some free time tomorrow. If I give you directions, could you come to my place at about lunchtime?'

Diana. At the time she was studying journalism at the Catholic University in Santiago.

'Yes, of course,' I said, a bit taken aback by her assertiveness.

The next day was a Sunday. I was living on my own in a very small apartment in the basement of a tall building in the Providencia area. I drove my 2CV to the area where she lived, in the old part of Santiago, where my family used to live from when I was born to until I was about four. It was a four-storey 1930s apartment building in Gorbea Street. She lived on the first floor. She opened the door and met me with a broad, beautiful smile, without the seriousness of the crisis days. Even her hair was more loose, partly tied up with a band. She looked so beautiful.

There was also a very fair young woman in the flat with her daughter, who looked exactly like her. She introduced her as her sister, but they looked very different, not like sisters at all. Diana cooked and we sat at a small table to eat. We talked and, when we finished, her sister and her daughter left. It was very strange. When her sister was with us it was as if everything was so normal, as if we knew each other from before, and when we were left on our own it was as if we were strangers again. We looked at each other with apprehension. We sat and started to converse. I apologised again for my failure to attend the last meeting. We laughed at our clumsiness and started to get to know each other. I thought that I was in love already. I was captivated. She was one of those people who smiled with her eyes.

She came from a Jewish family. Her father was of Spanish-Jewish descent and her mother Polish. She also had a couple of aunts and uncles in Chile who I would later meet and who had survived Nazi concentration camps. She had the air of a well-bred, educated young woman with a certain air of innocence, as well as of frankness. We agreed, each pretending that we were not interested in the other, that it would be a good idea to meet again. We looked in our diaries and found that we were both very busy. She worked full time in a publishing company and the rest of her time she dedicated to party work. I worked part-time, studying and doing Party work. We both agreed that we had no free time to meet for some weeks except, coincidentally, the next evening!

The following day we met at her place early in the evening. Later, I was about to leave when we both agreed that it had been a lovely evening and that it would be an excellent idea to meet again. The problem was when? Again, we looked in our diaries, in my case without really looking, since it was clear to me that I wanted to meet her again as soon as possible. Surprise, surprise . . . neither of us had any free time except the following evening! We agreed to meet at her flat again. We had a meal and late in the evening I said that I had to go; that I had to get up very early the next morning and so we arranged to meet in two days' time. She came with me to the main door of the building to see me off. Reluctantly I started to walk. I crossed the deserted road, darkened by the trees. I reached the street corner and turned around. She was still at the door with her arms crossed and a look in her face as if not understanding why I had to go. I hesitated, and then started to run towards her as if propelled by an outside force; she started to run towards me. We

Diana's class at university. She is the smiling woman in the front row wearing a white shirt.

met in the middle of the road where she jumped into my arms. I lifted her in the air and spun her around. We were both crying and laughing at the same time. We were kissing each other as if to make sure that what was happening was really happening; that I would not go away this time. We walked towards her building and climbed the stairs looking at each other, smiling and kissing, hands locked together. The full moon shone through her bedroom window, its light caressing her face as we lay together in tears, in happiness, in love. Her name was Diana, Diana Aron. I would find out that Diana was truly a remarkable woman.

★   ★   ★

About six weeks after I had arrived at the torture centre, the interrogation stopped for me. All that remained were the daily beatings by the guards, the insults, the humiliation, the sleep deprivation, the hunger and the witnessing of so many atrocities being committed against so many people. People would vanish in the middle of the night, taken away in big refrigerated lorries. We were told that these people, since they were not needed any longer, would be released. We would later learn that almost all of the people that were taken away during the dark hours in the refrigerated lorries disappeared forever.

Sometimes, whispering, we would learn about each other and give our names. As soon as one arrived at Villa Grimaldi, or Terranova as the DINA used to call it, one was given a number and was addressed by that number all the time. The use of names was prohibited and any breach of this rule was severely punished. We would talk a little about our lives. Only a little, though, because you could not trust anyone. So it was a great risk to talk to one another, apart from the risk of being discovered doing so by a guard.

One day they were interrogating this man who was a big, strong, young man. But, in my view, he was being quite cowardly under not much harsher treatment than was usual at the average interrogation. He hadn't even been stripped of his clothes but he was sobbing like a child and, with very little pressure, he would come up with the name of his former teacher or neighbour who he believed might have had left-wing inclinations. Even a former girlfriend of his was brought in for interrogation.

The next day, in between interrogation sessions, he was placed in the room were I was. After he calmed down, I asked him why was he unable to resist a little and not give the whereabouts of so many people, most of whom were only brought in for the sole pleasure and amusement of their tormentors. Young, pretty women would be sexually abused by many torturers at a time. He said that he was scared that he was going to be killed and that he could not bear even the smallest physical pain and that he did not know what to do. I told him he could do what we all did when the pain was no longer bearable, and that was to invent meetings in the street with fictitious people. They will take you to the chosen location and the fact that nobody turns up to meet you won't be your fault. Your comrades might have realised that you have been detained. Invent, brother, invent! And so he did. But when he came back from his first trip without identifying anyone it was too late, and they did not believe him. He was viciously tortured and he confessed that he had invented the whole thing. During the torture they asked him why he had done that, when he was doing so well cooperating with them? He told them that I had told him to do it. They came straight to get me and dragged me out of the room hitting and kicking me all over and hanging me from my arms again. To my surprise, I heard a voice saying that there was no point in wasting time on me. I was a bastard son of a bitch, a traitor to the fatherland who would not change and the only remedy for those like me was death. Ha! He added that it would happen very soon. I was left alone without further punishment. I was getting away with it pretty lightly, I thought. Perhaps they will kill me, without any more torture.

★   ★   ★

Tano was captured on a street corner; they were waiting for him in ambush. He had no time to shoot, only time to move his hand towards where he had his pistol. He was shot twice, in one hand and his abdomen.

When you are pitted against killing machines, you have very little chance if you have not transformed yourself into one. History is flooded with the blood of heroes who dared to stand against overwhelming power and who did not make that choice. One has to be prepared to shoot first, not always to try to double check, to understand the situation, to be absolutely convinced that the fellow human being facing you is really intending to kill you. You do not want to cause unnecessary damage, but when you have finished your thinking process it is already too late, there are already too many bullets in your body and you know there is not much time left. Thus, the daily account of dozens of detainees showed people being shot long before they were able to use their often unreliable Second World War pistols. This was how it was for those few people that had access to guns.

Tano was savagely tortured, especially in his wounds. They wanted to capture his girlfriend. He lasted for about five days before he was left to die, lying on the patio floor next to the toilets. One late afternoon, when a group of us were being taken to the toilet, I saw the long body of Tano lying there. His skin had a greenish colour, as though blood was no longer running through his veins. But in response to the noise of our chains and shuffling feet, Tano opened his eyes and looked up at me.

He seemed to recognise me and, as if he had just drawn his last breath, and in surprise, said: 'Luis? What are you doing here?'

It was the same feeling I had experienced myself just after I had been captured and was able to have my first glimpse of the wretched population of the place: disbelief, unable to accept the vision of comrades so dear and respected by myself, so admired by many, reduced to chained and blindfolded skeletons in rags, with defeat, humiliation, despair and fear imprinted on their faces. What can one answer to such a question in such circumstances? I wanted to say, 'You do not want to know, comrade.' Instead, I said, 'You do not look well, my dear child.'

Tano died that evening, other prisoners told me. Deep inside, I felt a bit envious of him. His had been a brief experience in that place of horrors, though a very brutal one. Also, because his brother was a military officer, he was treated with some kind of dignity; he was not abused or humiliated. But for me, more than anything else, what remained after more than a month in the torture centre was the fear of what was to come. The fear of more horror and degradation, together with the fear of going mad, of reaching the point of no return and losing all control over my actions and the situation I was in as a whole. If only I could kill myself! But they made sure I could not do this. Handcuffed most of the time, blindfolded and with chains around my ankles, there was very little I could do. Not to eat the meagre food would lead to physical weakness and loss of control, leading to my ultimate fear of going mad.

★   ★   ★

Nano was working in the same section of the Party as I was, intelligence and counter-intelligence. We worked long hours then, at the end of 1972, beginning of 1973. I was living with Diana in the old part of Santiago and Nano and Anita lived a few blocks away from us. Almost every weekday Nano would ask me to come to his house between nine thirty and ten in the evening. I would arrive punctually and wait for him, talking to his partner, who at the time was in an advanced state of pregnancy. I saw that it was difficult for her to move in that state and I developed a habit of preparing a hot drink for her. Only once did Nano arrive before I had left, which was usually at about one in the morning. He would say that it had been a very busy day and that he could not escape from the last meeting. This practice became a pattern and I ended up looking after Anita throughout her last weeks of pregnancy.

We would talk, and talk, and talk. We were living intense times and our conversations followed the same trend whether it was the present political situation, art, literature, theatre (she was an actress), child rearing, love, life itself. Soon we ended up talking about ourselves, our dreams and desires, our personal principles and values, our way of life. There was something very coquettish and flirtatious about this woman that I

Anita Maria – an intoxicating mixture of confidence, passion and coquettishness.

found hard to grasp at the time. It did not occur to me that her coquettishness and flirtatiousness were directed at me. I just took it as the way she was. The fact that she was in her lasts weeks of pregnancy made her look more like a girl, a bit cheeky, and she behaved the same way. She smiled all the time. I began to discover her. She had a wonderful voice, slightly deep, and she used her long, straight black hair as an accessory to enchant. The need to move it away from her face every now and then gave her an air of glamour and an excuse to look at you as if inviting you to join her in her dance. Her almost childlike interest in everything I had to say made me feel important to her.

Thus, the days and the weeks went by and Anita Maria now seemed used to my visits and showed great happiness at my arrival. I found myself looking forward to seeing her at the end of the day, becoming more attached to her big round belly and probably to the baby inside. However, I became worried that Anita Maria had to spend most of the time on her own in her condition and that I was turning into a surrogate partner for her. I decided to discuss my concerns with Diana. She said that she too found the situation a bit strange and that Anita was probably getting too dependent on me. She thought Nano irresponsible for not turning up earlier in the evenings and dedicating more time to his pregnant partner.

'Haven't you thought that Nano may be having an affair? That may be the reason why he has no time for his wife, particularly late in the evenings.'

I was shocked. Of course I did not think that Nano might be having an affair.

'No,' I said, 'that is not possible. It's just that there is too much work, too many meetings and emergencies.'

'Well,' said Diana, 'it's well known that that comrade is a flirt and that he is careless. And the worst thing is that he is using you. He feels less guilty knowing that you are there, looking after her, all caring, while he is with another woman.'

'That is typical,' I said. 'Is there anything that does not follow the same old pattern? Aren't we supposed to be different, to be part of a revolution, a change? It's pathetic, exactly the same as the bourgeoisie we criticise: make your wife pregnant and find a substitute as soon as possible.'

I felt cheated; so I decided to confront Nano about it. He listened to me with a cynical smile on his face.

'OK, comrade,' he responded calmly. 'I'm sorry I offended you. We won't meet at my house in the evenings anymore.'

'You explain to Anita Maria then,' I said. 'And say goodbye to her, and all the best with the birth.'

About two months after I confronted Nano and stopped seeing Anita Maria I attended a meeting with the people in charge of the different sections of information and intelligence. It was held in a big colonial house in the outskirts of Santiago. There were meetings being held in different rooms of the house. At one point, at about midday, I left my meeting to get some water. Along the corridor, another door opened and I saw Anita Maria, wearing black trousers and a black woollen polo neck, without her big belly. She looked less girlish and somehow more beautiful for it.

She smiled and we hugged. Then, holding my hand she pulled me along the corridor to another door. She opened it and pulled me in. There was a bed in the room and she sat on the edge of it. Tenderly she picked up her baby, who was awake, put her face to his head and smiled at me. Soon, tears were running down her cheeks. She was crying and looking at me. I did not know what to do. I walked towards her and embraced her.

'It has been so hard,' she said.

'Are you back with Nano?' I asked.

'No, not really,' she said.

'I am very happy for you and your baby,' I said, overwhelmed by emotion. She sat on the bed with the baby close to her chest.

'It is feeding time,' she said, lifting her sweater to uncover her swollen breast, which the baby immediately grabbed and suckled.

How much I wanted to stay with her and the baby, to embrace them both and keep them with me forever. Anita Maria and her baby, the wife of a superior who I had grown close to, and began to love without even noticing it. Seeing her crying in that room with her baby, the baby she wanted me to see as if it was also mine, I felt an enormous force pulling me towards her that I found difficult to control.

It is these kinds of moments in one's life that trouble me: when there is so much tenderness and love. When there is fondness and understanding, when there is so much communion of purpose. When there is a desire to embrace and melt in each other's arms only thinking about eternity. When one knows that that is the only act that would solve everything, that would move mountains and let us pass to the other side where we could look into each other's eyes forever. I stopped myself. I cannot do this, I can't commit myself; I am with Diana, and she'll be heartbroken. How can I make Anita Maria happy and at the same time inflict pain on another loved one? Why does the other loved one have to feel so bad, so betrayed, so hurt in the face of an act of love? On the other hand, what is it that Nano has done wrong to Anita Maria if it was not to succumb to a moment of tenderness, love and communion of purpose? Or was it? But, on the other hand, I remembered my grandmother saying to her sister 'no man should ever abandon a pregnant woman. Most animals do not abandon their partners when they are pregnant. It is something that it is just not done!'

Those are words that stay with you forever, not just because they were spoken by the voices of eternal wisdom, but because, once heard, they echo inside you until they become part of your soul and your instincts. The sight of a pregnant woman then triggering strong feelings of tenderness for her and the little human inside her belly. The impulse to caress that belly in order to caress the little human. To tell the baby that she or he is expected, to welcome, to tell him or her that it is OK out here, that there will be love. To ensure that mama feels like the most precious being under the sun performing the miracle of birth.

I know that Nano was sleeping with another woman while I was his partner's minder during the last weeks of her pregnancy. The fact that he was sleeping with someone else did not bother me so much as the fact that Anita Maria and the baby were deprived of the care and devotion they deserved. Also because Anita was lonely and upset at a time when she should have had all the attention in the world.

★   ★   ★

The summer of 1973 was a miserable one. Although the nice weather made things look brighter, sometimes the heat made fear feel colder still. Walking in the streets of Santiago was a stressful activity. Taking care to spot anything unusual, checking if one was being followed, trying to go unnoticed. The Party was already in full underground emergency operation. Communications were difficult since every meeting had to be prepared well in advance to make sure that one met the right person and that the person had not been caught and forcibly taken to the meeting place. Thus one would receive several notices of meetings every week from the coordinators, apart from one's own regular meetings with cell members.

It was not an unusual arrangement, then, to have to meet a woman comrade walking in the opposite direction on a quiet street. She would be carrying a net bag, popular at the time, of oranges, making sure that the oranges were visible. She would respond to a certain coded question. It was midday and although beautiful and summery, people looked sombre and worried. The young woman with the bag of oranges was walking too fast towards me, as though she was too eager to arrive at her destination, not really trying to find anybody. It cannot be her, I thought, and although I was showing the right magazine under my arm she did not look at me when we were close. That this was the wrong person became apparent when I noticed that it was Anita Maria. Now she recognised me and tried to smile. You are supposed not to greet or acknowledge any known comrade in a public place. We passed each other and after a few steps in the opposite direction we both turned around at the same time. I looked at her oranges; she looked at my magazine. We smiled and walked towards each other.

'Your paper is under the wrong arm,' she stated, kissing my lips. The summer version of Anita Maria was very different but no less beautiful. She was wearing a sleeveless top and a long, loose, flowery skirt. Her long hair was tied loosely at the back.

'What are you doing here?' I asked.

'I wanted to see you, and I thought that this was the only way to meet these days.'

After a while we were walking carelessly on the streets, turning here and there until we found a half-empty café. Soon I realised that this was not a formal, Party-related meeting. She told me that her baby boy was fine, being looked after by her mother, and that her five-year-old son had been taken out of the country by the boy's father.

'He was a liability,' she said. 'Every time he saw a military patrol in the streets he would pretend to shoot at them and shouted that his mum would give them a hard time because she was a member of the resistance. There was no use in trying to convince him of the dangerous situation we were living in. He just would not listen.'

She desperately needed to talk because she had been locked up somewhere on her own, and we talked about anything and about everything. Quickly, in desperation, she suggested we should go to a bar in a secluded road that used to be frequented by artists. It was very discreet and the wine was good. The place was small and dark. We sat at a small table and ordered tapas and a bottle of wine. Anita Maria acted with pride and confidence in that place, as if it was a sanctuary from the streets for her. I listened to her attentively, finding her very seductive, displaying all the charms she was capable of. She talked about her relationships and how she ended up with two sons and on her own. She talked about her career, about the street theatre in the poor neighbourhoods where she and her group used to perform just a few months ago. She talked about how weird Party life was for her and how difficult she found it to adapt to, even more so clandestinely. She talked about the pain of not having her little boy with her, of being on her own and about being an only child.

I talked about my family, my daughter, dreams and aspirations, visions of the world around. It was as if we had to compress everything in one moment because there would be no tomorrow. It was like we had a premonition, as if we were saying: 'This is the last time; this is the only time.' As if there was a death sentence hanging over us.

'You are handsome,' she said.

'And you are so beautiful. I like your voice and the way you look at me,' I replied.

'It is getting late, shall we go?' she said.

'Yes, let's go,' I answered, without really wanting to get up from the chair.

We walked through a park towards Plaza Italia. She took her sandals off and walked barefoot.

'Walk me home,' she said, and added, 'I want to buy a bottle of Pisco from the posh market in Plaza Italia. I need to get drunk tonight; there have been too many emotions for one day.'

We carried on talking as though there was a pact between us not to speak about the future, probably because it was too painful. We had no future to speak of.

We were nearing her place when we fell silent. There was nothing else to talk about apart from talking about the future, and that we would not do, as all the roads that led there were closed. We walked in silence, reflecting on what we had done. We had opened ourselves to each other in a dramatic way, had crossed a path that would seal things between us forever. It was as though we had made love and we were now exhausted and sad because we had to leave each other.

'I am staying with other people in this house,' she said, 'and I am not allowed to bring you in. Security reasons.'

'I understand,' I said. 'The curfew is only minutes away and I have got to go too.'

We looked at each other for a long time; we were in pain and there were no words for what we were going through. Slowly we moved towards each other and embraced and kissed for a long time, tears rolling down our cheeks. We left each other and I managed to get my last bus home.

Later, much later, two days after I had abandoned the house where I lived with Diana when she failed to return, I had nowhere to go and decided to use one of my emergency recovery meets with Nano. The situation was too serious not to report. The meeting had been arranged to take place in a pizza place in one of the rich neighbourhoods. The place was almost deserted when I arrived at lunchtime. Outside the sunlight was blinding so that the place looked darker than it really was. I stood at the entrance scanning the place and waiting for my eyes to get used to the darkness. Suddenly, I heard steps behind me and, before I could react, a hand grasped my right hand from behind. I turned my head to see Anita Maria's face. She held my hand without a word, just looking at me. I could not speak; I just looked into those beautiful dark eyes and saw a vast lake of cool, refreshing, dark waters. It had been nearly a year since we last saw each other.

Nano, who had been parking his car, joined us and we sat at a table. They ordered food, but I was in no state to eat. We talked about Diana's last moments with me, about our house, about her book of codes and so on. I was like a zombie; my eyes were fixed on a remote point where Diana had been. I do not remember the rest of the conversation, only that we were frantically trying to decipher Diana's codebook, one of the few things I had rescued from the house. We managed to decipher quite a lot, enough to recover most of her emergency meets. Anita Maria looked very sombre and I thought it was unfair to make her feel bad. She kept saying that I should make an effort and eat something.

'I am not able to,' I said.

Nano looked as if he was containing his anger.

'I know it is bad, comrade,' he said, 'but we have to continue.'

I could not answer. I was numb.

After a couple of hours we were ready to leave, Nano taking with him most of the deciphered notes on Diana's meets. He gave me a couple of safe addresses where I might stay. He also told me that I should expect to hear from him soon as it had been decided that we were going to work together. He was looking forward to it, but I did not answer. On the way back to the city in Nano's Peugeot 404, Anita Maria, who was sitting next to him, kept turning her head to check on me. She did not smile; she looked concerned. When I got out of the car she gave me a kiss and stroked my head. That is my last vision of Anita Maria. She must have been twenty-seven or twenty-eight and I loved her.

Three weeks later, when my torturers showed me the blood-splattered inside of Nano's car, where he and Anita Maria had been machine-gunned on 6 December 1974, they were boasting about how they had prepared their ambush and about how large Anita Maria's hips and vagina were, referring to her as 'that whore'. Although I was devastated, I was determined not to give them any chance of seeing what I was feeling inside. They do not deserve access to any feelings of mine, I thought, least of all my feelings towards Anita Maria. I felt as though yet another part of my being had left me that day, making me wonder when the whole of me would leave.

# Sweet voices singing 12

Blindfolded, I was shoved into a refrigerated van. This was it then, the last journey of my life. People were crying. The journey was short but we were thrown about as the van bumped over the unknown terrain. We arrived at our destination and the fear and crying intensified. I prepared to die. But, no, no mass execution for me. Instead I found myself in a new cell, a new prison. Solitary confinement.

Late one night they took everyone away and my section of the prison was left almost empty. Where were they taking them? About a hundred men and women. The women were held in the same part of the building but on the other side of the lavatories, with empty cells in between. There was a lot of shouting, screaming and crying. Some people were shouting their names out loud so as to let the others know who they were, in defiance of the prohibition against using names, as if the prisoners were already predicting what was going to happen to so many of them. They would disappear. Swallowed by the night.

Very early the next morning I could hear the voice of a young woman calling my name. It was a very soft voice. I thought I was dreaming and turned over on the mattress to carry on sleeping. The voice continued calling my name and I started to believe that I was deluded. I thought it was Diana calling me from some place. Maybe she was not dead; maybe she was somewhere in this place and had heard my name and was calling me now. I tried to wake up but I couldn't and the voice kept calling my name. Suddenly I realised it was not Diana's voice. It was a very different voice with a higher pitch. Diana's voice was deeper. I stood up from the mattress as if to make sure I was awake and walked towards the barred window. It was a sunny day and the voice called my name once more. The voice came from the women's section and I decided to respond.

'Yes I am here,' I said, without raising my voice too much in case the guards came.

'My name is Carmen and I am Argentinean,' she paused. 'I am very frightened . . . they took everyone away last night . . . I am the only one left. I think they are going to kill me. Are you on your own too?'

'Yes I am,' I responded.

'Are they going to kill you too? I think they will because you were singing. I heard you singing and if I heard you the guards must have too, and I don't think they liked your singing.'

'I know,' I said, 'but I don't care. I did not sing for them.'

She was crying now and I said that she was not going to be killed, that perhaps she was going to be sent back to Argentina and the others had been taken to concentration camps. She calmed down and silence fell upon us. The place was really empty. She broke the silence again with her sweet voice and asked me if I would sing 'that song' for her. I said that I would sing for her. It was a beautiful song from one of Garcia Lorca's poems that I had learned from Diana, but I did not know where the voice came from within me. It was too nice, too easy to sing the high notes. I wondered how my voice had learned to sing in such a way. It didn't sound like my voice. Well, mysterious things have happened in this place. The distortion of life.

When I finished the song, I was shocked to hear somebody clapping; they were male hands. I could not guess where the clapping was coming from. After a while I realised that the person clapping was in the cell next to mine.

'Well done, it is really a very beautiful song,' said a deep voice with a strong foreign accent. 'I am a Belgian priest. I was detained a week ago; do you think they are going to kill me?'

'No,' I responded, 'you are a European. It would be more difficult for them to kill you I suspect.'

The Belgian priest gave me his name and started to describe himself. 'I am tall, with brown hair, and I have a beard.' Then the Argentinean girl, in her lovely Argentinean accent, said that she was feeling better after my song and started to describe herself too. The truth is that it did not matter how she described her appearance, for me she was the most beautiful girl in the world. Years later, while in exile in England, I learnt that she had survived and was living in France.

Of the people they took away that night, about a hundred of them, only a handful would survive the concentration camps, the rest were taken to secret places to be exterminated. I could not see their faces, nor could they see mine. Most of them were together in a big room at the end of the building. I could see their hands when they were stretched out through the bars of the windows and we would communicate, making each letter of the alphabet with our fingers. It was a lengthy process but it worked. We would tell each other our names and where we came from, where we had been detained and who else we had seen in our common journey. There were people from all over the country, from the far north on the frontier with Peru to the extreme south on the last frontier with the Antarctic continent.

There was a young man who used to sing with another prisoner in a different cell, and they would sing in perfect harmony. Only one of them survived; the one who created the songs 'disappeared'. One of the songs, the one that impressed me most, would never leave me and is still with me now. I sing it still on every occasion when people ask me to sing. Even people who do not understand Spanish like the song very much; it has got something in its tune that moves you. I have to sing it because he cannot, because they silenced his voice. He has to sing through my throat. I hope he is not too disappointed.

> Estaba yo un día sentado
> Conmigo en una mesa
> Estaba satisfecho de mi mismo
> Mi vida su miseria y su grandeza.
>
> No era un día de tantos
> Era un día
> No eran viejos amores ni cerveza
> Era un día de tantos el que yo amaba
> Su vida, su miseria y su grandeza.
>
> La agarré con las piernas, con los brazos
> Con la boca, con los dientes, con la lengua
> La agarré, la besé, la quise tanto,
> A esa 'sudestada' en mi cabeza.

I was sitting one day
alone at a table
I was content with myself
my life, its misery, and its greatness.

It was not just any other day
it was the day
it was neither about old lovers nor about beer
it was a day of so many other days, the one I was loving
its life, its misery, and its greatness.

I grabbed her with my legs, with my arms
with my mouth, with my teeth, with my tongue
I grabbed her, I kissed her, I loved her so much
that one, the wind that blows from the South.

We were not the only ones singing; others used to sing in the evenings, one by one or in pairs. In the mornings, though, there was a choir of women who sang beautiful songs that made us cry with longing. I was surprised they were allowed to sing such songs, so loud, so many times a day. From where I had come from, the only other human sounds you could hear were those of the pain and terror of the prisoners or the voices of the torturers in their frenzy. The women's choir sometimes frightened me. What are they doing there? What are the security forces doing to them? What is the purpose of their singing? Are they trying to tell me something? Do they know I am here? Are they trying to drive me mad, making me want to cut the bars on my window and jump the high wall with barbed wire to get to them? Is Diana among them? If not, why are they alive and Diana isn't? Carry on singing, sweet voices; it makes me feel that none of this has happened, that the nightmare is about to end and I am going to embrace you soon. We will sing so many songs then.

In this detention centre we used to get two meals a day and although we were harshly treated we were not beaten or tortured. There was bread twice a day too and I managed to make a set of chess pieces by mixing the bread with water and toilet paper. The black pieces were mixed with blue paper. I encouraged other prisoners in separate cells to do the same and so we managed to play chess with each other by shouting the movements through the bars of the windows. It all ended when my cell door suddenly opened one evening and the two guards accused me of passing coded messages. It must have been a strange sight, me sitting high on the windowsill hanging from the bars and this weird construction on the floor.

'What the hell are you doing up there, and what the hell is this on the floor?' they shouted.

'I am playing chess,' I told them.

'Come down from the window,' they ordered and proceeded to destroy my chess set and to search every cell. They did not punish me any further, apart from taking away my bread ration.

They must have thought I was mad. Also, perhaps they even took pity, because when I first arrived I was in a very bad shape and could not walk properly due to injuries to my kidneys and back. I had lost a lot of weight and had nasty infections on my hands, in between my legs and on my feet. As I was placed in this small cell on my own, I took all my clothes off and waited until the guards took me to the bathroom. There were showers there and the guard gave me some washing powder. As I was supposed to be in solitary confinement, I was in the bathroom on my own, with the guard close by pointing his machine gun at me. I showered myself for a long time, as if trying to wash from me all that had happened, especially the memory of their hands on my body. I then proceeded to wash all my blood-stained clothes including my jacket. During the days that followed I stayed in bed almost all the time. At mealtimes, the guards would open the door and slide the food along the floor and leave. One day there was a different guard who asked me to stand up from the bed. I said to him that I did not want to stand up, to which he shouted that the point was not whether I wanted to or not. It was an order of his and I should just obey. I told him that I had had enough in the past few months and that he should leave me alone. He shouted louder still, at which point I stood up from the bed and showed him my naked body.

'Why are you naked?' he asked.

I told him that my clothes were all wet and I was waiting for them to dry. I must have washed my clothes every day for a week and when they eventually dried out I only wore my underwear.

'They will never dry if you wash them every day,' he pointed out.

'They need a lot of washing, sir. They have been through a lot.'

'Get back into your bed,' he ordered and left the room.

Eventually my wounds began to heal, my right kidney was less painful and so was my back. Little by little my strength was coming back. Still I had to remain very alert. Every single noise had to be registered and analysed. It was a matter of life or death. One has to know what is going on, who is coming, whose steps they are, what mood the person is in, what authority the person has. There is very little time, sometimes a fraction of a second, but it is like an obsession, one has to know who is coming and what his or her intentions are. It is as if one's body needs this information to get ready, to prepare itself; it is a reflex, the need to know in anticipation. One's system gets flooded with adrenaline in the hope that there will be the time and opportunity to do something, anything, even if that something is to switch off the system, to give up and get ready to die. This is very taxing; one gets very tired and sad. Too often, the anxiety, the panic, wins through. There is no time to relax; it is dangerous to relax. The muscles remain tense, always ready for action, even if that action is not an external one but the opposite, an internal one, tensing like a spring, a spring you know one day, very soon, will snap.

The prisoners they took that night were soon replaced by new ones who we had to learn to trust and teach the rudimentary sign language which, after a few days, would be used frantically by everyone with access to a window. One could see, in the distance and if looking obliquely, the hands and fingers dancing in the air, communicating personal details and histories. The hands and fingers were giving names back to people who only a few days before were numbers.

I do not remember how long I remained in solitary confinement, maybe several weeks or perhaps an eternity. One day, at noon, I was ordered to get dressed in a kind of denim jacket and trousers that were about three times my size, because it was time for me to go, to be taken somewhere else, to another part of the camp as it turned out.

I had got used to my cell. There I was able to take a cold shower daily, until I was satisfied that I did not smell of torture anymore. I could also mend my torn trousers and my shoes with a needle I found in a tiny hole in the wall under the bed where I also found a very small piece of a plastic bag with salt in it. Strange things to hide, I thought and curious things to smuggle in too. With thread taken from the edge of the blanket, the use of the needle, and lots of patience, my trousers became as good as new and so too did my shoes. I also learned that beautiful song from another prisoner and got to know an old coal-miner from the south who occupied the cell next to mine for a few days. I learned to admire and love this old

# Tres Alamos                                          13

We walked a short distance through various corridors until we arrived at a very tall, painted, grey steel door. The guard, who was wearing the uniform of the Chilean police force, opened the door only a little, letting one prisoner go through at a time. I was the last one, and when the door opened I was suddenly blinded by the midday, end of summer, sun. I could not move; I hadn't seen the direct light of the sun in almost three months. My eyes had been badly infected by nearly ten weeks of wearing a blindfold and I could not see properly. The guard pushed me from behind and I desperately tried to see what was happening. Suddenly a deafening roar startled me. It was the sound of people clapping. I tried to see, my eyes too used to the darkness to respond to the intense light. It was the sea, a navy blue sea slowly coming towards me. I could see faces, all kinds of faces, unknown faces, but at the same time they were familiar. The sea was in fact hundreds of prisoners in navy blue fatigues. They were clapping, louder and louder, making no other sounds, just a roaring sound, like the waves on the rocks. It was like a dream, they were applauding me because I was there, because I had survived, at least up to that point. We were hundreds and we would not now feel alone. No, we would not allow it; we would give each other company, whatever the cost. Two or three prisoners came up to me and embraced me saying, 'Welcome *compañero*'. Then others came and one gently led me away from the steel door and into the navy blue sea that was now all around me.

'Well done *compañero!*' one shouted, offering his hand. Tears were rolling down another's cheeks.

'What have they done to you *compañero*!' yet another one said.

There were blotches of red in the blue sea. Some well-wisher had been allowed to dump a lorry load of watermelons in the camp and many prisoners had their heads buried in a half or quarter of a watermelon. I was offered a piece of the delicious fruit and some familiarity with life came back to me. This was the fruit of the grandmothers, of the country, of childhood, of hot summers by the river with my family. This was fruit with sweet, fresh water and a rich taste from the generous earth. This was the fruit of welcome to the visitor, the traveller, the one who comes from afar and is thirsty. This is the fruit that is the same for everyone, guards and prisoners alike, their lips, teeth and mouths enjoying the huge, smiling watermelons.

The camp consisted of a barracks-like building in an 'L' shape with a yard in the middle. At the back there was a big room containing bunk beds. In the long section there were about twelve small cells. The four toilets and two showers that served the entire camp – some 600 or so people – were in this section. Inside the cells there were two bunk beds, shared by two men per bed, with two or three others sleeping on the floor. Thus, in a cell designed for one or two people – since this had been a place of meditation for nuns – there were ten or eleven prisoners. In the big room, on the short section – which must have been the classroom – there were about forty bunk beds with two men per bed, plus two sleeping on the floor in the space in between. Still more slept in the space between the two rows of bunk beds. There were about two hundred men, and a number of rats, in a room no bigger than a normal sized school classroom, designed for thirty seated people. The four toilets were constantly in use and constantly blocked, as were the two showers, with a permanent queue of about twenty people. It was impossible to do anything unless it was late at night, before the doors of the cells were locked or very early in the morning when the queues were shorter.

During the night there would be all sorts of noises, from people snoring or crying to people waking up from nightmares. A mouse or a rat getting into their sleeping bag would awaken some, which in turn would inevitably wake two hundred others, while some could not sleep due to an illness or injury caused by torture. Still more would talk all night in their sleep.

I was assigned a space on the floor in between two bunk beds in the big room by a representative of the 'Council of the Elders', an elected body which represented the prisoners before the camp authorities and which tried to manage the chaos as best it could. On the evening of my arrival, after the watermelon and a few introductions, I was taken by members of the council to one of the cells where I was offered a seat and a cup of tea. The cell was very crowded with beds and people's possessions. I was introduced to two other prisoners and a young man who, with a grave attitude, started to talk.

'You have been in the torture centre the longest of those who are still alive and must have been through indescribable horrors. You must have also witnessed and suffered other people's pain and despair. We are very interested in knowing if you have seen a young woman who disappeared in November last year. We happen to have her photograph, as her father has managed to smuggle it into all the known concentration camps in the country.' He carefully took the black and white photograph of a beautiful smiling woman from his chest pocket and said: 'Her name is Diana Aron, also known as Ursula or Alba.'

My already bruised heart sank once more and tears flooded my eyes.

'I am very sorry comrade,' he said. 'Do you know this woman? It is OK, take your time, but we need to know.'

I struggled to get the words out. 'She is my wife,' I declared. The three men looked at each other and one of them, putting his arm around my shoulders, asked me what I knew about her and if I had seen her.

'No *compañero*, I haven't seen her, but I fear she is not alive.'

'What do you know *compañero*?'

I told them what I knew from Villa Grimaldi and asked if they knew where her father was. '

'We believe he has gone back to Israel,' one of them replied. 'We are very sorry *compañero*, we are sorry we had to ask you, but you must be strong now.'

'Do not worry,' I said, 'I think I know how to be that; it is just that I am a bit tired of it.'

The prisoners had to eat outside on long wooden tables placed near the walls. There were two meals a day, which were prepared in the camp's kitchen and some prisoners were called daily to help with the cooking. The food consisted mainly of boiled potatoes, beans or chickpeas. Huge quantities of lard would be added to the water that these were cooked in and sometimes beef fat would be added. Bread was also distributed once a day. Seating was mainly organised by political party, although other factors, like place of origin, being in the same cell, or simply friendship were also possible.

The day after my arrival at the 'Tres Alamos' concentration camp, I was invited to share the table of the man I had briefly talked to in the cell next to mine in the solitary confinement section: the old coal-miner from the south. He greeted me with great affection and introduced me to his comrades as his friend. He was a short man who looked as if he was in his late seventies, although he could have been a lot younger because coal-miners age much faster than other people. The other comrades were more or less the same age as him. They were all coal-miners from the same region and they all belonged to the Communist Party. I would spend long hours with them, talking at their table.

I belonged to the MIR, whose political stand was to the left of the Communist Party. There was a lot of animosity between my Party and the communists at the time of Allende and this was still the case in the concentration camp; each side blamed the other for the failures of the Popular Unity Government. But these men were different. These were hardworking miners who did not need lessons about politics to know who the enemy was, to know who was torturing and massacring the people. They had seen it all before, had suffered themselves as a community from the thirties onwards. Every single government for decades had sided with the mining companies, ordering brutal repression when the workers had protested about conditions and pay.

The next day I was invited to join another large table used by other young MIR comrades and socialists, among them an ex-minister of the Allende government. I was greeted and welcomed warmly. Nevertheless, I would spend more time with the group of coal-miners. Somehow I felt more comfortable with them. The young comrades of the MIR seemed, most of them, jolly and cheerful as if what had happened and was happening was just one more adventure; they kept cracking jokes as if trying to cheer me up. The jokes were usually in bad taste or just plain silly. I could not understand this behaviour; it was very disconcerting and started to irritate me. It took me some time to work out what was going on. Then I realised – none of the survivors here had spent more than two to three weeks in a torture centre or in solitary confinement. None of them had been injured. Their survival was testimony to this –

had they shown physical signs of brutal treatment and torture they would have been made to 'disappear'; evidence destroyed by the junta. During my stay at Villa Grimaldi, from early December 1974 to the end of February 1975, I saw four people brought in with bullet wounds and I heard of at least another three; they are all on the list of missing prisoners. There were others who had been seriously wounded during torture, with broken ribs and internal bleeding, broken legs or arms, mutilations, or who had been raped and abused or who were comatose due to suffocation, drowning and madness; none of those prisoners survived. They remain on the 'disappeared' list.

The concentration camp prisoners – with a few important exceptions – were more 'lightly' treated, and their experiences, though highly traumatic, were comparatively brief. Nonetheless, they were in denial – the humour and laughter was just a mask to hide the unbearable pain. But they looked fragile. The serious consequences of the torture regime they had endured would lie hidden for a few years but would come back to haunt them. And there were two years of concentration camp life still ahead of them, two years of harshness that would wear out any defence mechanism, including their humour.

Being a coal-miner in Chile amounted to everyday torture, without the torturers themselves being present. Hunger, cold, malnutrition, exhaustion, silicosis, extremely long working hours, working with dangerous ancient equipment, abuse and degradation, no prospects of betterment, blindness and early death were all part of their daily working life. And yet these were the kindest of men, their warm body language and the way they spoke, their attitude to life and death, their simplicity, their calmness, their solidarity, their lack of bitterness towards their tormentors. They were wise men too; that kind of wisdom you know has been transmitted from generations before them. The knowledge of how to relate to another human being, the unspoken language that is just a gentle stare, a silence, a hand in the right place at the right time, an action rather than an explanation, their openness and availability, their humanity.

No silly jokes nor trying to be cheerful at their table, just acknowledgement, recognition and acceptance. 'We know what happened to you comrade. They are bad things comrade, they are terrible things and they are very sad things comrade. Sometimes it seems there is no limit comrade. Finish your tea comrade,' one of them would say. I felt comfortable and safe with them. Apart from the fact that they could have been my grandfathers (I was twenty-seven at the time), with them I could be myself. I did not have to pretend to be cheerful and strong and to play the role of a Party leader who had endured the most atrocious torture treatment without compromising the Party's security. I could sit in silence, for long, very long periods, within myself. I could fly away and disappear, and that was OK by them.

The coal-miners all belonged to the Communist Party and one of them, the one who for a brief period was in the cell next to mine in solitary confinement, was severely beaten, according to his tormentors, for being stubborn. He was no longer working as a miner because he had been sacked after the military coup for being too old and infirm. Since there was no pension and no state benefit, he had to work to support himself and his wife. So he and his wife sold men's underwear at the mine gates as well as distributing Party pamphlets hidden in each piece of underwear sold.

They came for him at the gate and brought him from Lota – about 500 kilometres south – to Santiago to be interrogated. They had information that there was an arms deposit belonging to the Communist Party there and that he knew where it was. They had another prisoner – an eighteen-year-old boy – who had confessed these facts. The miner, realising that the boy (whom he had met before) would have confessed to anything in order to avoid more pain, did not want to contradict him and declared that yes, there was an arms cache, but that he had lost the instructions as to how to get to it. He was badly tortured before they realised that the story had been made up. Later, when they discovered that his wife was also a Party member, they started to torture him to reveal his wife's whereabouts,

'Where is your wife, you old bastard?' they would ask.

'I haven't got a wife,' he would answer.

This went on and on for hours with the torturers producing his marriage certificate and telling him, 'Look, you are married, you have got a wife, here is her name.'

He would answer: 'I haven't got a wife, you bastards, I have a "comrade". When you are born in the mines and live in the mines all your life, you haven't got a wife, you have got a "comrade" you stupid bastards.' He did not give up until the torturers asked for his 'comrade's' whereabouts; and then his answer was 'I don't know.'

Then, when he was being enrolled at the entrance of the concentration camp and the guards were giving him back some of his personal belongings, his watch and wallet, he asked for his ID card. The guards told him that he was not allowed to have his ID card because he was a prisoner of war, and prisoners of war could not have IDs. Being the way he was, he persisted until the guards gave it back to him, whereupon he replied: 'No, not this one, I want the "red one" back. I am not interested in the "national" ID card, you can keep that one. Give me the "red one" back or I won't move, you will have to drag me along.' The guards shouted a barrage of insults at him, but in the end they had to give him back his Communist Party membership card, 'the red one'.

After a few days sharing the coal-miners' table and wandering around the camp during the day observing the different groups of people, their conversations, their different accents, I thought I should join the comrades from my own party, the MIR. People tended to group mainly around membership of a political party but also by their place of origin. Chile, being such a long strip of land, contains an incredible variety of people and cultures as well as races. The men from the north, for example, were darker, while the ones from the extreme south, from Punta Arenas, were mostly from Yugoslav descendants. They could not speak any of the Slovenian languages of course, but they had the distinctive southern accent. This group, of about fifteen men, were all Communist Party members, but apart from that, they had very little in common with those members from other parts of the country, or any other person, for that matter. Punta Arenas, being very far south, is the last city on the tip of the South American continent and is extremely isolated from the rest of Chile. The only access to it from Chile is by sea or air. To get to it by land you have to pass through Argentina. Thus Punta Arenas has more ties, commercially and culturally, with Argentina than with Chile. Having said that, the Argentinean towns on the other side of the border are also so isolated from central Argentina that they have more in common with Punta Arenas. Thus, it is safe to say that the people are a community of their own whether Chilean or Argentinean.

There was obviously a fair amount of mistrust among the prisoners. There were people who had been in prison for over a year, who formed a separate group. They had been in the concentration camps in the desert of the far north and they carried the scars of terrible and unspeakable experiences. They did not trust the new arrivals. There were others who had been army personnel loyal to President Allende. They were not to be trusted, though they desperately wanted to be.

There were people from most sectors of Chilean society, although the upper classes were missing. There was no discrimination inside the camp; an atmosphere of camaraderie existed, despite the fact that some groups did not trust others. But once Party membership was established, and after the ice was broken, solidarity and even friendship were the norm. Perhaps the most reluctant group was made up of people who had been in detention since the coup, among them those who had been in the infamous Chacabuco camp in the middle of the desert. Chacabuco used to be a nitrate-mining town built by a British company in the nineteenth century and abandoned when the Germans invented artificial fertiliser just before the Second World War. Thousands of male prisoners were sent there soon after the coup. They gathered them from all over the country, although the vast majority were from Santiago. Conditions were extremely hard there and the sense of isolation was made worse by the unchangeable climate: always a blue sky and an implacable sun with more or less non-existent air humidity. It seemed as if these men had had enough. They had seen and experienced too many horrors and most of them were, from the point of view of the new arrivals, quite disturbed. We looked at them in fear of what we would become in a couple of years' time. They had daily rituals that looked weird to us. Everything they did looked like part of a strange ceremony, from getting up in the morning, to eating, relating to each other, going to bed and even the way they behaved with the guards. One of these was Garcia Lucero, a tall European-looking man, with fair hair and blue eyes. A few days after I had arrived in the camp, he approached me in the yard while I was taking a routine walk up and down the camp, which all the prisoners did, as if it were a town square evening ritual. He introduced himself with a firm handshake.

'My name is Garcia Lucero. I came from the Chacabuco concentration camp in the Atacama Desert. I belong to the Socialist Party, but I am here to talk to you in my name and nobody else's.'

He was in his forties, wearing a white T-shirt and white shorts, his skin bronzed by the sun. 'I want to talk to you because I have heard a few things about you and want to warn you about the camp inhabitants so you know where you are and who you might prefer to mix with,' he continued. 'The camp is divided into the following sections. There is the informers and collaborators section, the stupid bastards section, the "big balls" (super stupid) section, the poofs section and the sons of bitches section.' When he started to explain why one or another prisoner qualified for one of the sections he was quite vague, and it seemed as though individuals qualified for membership of more than one section!

In essence, Garcia Lucero was an anarchist. He was one of those people who could never be reconciled to any sort of organisation or institution. He was constantly punished for non-compliance with the camp's rules. He would not get up in the morning for roll call, he would not wear trousers instead of shorts, and he would always answer the guards back. When they came for him, he would remain in his bunk bed shouting to be left alone. 'You have done enough damage to me already, now leave me alone,' he would cry.

Garcia described how the Commandant of the small garrison at the Chacabuco concentration camp decided that his soldiers should parade in front of the prisoners and the national flag in honour of the Armed Forces Day on the 19 September. He ordered his 'troops' to practise marching, formation, and infantry movements accompanied by music played by the military band.

Garcia Lucero watched these manoeuvres with interest. After a few days of observation, he decided to have a word with the Commandant. He requested an audience and told the Commandant: 'Your soldiers do not know how to march; it is a shame the way they do it, without energy or coordination, without enthusiasm or dignity. I believe that you, the armed forces, we, the prisoners, and the motherland deserve better than this. This is achievable, Commandant, with more effort, by working harder and by being led by a person who knows how it should be done. That person is me, Commandant, with years of experience and with the gift of command. Allow me to direct the practice operations and you will be able to appreciate the transformation in these young soldiers.'

The Commandant thought for a while and decided to give orders to the soldiers and their band to place themselves under Garcia's command, without delay and with enthusiasm.

Garcia started work immediately. 'Left! Right! Band, music! Forward, maaarch!' And so he led 'his troops' through the dusty roads of the abandoned nitrate mining town turned concentration camp in the middle of one of the driest deserts on earth. Dressed in rags, shorts and a dirty T-shirt, his tall figure gave him the air of a European conquistador in some quixotic adventure.

After a few days, this incongruent group became a familiar sight for the inhabitants of the camp, prisoners and soldiers alike. For some, Garcia was an eccentric who had been turned mad by the torture, the heat and solitude of the desert. Others were suspicious of his friendship with the Commandant.

Having assured his command and the respect of his 'troops', Garcia headed one day, full march forward, with drums and cymbal, trumpets and triangle, towards the main gates of the camp. A few metres before the gates Garcia raised his command stick and shouted as loud as he could, 'Oooopen the Gaaates!' The guards at the gates looked at each other and then towards the guards on the towers, but no one knew what to do before the thundering and determined commanding voice other than open the gates.

Before anyone in the camp noticed the gravity of what was happening, the soldiers, rifles on their shoulders, started towards the desert like an absurd troop marching towards the edges of the infinite, with no other destiny than Garcia's own freedom. Garcia free and at the same time trapped in his own dream. On the other side of the barbed wire surrounded by hundreds of kilometres of sand and a merciless sun, the ghostly desert vision was disappearing into the distance when the guards realised that Garcia had no intention of coming back to the camp, at least not yet. Garcia was absorbed in a dream, where he was seated in his garden, cool under the shade of a tree, where he could watch his beloved Francisca, his young daughter. Machine-gun shots, the engines of the military vehicles and the cries of the soldiers awoke him from his dream. What was he doing there, in the middle of that deserted furnace in front of a handful of recruits whose command did not belong to him? He remembered the day of the coup d'état, with gunfire, uniforms, screams, and jeeps, still unable to understand the whys of everything.

His ephemeral triumph ended abruptly when he was hauled up in front of the Commandant. 'Do you know, you son of a bitch, what the penalty is for attempting to escape? The death penalty! My soldiers have orders to shoot to kill. It is a miracle you are not dead.' Garcia was breathless, but still managed to speak.

'How could I have escaped when marching in front of about thirty armed soldiers? And where do you think I was heading to, Commandant, to Santiago? I only needed more space to practise the marching.'

'Take him out of my sight!' shouted the Commandant.

'I only wanted to demonstrate that I was cleverer than them, Luis, that I could have escaped if I wanted to,' Garcia told me.

'Had you any idea where you would go?' I asked him.

'No, I only wanted to carry on walking in any direction, but free. The desert would have killed me, but it would have been in freedom, Luis, in freedom.'

Like Garcia, we all, in one way or another, while in prison, travelled to where they could not find us, only to wake up again. That is why I played a non-existent grand piano next to the torture chamber. We sang, we wrote poems on the walls, we read books and we even managed to perform a few plays. Although some books were made available by the authorities, they were heavily censored, but we did manage to obtain others that were smuggled in by relatives visiting the camp. Among these were two short plays by Bertolt Brecht, which were a great success when we performed them, and *Marat/Sade* by Peter Weiss, a play set in a lunatic asylum. This turned out to be our major production.

The focus of the play is a debate between the Marquis de Sade and Jean-Paul Marat which considers politics, philosophy and the place of the individual in society. I played the role of the disillusioned, deluded and fevered Marat, a part that came easily to me given my state of mind and poor health, while De Sade was played by a lecturer in history who possessed a Mephistophelean face and seemed to relish his role as a sadist. The parallels between the play and our situation were obvious and my fellow prisoners had no difficulties in capturing the essence of their roles as mentally ill patients. It was a memorable performance.

While we, the fairly new prisoners, related to each other with respect and preferred to stay at a distance from the guards, the old contingent were very familiar with each other and uncomfortably familiar with the guards and the camp's Commandant. While we were new to the brutal horrors of the torture centres and were concerned about the fate of so many men and women whose whereabouts nobody could tell us, they were cynical about it. It was as if they were saying 'We have been there, we know what it feels like, we don't want to know about it any more; all we want is to get out of here as soon as possible.'

In their relationships with each other they were like a dysfunctional family, fighting over trivial things one minute, friendly the next, performing each others' little rituals and gestures. It was irritating for us. I found this incongruous when something so horrific was taking place out there, something so close to the horrors of Nazi Germany, something very similar to their extermination programme, only without the gas chambers, but with the inaccessible Andes and the bottomless Pacific Ocean providing the hidden mass graves.

They were also reluctant to talk about themselves, about their experiences, and when they did it was as if they felt ashamed of what their captors had done to them. They felt ashamed of the way they reacted, accommodated and learned to live with what had happened to them. Perhaps they felt guilty for having been captured in the first place and for being alive when so many were not. It was, in any case, sad to see these fellow Chileans reduced to the state they were in and realising that perhaps in a year or two we, the ones who had just arrived, would develop the same syndrome: the concentration camp syndrome.

The concentration camp syndrome was made worse by the uncertainty of what the future would bring and the horror stories that reached the camp, brought by the prisoners transferred from the torture centres up and down the country. The majority of the stories were true, but others were reality mixed with the prodigious fantasy of some of the prisoners' minds. After listening to so many of these accounts, I began to believe that my reality was probably not as real as I believed but was of another dimension. Or maybe this was what I wanted to believe.

There was the possibility that Diana was alive, for instance, somewhere in one of the hundreds of detention centres up and down the country. Someone was certain that people who had been captured in the north of the country, had been transported to the extreme south, to a deserted island. I allowed myself to entertain the idea that this could have happened to Diana, and began to listen with great interest to the stories being told during mealtimes or while we were getting ready for the night. The stories would then inhabit my sleepless mind and I would find Diana in the most incredible places, in different states of health or mood. This activity, in turn, fuelled my daily interest in listening to as many conversations as I could, discarding the ones I found less interesting and leading me to look for the ones that had some degree of feasibility.

One evening at the end of April 1975, when I was in Camp 1 of Tres Alamos, I was called to the gate. I had to bring 'all my things', which was the euphemism for when they took people for re-interrogation, many of whom later disappeared.

The Council of the Elders tried to intervene on my behalf and told the guards that they had my personal details and that they were in touch with my family and the church authorities. All this was not true, but they believed that if the DINA knew that the church knew I was there, it would be more difficult for them to make me disappear. The guards responded that they did not know and that it was not in their hands; they were only following orders. Thus I was transferred to the solitary confinement block.

They kept me there for that night and the next day. Late on the second night I heard the sounds of people approaching my cell and then the door was unlocked. There were two men and a young woman standing there. The woman was Luz Arce.

She was a striking young woman who had belonged to the Socialist Party before being captured very early on in the extermination campaign launched by the military junta. At the time she was collaborating with the secret police in Villa Grimaldi. Many prisoners seemed to have known her in the past and quite a few others had met her at the torture centre helping the interrogators with their questioning. Still others had heard stories about her that ended with a shrug of the teller's shoulders, as if she was a mythological being whose actions could be one way or the other, good or bad, true or false, but had to be accepted.

Without talking to me the men proceeded to attach electrodes to my hands and fingers. This was done in a very matter-of-fact manner, without even taking the precaution of blindfolding my eyes. They sat me on the bed while one of the men took an electrical instrument from a bag and the cables that were connected to it. Luz Arce took a notebook from her bag and started to question me about a man they wanted and about the same things they had tortured me for during the previous three months. As I refused to answer, she started to shout and swear at me while the men worked at the electric shock machine. My body started to convulse and I managed to say to Luz that it was a waste of time because I would not open my mouth – unless screaming from the pain – while the electrodes remained attached to my body. She agreed and asked the men to remove the electrodes. She began with the questioning again and I told her that I had nothing to add to what I had already said in Villa

Grimaldi and that she should ask her superiors because I could not remember what I had said. She was furious, of course, and started to swear at me, arguing that she had agreed to the electrodes being taken off because I was going to talk. I had lied to her and she could not trust me anymore; she would have to take me back to Villa Grimaldi. I responded that if she had to do that, well . . . she had to do it, but I had nothing else to say.

The thought of going back to 'Terranova' chilled me to the bone. By now I had been away from Villa Grimaldi for almost seven weeks and what were before only rumours had now been confirmed: they were killing people as if there was an official policy to exterminate the opposition. Prisoners were regularly taken away and not seen again. People were disappearing in refrigerated lorries and there were relatives outside the concentration camps looking for them. The images of Nazi extermination camps came to my mind, the piles of bodies, the mass graves, the incineration ovens and the experimentation with humans. The experiments with humans: that was what terrified me most. But so did the realisation that we could all be exterminated and that we would all end up in mountains of dead, naked bodies, with our parents and our children; the realisation that the survivors of what had been the noblest social movement in Chilean history were already outside the country or inside the overcrowded foreign embassies in Santiago. And we, the concentration camp population, were held as ransom, ready to be exterminated. From now on, there would be no escape.

Luz Arce stepped outside the cell with her men for a few minutes. Then she came in to say that she would not take me back with her to Villa Grimaldi this time, but that she was sure there would be another time. This was the face of the new Chile that had just been born; out of horrendous atrocities and terror, the past had been erased and a new kind of person had emerged in power, devoid of feelings towards fellow humans, ready to hurt and kill if they could not get their way.

Disbelief, incredulity, astonishment, shock, words that attempt to describe what is beyond description, beyond words, beyond concepts. The world so far had been one with values, morals and principles that seemed to have been in place for ever, so deeply rooted in the fibre, not only of our society, but in the whole of human kind. They were not concepts that had to be profoundly analysed or exhaustively taught in order to be integrated by the individual and the society. In the words of my grandmothers, 'Things are the way they are, because they have always been so'. 'Things' were taught without words: tenderness, respect, fraternity, solidarity, tolerance, love, were things that emanated purely from the act of living.

Horror, fear, pain, suffering, extreme cruelty and sadism inflicted by fellow human beings, and more so by fellow countrymen, is something that one thinks, perhaps, could only have been perpetrated by an insane mind, by an individual who had gone mad. This was different though: this was a calculated and massive extermination of people carried out in the name of the state; atrocities, terror and plain butchery in the name of the state. This gave free rein to the expression of the most outrageous mental pathology until then locked up in the minds of the members of the Chilean armed forces.

I was sent back to the camp with the other prisoners three days after the interrogation with Luz Arce. Some of the 'elders' in the camp approached me with concern; others asked me what had happened, fearing what I had to say. There were no limits; nobody was safe anywhere and the usual rules did not apply anymore. There was nothing one could do, nobody who could help us, protect us from the savagery. There were no institutions, no law, and no sense. We were all alone, like the prisoners of the German concentration camps in Poland, surrounded by people but a population so terrified or indolent or both that we would remain alone until the end.

Strange things were happening, things that only helped trouble our already tormented minds. After a few weeks with what could be called 'my generation' of prisoners, I was transferred to a different section of the camp, with the 'old generation' of prisoners who were isolated from the 'new generation'. A huge wall separated the buildings. It was strange because amongst the old prisoners in what was called 'Camp 1' were also those prisoners who were going to be expelled from the country and were awaiting visas and flights. Many of them had occupied positions in the Allende Government and were being exiled to countries such as Mexico, Cuba and even Russia, under a reciprocal agreement that resulted in the release of foreign political prisoners.

'Camp 2' was empty, the prisoners having been transferred to a concentration camp near the coast, north-west of Santiago, in a very isolated place called Puchuncaví, the camp taking the name from the local village. We were transferred to Camp 2 while Camp 1 was filled with women prisoners who until then had been suffering in an even more isolated camp called Pirque south-east of Santiago. Soon after a number of prisoners had been expelled from the country – or so we were led to believe – Camp 2 was filled with more prisoners brought in from all over the country. The torture machines were working full time, devouring human flesh and discarding into the camps an endless flow of zombie-like people.

If one followed the regime's own logic, I should have been transferred with 'my generation' of prisoners to the Puchuncaví camp. What was I doing in the camp for those to be expelled from the country, the 'foreigners'? In any case I knew it was not good: for some sinister reason they wanted to keep me there, close to the torturers and the torture centres. Sure enough, one cold winter's day I was taken to the office of the camp's Commandant. It was a spacious room with a big window. There was a huge mahogany desk and a big leather chair behind it. Looking out of the window, though the view was blocked by one of the camp's walls, was a tall man in a navy blue jacket and grey trousers. After a few seconds he turned around; it was Captain Miguel Krassnoff, with his big, angry-looking blue eyes. It reminded me that although I was in what was called an open concentration camp, where one was allowed visitors, I was still in Krassnoff's hands. We were on our own, since he had ordered the guard to leave the room. The camp's Commandant had also been told to make himself scarce: no witnesses.

As I had already found something useful to do in my new life as a concentration camp detainee, I feared that my activities had been discovered and here was Krassnoff to give me his sentence for my new 'crimes'. I had managed to befriend a prisoner that almost everyone in the camp believed was an informer. I had found him secretly crying one night on his mattress on the floor of the large room. He had told me how bitter he felt towards the camp's prisoners for calling him an informer, that if he was so often called to do odd jobs for the camp's authorities, this was because he needed something to do and also because he had been told that if he did not do as he was asked, his beautiful wife would suffer. Although he was not an informer, if he was pushed he said he would become one, and would report on those 'extremists' that were mocking him. Those 'extremists' were some of my best friends.

I told this big man that I believed him and that I thought that those comments about him would soon be over, since prisoners were moved all the time. I gave him my pipe tobacco and a couple of chocolate bars. Our friendship was sealed. Soon after that, I had urgent secret meetings with my comrades and told them of my plan: almost every day, I had seen this man sweeping and cleaning the no-man's land between the camp's walls and the barbed wire fence. There was a passage leading to the solitary confinement building he also frequented; sometimes he had been asked to help with the distribution of food there. We knew now that this segregated area was the gathering point for prisoners coming from the torture centres that were going to be made to 'disappear', as well as those who were going to be sent to concentration camps. This man also helped with minor chores in the guards' quarters. In short, he was a rich source of information and so should be nurtured by us in order to extract information from him. It was important that we should stop accusing him, publicly, of being an informer, without arousing suspicion from the guards and the Commandant. As far as the camp's authorities were concerned, he should remain 'one of them' among us. They trusted him because the prisoners treated him as a traitor. He should remain that way without him feeling too bad about it, I told them.

I personally would remain his confidant, and that would require me not being seen to be too close with the so-called 'extremists'. Our meetings should be secret. Only the more senior members of the other parties should be informed of the true nature of my relationship with this man. My plan was accepted with the recommendation that I should be extremely cautious not to fall into a trap.

The 'informer' started to produce highly valuable information for us almost immediately, especially about who was in solitary confinement. He even managed to pass messages to and fro. I would tell him that I was interested in a certain friend of mine who had nothing to do with politics but had been arrested and nobody knew his whereabouts. He would make enquiries and tell me anything he found out. When I felt confident enough to ask him about the number of guards and their weaponry, the administration, logistics and real size of the camp and its surroundings, he did not hesitate and always came back to me with answers. I would then smuggle information about prisoners in solitary confinement out of the camp by way of visiting relatives. That information eventually reached Chileans in exile and the international solidarity movement.

So, standing here in front of Miguel Krassnoff, I was in no doubt that my secret activities in the camp had been discovered. For some reason I did not suspect the 'informer'. I feared that the leak, if there was one, came from outside the camp. One of the prisoner's relatives, who were allowed to visit their family member, might have been caught with a smuggled piece of cigarette paper and mentioned me as the source. Silence.

'I wanted to know how you were coping.'

Silence. Thirty seconds? Five minutes? An eternity perhaps? Does he really expect me to believe him?

'I wanted to know if the sadness is still with you.'

Silence; another eternity. What is he waiting for? Why doesn't he just tell me that I have been found out and that he will take me back to Villa Grimaldi? After all, he came with his dog handlers. I can hear them outside, opening and closing the car doors and shifting their machine guns on their shoulders. He is looking out of the window.

'How is life inside there?'

Silence; eternity; no answer again, I am waiting for the blow. I can recognise the dogs' barks outside, just a few yards from us in the parking space. They are the dogs from his team, 'Troglo', 'Romo', brutal torturers and murderers. He is going to give them the order now, I am sure, 'Take him into the car! Blindfold him!'

Instead he says, 'Who comes to visit you?' This is it, I thought, I have been found out. He knows I have been passing messages. He knows they are hidden in the heels of shoes and in cigarettes. No more silence, I have to defend myself, I have to attack.

'You know who is coming,' I said, breaking the silence. 'Your guards know everything, and they photograph everything, I have seen them, ask them.'

'Yeah,' he said, 'I have seen your sister.' This is it. Come on, jump at me, bite, you dirty dog, I can see your saliva!

'Who else comes to see you?' I had broken the silence, now I had to answer. I could not remain silent any more. I had fallen into his trap.

'Ask them,' I said, nodding towards where the guards would be.

This is it now, I have damned myself. Nothing will now save me from Villa Grimaldi. I feel cold with fear. I think about my poor body; no, not again, not that again. Silence, a long, unbearable, silence, and then suddenly, 'I came here to see if you needed anything.'

'If it was up to you, you would not come here to ask me what I needed; that is not what you are here for, is it?' I almost shouted at him.

'What would you do if you were set free today?' Silence. What is he playing at? Cat and mouse and he is beginning to enjoy it.

'I would carry on with the struggle,' came the answer from deep down in my being, almost involuntarily.

'By different means, I suppose,' he said.

'That would depend on the circumstances,' came my reply, when the truth was that I would have tried to reach the most deserted corner of the earth and stay there, cultivating the land in the company of a few animals. Silence. Long, thick, silence.

'I think we will meet again,' he said, and I thought that was enough and the grandmothers and all the ancestors and their anger came to me.

'Look, I am your prisoner and you are my captor and my tormentor. A guard brought me here in front of you without asking any questions. If the guard had said "Mr Muñoz, would you like to see Captain – or is it Major now after all your heroism? – Miguel Krassnoff?" Have no doubt that my answer would have been "No Thanks!" So, of course you can be sure we will meet again, because I have no option.'

Silence . . . and then, 'Guard! Take this prisoner back.'

# Puchuncaví 14

One crisp spring day in 1975 I was called to the camp's gates together with a group of prisoners. We were instructed to get our belongings as we were going to be 'transferred'. Nobody would tell us where we were going to be transferred to. We got on to the military bus in our rags. There were about twenty of us but we were not allowed to sit on the seats and had to lie down on the floor of the bus as best we could. Some of us, including myself, were handcuffed to a seat's leg. What a pity, I thought, it's such a beautiful spring day. It would have been nice to see the trees, flowers and mountains if we are going to die. Of course they wanted to conceal their cargo. Nobody could be allowed to see the ones who were about to be executed. So this is why I had been left behind in the previous transfer – I had been chosen to be executed together with these people on the bus.

The journey was frightful. The metal floor of the bus was not only hard and cold but bad roads full of potholes transformed it into a body-battering instrument. We drove for about three hours non-stop, the guards seated separately in the bus. We were not allowed to talk, sit, stand or make sudden movements. Somehow, though, some people recognised the route and whispered that it was the road to the coast. This meant that we were heading to one of the two known concentration camps situated on the coast near Valparaiso. In that case, perhaps we were not going to be executed, at least for the time being. The camps were called Ritoque, nearest the sea, and Puchuncaví, further to the north, in the hills; but we also knew that Tejas Verdes, an army unit nearby, was a torture and extermination centre. There was nothing we could do . . .

just let the body feel the fear bit by bit . . . get used to it . . . the fear of dying without knowing how, without knowing which would be the last blow, the last army knife somewhere in the back or stomach.

With our bodies all bruised, we arrived at about midday at Puchuncaví concentration camp, a scaled-down version of a Nazi concentration camp. The main differences between this Chilean version and the German one was that ours was made entirely from wood, including the high watchtowers, where guards with machine guns kept us under surveillance.

The camp was situated in a depression between low hills. This special position made the camp itself invisible from a distance since it was protected from view by the surrounding hills. Conversely, once in the camp, one could not see beyond it unless it was from the top of one of the 12-metre-high watchtowers. The A-shaped barracks, containing about six rooms each, were asymmetrically and unevenly distributed in about an acre of land.

As we got off the bus we could only see a series of large wooden bungalow-like constructions. These accommodated, to the right, the army personnel with their facilities, and to the left, the camp's kitchen, eating and 'leisure' facilities. At that time there were between five and six hundred prisoners living in nine barracks. The six small rooms in each contained between eight and ten prisoners. Two high barbed wire fences surrounded the camp with a no-man's land between them.

The soldiers, who I later learnt were marines, led us through a series of gates to where three prisoners in camp fatigues waited. A sergeant gave us a spoon, a fork and a plastic mug; we were told never to lose these items since we would be held accountable for them. We were finally allowed into the camp where the prisoners in charge of the different sections sent us to various rooms.

The atmosphere was less welcoming here. There was a sense of weariness under the burden of camp routine. The isolation of the camp and the lack of information from the outside world (radios were not allowed) contributed to the sense that our destinies were sealed: there would be no way out of here, not alive anyway. Another peculiarity of this camp was that the navy ran it and the regime was more militarised, with more interference in the prisoner's affairs. As before, there was a 'Council of the Elders', prisoners' representatives who went before the Commandant to represent the prisoners' demands. Since all the prisoners here were political, almost all the demands put to the Commandant had a political content or obvious double meaning: demands with a political sting attached.

Soon after being introduced to the other prisoners sharing my assigned room, the prisoner in charge started to read from a small piece of paper outlining the camp's rules. Then he took another piece of paper from one of the pockets of his fatigues and gave it to me.

'These are marine marching songs. You have to learn them because they have to be sung every day, twice a day, on our way to where the Chilean flag is flown. The flag is raised in the morning and lowered in the evening. During this ceremony the national anthem should be sung, including the new verses introduced by the junta.'

'Comrade,' I said. 'You are not serious, are you? I have never in my life learned or sung a military song other than when making a mockery of them. I truly loathe them. I am not going to sing them.'

'I am deadly serious comrade. The punishment for refusing to comply is pretty bad, and it would not just be you who would be punished but the whole section or even the whole camp,' he said with fear in his voice. 'That is enough for the moment; the call for lunch will be soon. And another thing,' he added, 'you may have already noticed from the smell that the meal today will be lamb in some shape or form, and tomorrow, and the day after tomorrow and so on. You see, there is an overproduction of lamb in the extreme south of the country. The navy has to patrol the coast and their ships get the lamb almost for free. It is distributed along the coast; it is cheaper than fish. So, lamb every day.'

'I hate lamb, comrade, it doesn't agree with me,' I replied on our way down the slope, past one of the gates, to the dining quarters.

The prisoners had to pick up a tray, a small plastic bowl and mug and collect their rations, then go back to long tables and benches to eat. The bowl and mug were sticky with lambs' fat and everything smelled of cooked lamb. The meal was lamb soup, with a small piece of boiled lamb. The mug of watery black tea was like a milder version of the lamb soup. This was because the dishes were all washed in the same water with almost no detergent, so the lamb fat got recycled there.

It was a strange experience to be there in the evening when the national flag was raised and the national anthem sung. First, there was a trumpet at 6.00 p.m. To my astonishment, everybody stopped what they were doing and stood to attention looking in the direction of the flagpole, even when this was not visible. It was like the children's game of 'statues'. But the problem for me was to witness the prisoners, fellow proud Party members, performing this ritual like robots. There was more to come. A few minutes later the prisoners had to form in sections around a perimeter in the centre of the camp with military precision, standing to attention. Then we had to march to the flag singing one of the marines' marching songs, closely observed by the guards, march back to the perimeter, perform a few more military antics and sing one or two more marching songs.

I could not believe it. The prospect of me being required to perform these acts made me sick. It was weird to see comrades forced to obey and humiliated in this way. Why didn't they rebel against this treatment? Why didn't they stand up to the Commandant and tell him we would not obey; we had suffered enough humiliation already and would not take anymore. My first night in Puchuncaví would answer some of these questions. After being locked up in our rooms (in mine there were ten prisoners, six sleeping in bunk beds and four sleeping on the floor), one of the prisoners, a young man, began to cry; he was shaking with fear. I could not understand what he was talking about but it looked as if he was having a panic attack. One of the prisoners came to me and began to explain what took place in the camp every two weeks or so, in the middle of the night. The military called it *zafarrancho*, an attack simulation. The machine guns from the four towers would open fire towards the camp; the room doors would be unlocked and soldiers in full combat gear, faces painted black, would attack the prisoners, drag them out of their rooms and beat them up. Others would be thrown against the barbed wire naked while being shot at, the bullets ricocheting on the ground. This form of torture would last a couple of hours. Some prisoners would end up in the infirmary. So I began to understand the 'docility' of the prisoners in this camp. That night, the man having the panic attack was convinced that there was going to be a *zafarrancho*, since he had seen some soldiers with painted faces. The others were trying to convince him that an attack was not due yet. I could not sleep that night, waiting for it to start.

During my first sleepless night I had decided that I would not march, sing military songs, or eat the nauseating lamb twice a day. Well, at least I would try not to, I thought. As a consequence of the torture, I was suffering from severe back, chest and kidney pain. One of the four doctors imprisoned with me believed that my kidney had become detached from the tissue holding it. Another thought that the urethra might be kinked. They also diagnosed that my chest pain was due to ribs being displaced, fractured, or both. My stomach was very sensitive, too, giving me a lot of trouble with the camp food.

The next morning at inspection and roll call, we had to 'throw' the right foot, to give the impression of a line of toppling dominos. When the order was given, I 'threw' my foot and fell to the ground in pain. The guards paid no attention and ordered the prisoners to keep in formation. I thought that I had to go for all or nothing, so I lay on the floor writhing in excruciating pain. Eventually two guards came and asked me what was the matter and if I could stand up. I answered that I did not know but that I was unable to stand up on my own. The guards and two other prisoners helped me to my feet and led me towards the infirmary. Once there I was given painkillers and sweet, fresh water. I spent two days in the infirmary. I did not march again or sing military songs, except when we gathered to salute the flag and sing the national anthem. I rarely had to eat lamb either, since I managed to convince the nurse that I needed a special diet for my condition: 'gentle food'. It was not difficult for me to exaggerate my pain since it was constantly there in varying degrees during the day. I did feel guilty, though, as the rest of my fellow prisoners would have to carry on marching, singing military anthems and, with few exceptions, eat lamb almost every day.

When I explained to my comrades what I had done, they were not impressed. 'Very clever,' was their comment. But I had to understand that not all the battles could be fought so quickly. Slowly and patiently the singing and marching would be abolished, they said. I told them that my body, indeed my whole being, could not wait; that I was used to a little bit more dignity in the previous camp. One comrade, who had been in this camp since it was opened, started to tell me the story of Puchuncaví. Prisoners were used as forced labour to build it, from the architects to the engineers and labourers. The prisoners were regularly terrorised and tortured, living in fear; there was nothing for them to do but obey. There were many of those prisoners still in the camp, many of whom had been in the camps in the Atacama Desert and who knew what had happened there. Many of them belonged to the Socialist and Communist parties. We could not force them to stand up against camp rules since this would certainly bring punishment from the Commandant. I had acted selfishly and without consultation with my fellow comrades.

I had also exposed myself to punishment, 'because once the camp administration takes notice of who you are, they will not want to believe your illnesses or your condition.'

I could see their point, but deep inside me I felt that the ultimate punishment had already been inflicted on me and I would not budge for anything less. I had not given in under the most abhorrent torture. I had even risked my little girl's life just for not wanting to give in. They could not expect me to be humiliated further under the threat of beatings, of being thrown against barbed wire or soaked in the middle of the night. It's true, I did not stand in front of the guards and tell them to their faces 'I will not sing your songs or march because I find it humiliating. I will sit and watch instead,' and face the consequences. But in a way I used a by-product of the torture, my ill health, to get better food and avoid further humiliation. Two weeks later a *zafarrancho* took place. There was shooting, shouting, verbal abuse and banging of dormitory doors. Although a terrifying experience and a sleepless night, nobody received beatings or ill treatment.

My sister managed to bring my little daughter to visit me in the camp a couple of times. It was a long journey for them, uncertain of whether or not they would be able to see me. We were allowed a once weekly, twenty-minute visit, but this could be revoked for the most tenuous of reasons. They travelled in a hired bus with a group of relatives for whom it was a whole day's trip to the coast for a few minutes with their imprisoned relatives. My daughter Dalia was cute, with big green eyes, fair hair in a pony tail, bubbly and sociable. She was known by most of the prisoners, standing out as a confident, carefree, smiling, little thing. She was adorable. During one of her visits, she went to play in a sandy patch next to the dining quarters. I sat on a bench just looking at her playing in the wet sand, as it had rained earlier on in the day. Immersed in my thoughts I wondered how one could explain to a four-year-old child that her father was in prison and that he was a political prisoner, not a criminal. Should I try to explain it to her then? And if so, how? I could see her hopping in the wet sand when suddenly she shouted: 'Political prisoner, come here!' I could not believe my ears, but she carried on calling me political prisoner. There was nobody around. I stood up and walked towards her. 'Look here, papa,' she said, 'I am going to leave my footprints here for you to come and visit when I am gone; they will remind you of me, as they are a bit of me.' Is there anything to explain to this child? I thought. I just picked her up in my arms and kissed her as much as she would allow me to.

It was the winter of 1975. The news was published in two bogus magazines, one in a remote city in Brazil, the other in Argentina. The bodies of 119 comrades had been found in different parts of these countries. 'They were killed by their own comrades as a consequence of the internal fighting of *terrorist* organisations.' All the major papers in Chile reproduced the news. According to the junta, this proved that 'our forces have not kidnapped people; most of them have fled the country and are sorting out their differences in fights amongst themselves.'

We were horrified by the news; most of the assassinated comrades in the news reports had been in various torture centres run by Pinochet's secret police, including Villa Grimaldi. There were at least fifteen people I had seen or been with during my three months stay at that torture centre. Several other prisoners now in the camp had seen the others. Pinochet and his cronies staged it all. But more than anything it demonstrated to what extent the junta was prepared to go; killing the prisoners it had been accused of kidnapping, mutilating their bodies and dumping them in the middle of nowhere with absolute impunity. There was also a very clear message: we, the ones in the concentration camps, could be next.

A group of us in the camp felt that we had to somehow make people understand that the story had been fabricated, probably by the junta itself. We had to tell our side of the story: that we had been with the assassinated comrades in torture centres, that the press had been eager to publish an uncorroborated story when a very superficial enquiry would have revealed that the story was a lie. We wanted to let the world know that what was happening in Chile was an extermination of dissidents by the Pinochet regime. The only weapon at our disposal was the hunger strike and we decided that it was time to use it. There was a lot of preparatory work to do. First, to discuss the idea with our comrades and agree a plan. Second, to put the idea to members of the other parties and reach some kind of agreement for them to participate and support the action. Third, to discuss the idea with the organisations representing relatives of political prisoners.

One of the main problems was how to break out of the isolated situation we were in. Miles away from the capital with no means of communication with the outside world, any concerted action would bring a furious reaction from the junta and the military in charge of the camp. The slaughter of prisoners was a serious possibility. To minimise this, we had to use the visiting relatives as our voice before, during, and after the action. If the military decide to kill us, we had to make sure that the outside world knew, as soon as possible, why and how we had died. Good coordination with the relatives was essential. The relatives would be in contact with international organisations, foreign embassies, the press, and relatives of prisoners in other concentration camps and detention centres.

Our demands were that the junta should: (1) clarify the situation and order a public inquiry that would hear the testimonies of the surviving prisoners; (2) explain why it had fabricated this story of internal fighting between Chileans abroad; (3) arrange for the Archbishop to visit the camp to meet the prisoners on hunger strike; (4) allow the international Red Cross access to the camp and the striking prisoners; (5) guarantee the safety of the striking prisoners and their families; (6) legalise the detention of thousands of political prisoners by a process of legal trials guaranteeing internationally recognised processes of law; (7) guarantee that there would be no reprisals once, and, if the strike ended; and (8) make our demands public.

It was a long shot. We were risking everything and we knew it. We had to make the necessary internal arrangements to be prepared for any eventuality. We knew that the first reaction of the Commandant and the people in charge of the camp would be to threaten and terrorise us in the hope of breaking the strike, to separate the strikers from the rest of the prisoners, to isolate them. We needed as many prisoners to go on strike as possible, but we also needed hard and experienced comrades who were not on strike to be in charge of communications; others had to maintain the support of the camp's population and organise other ways of demonstrating in case strikers were killed or died as a consequence of their action. The hunger strike would be indefinite and would only stop when our demands were met or if we were certain that prisoners of the camp, strikers or not, had been killed.

About one hundred and fifteen prisoners, out of about five hundred, volunteered to go on hunger strike. It wasn't a great number considering the size of the camp's population but it was a significant number all the same. Finally everything was ready and the time came for the 'Council of the Elders' to meet the Commandant and present him with our demands. There was the possibility that the Commandant would decide to punish the council members there and then and that they would not return. The council would tell the Commandant that the rest of the camp would be waiting for their safe return an hour after they entered his office. If they did not return safely, the prisoners would not only go on hunger strike anyway but they would revolt. 'You would have to kill us all, Commandant, and the world will know.'

The Commandant in charge for that particular fortnight was one of those rare officers in the Chilean armed forces that had risen from the lowest ranks. Although he was around fifty, he had only reached the rank of lieutenant, his promotion being prevented because he had not attended the select officers' academy. His name was Avalon and he was a lean, handsome man who made an effort to appear firm but fair, understanding and reasonable. He always listened to what the prisoners had to say with respect and tried to reason with us in matters of politics. It was probably a good thing for us that he was in charge that day. Once our intentions were put to him, he was visibly disappointed. As far as he was concerned, he had tried to be reasonable and had developed good relations with us within a framework of mutual respect and understanding. How could we respond in this manner, undermining his authority? He would have to contact his superiors; the matter would be out of his hands and then we would see that the others would not be as reasonable as he had been.

It was explained to him that our intended action was not against him, nor even against the navy. We appreciated and acknowledged his integrity as a marine, an officer and as a man, but that he should also try to understand our position: our comrades had been brutally murdered by the secret services and now they were trying to wash their hands in this despicable manner. We were convinced that in our position he would have acted in the same way. 'No,' he said, 'you are acting as a mutinous rabble and mutiny is not accepted in the navy.' In any case he would have to call the intelligence department and a senior officer in the navy. 'There is going to be trouble, I can assure you of that,' he said.

Sure enough, that evening they arrived in force. Personnel carriers and troops surrounded the camp. A group of officers were introduced to some of us as being from intelligence. They stated that the situation would be classed as a rebellion. We were military personnel and would be treated accordingly under military rules and law. They wanted to know the extent of our external support network since they understood we were not fool enough to take this course of action in isolation. After that we were dismissed to wait for further information and news. After quite a long wait, an Admiral appeared. He started to shout insults and threats at all the camp's prisoners: we could be court-martialled; we could be sent back to the torture centres for interrogation; our families could suffer; we could be transferred to camps and prisons in remote parts of the country; we could be kept in solitary confinement; the leaders of the strike and the participants would never leave the camp alive, etc., etc.

After his speech the Admiral ordered all the prisoners to form lines. Then he asked the ones who, in spite of what he had said, still wanted to go on hunger strike to take a step forward. Of the initial one hundred and fifteen or so volunteers, about ninety of us took a step forward. The rest of the prisoners were dismissed. It was already dark when the Admiral's words started to thunder again.

'Most of your comrades have already abandoned you; they have seen the futility of your action and the detrimental effect on the camp's life. The prospect of releasing the "good prisoners" has been thwarted. And what do you think you are going to achieve? Do you seriously think that we are going to give in to your demands? Do you think that the political circus of the past is going to continue? Do you think that you lot, who have committed crimes against the nation, deserve to be heard and taken seriously? Do you think that your threats to security and political action are going to go unpunished?'

So on and so forth the Admiral's threats continued to escalate. After a while he stopped and announced that we, the ninety or so remaining 'stubborn bastards' should line up in the middle of the camp in four lines separated from each other by three paces each side. I noticed that the rest of the prisoners were already locked up in their rooms. We were not allowed to talk to each other and I was preparing myself and my body for what I thought was inevitable: we were going to be beaten up and tortured here. The Admiral ordered the soldiers that were surrounding us to come closer with their weapons pointing at us.

'Before proceeding,' he announced, 'my intelligence officers are going to interrogate every one of you individually and ask you your name and whether you still wish to continue your action. If your answer is yes, the officer will warn you of the military legal charges you will face. If your answer is no, you will be free to go to the kitchen, have your supper, and return to your room as if nothing has happened.'

So the officers wrote down the names of those who had decided to go on hunger strike in protest at the savage assassination of our 119 comrades. This time the number of volunteer strikers was further reduced to about 70 prisoners. The others were dismissed. Out of 500 prisoners, only 70 would go on strike. Still, 70 people on hunger strike is not that small a number. We were told that we would be separated from the rest of the prisoners with whom we should not attempt to communicate. Visits from relatives would be suspended. Should anyone wish to change his mind, they would be allowed to do so; a nice meal would be prepared for him immediately. We were taken to a building above the toilets and showers. This was separated from the rest of the camp by barbed wire; it had the advantage that, because of its elevated position, it was visible from the road below. Thus we were able to overlook the entrance to the camp to our right and some of the village's houses to the left. We could not see the rest of the camp behind us, only a few of the huts directly on the far right.

That first night was full of apprehension. After we were left alone by the guards we started discussing the events of the past few hours. We assessed the situation, thinking about the different possible courses of action that the government could take. They could isolate us completely, trying to prevent the news of our action reaching the media, and try to scare us with threats of reprisals, attempting to divide us and break our resistance. They could separate us by transferring us, separately, to different camps and prisons around the country. This was the most frightening alternative for us for obvious reasons. Divided into small groups, separated from each other, we would be completely powerless, totally vulnerable, and they would be able to do anything they wanted with us. They would have a few difficulties with this course of action though. One was a logistic problem. As long as we remained a large number of prisoners, it would not be easy for them to arrange quick transport and accommodation for us. Another thing for them to consider was the fact that our relatives would, by now, have started their planned actions. The Archbishop and the church network would have already been alerted and our demands made known to them. The press would have also been informed as well as the foreign diplomatic representations in Chile. Or the government could start killing us one by one, thus forcing us to abandon our strike, as this would certainly frighten the rest of the strikers. We would also lose the support of the majority of the prisoners not participating in the strike, vital for our communication system. It was odd, having to think again about how I was going to be killed. Would my comrades be around? Would it be with bullets? Would I be beaten to death, like I had seen others killed in Villa Grimaldi? Would I be drowned, dumped in the sea with an iron weight attached to my body? Who knew? It could be anything; anything could be expected from these psychopaths.

I could not sleep that night and I am sure I was not the only one. Not only was there a *zafarrancho*, where they searched room by room, there were also movements of the troops surrounding the camp, together with the landing and taking off of a helicopter.

Next morning we were woken up quite early for the roll call. The Commandant addressed us this time, announcing that the authorities were studying the possibility of bringing charges against us similar to those in times of war, especially against the leaders of this 'rebellion'. In any case, 'there was hot tea, milk and toast waiting for those who wanted to abandon the strike. Scrambled eggs could not be ruled out!' Needless to say, our stomachs rumbled furiously and our mouths watered profusely. But nobody took a step forward this time. The day went by slowly, full of rumours and theories. The comrades in charge of the forbidden transistor radio, who were not on strike, had already managed to contact us by mid-afternoon saying that nothing had been reported on the radio yet.

The second night was more difficult than the first one. We only allowed ourselves water, plenty of it, but nothing else. In fact the Commandant made sure that everybody on strike should have nothing else. On the third day we had visitors from military intelligence who, in the presence of the Commandant and other officers, started to 'informally' interrogate us, one by one, beginning with our representatives or 'leaders'. All the questions were directed to try to find out ulterior motives for our action, outside contacts and organisation, and the extent of our network abroad. By this time, in the winter of 1975, the junta's extermination campaign was rampant. People were still disappearing and mutilated bodies appeared sporadically in rivers, valleys and on beaches. On the fourth day some prisoners were unable to cope with the lack of food and began arguing with the rest. Although I was extremely hungry, I was feeling all right.

★   ★   ★

It reminded me of a period in my childhood when there was not enough food. My father was very strict about it: one could not have anything to eat until one had earned it. So there could be no breakfast, at least not for my brother and me. We would eat what we could at about midday after working hard, in the market, mainly carrying heavy loads to and fro. If we were lucky, we would eat a couple of *sopaipillas* (a small fried tortilla made from pumpkin, flour and lard) with butter and a small slice of ham. Other, more unfortunate times would bring only boiled sausage on bread and on some days there would be no cooked food at all, only fruit picked up from piles of discarded rubbish. Then there would be no more food until late in the evening, and never enough. After a while my stomach started to ache and I assumed that my younger brother was suffering the same. I then resolved that he should have priority when food became available. I did it just because he was my kid brother, and therefore weaker than me.

My brother had a good pair of shoes, mainly because his feet had not grown too much yet. Mine had grown and my only pair of shoes had developed huge holes in their soles. I kept them very clean, though, and always looked for the toughest cardboard from boxes of imported fruit like bananas or pineapples with which to patch the soles. The market floor was not a friendly place for my beloved shoes, permanently covered in rotting vegetables and fruit and always very wet. So I decided that in the market my shoes should stay in my back pockets, then only be delicately worn, almost without touching the ground, after working hours. Walking barefooted in that filth was not comfortable, but the prospects of new shoes were non-existent, and I needed them, most of all, for evening college.

There were beautiful girls there, from well-off families, since the school was situated in a rich neighbourhood. One of them had invited me, the first day of school, to sit next to her. She was so sweet to me that it almost made me cry. She said I should sit at her bench because she liked me, and she advertised the fact to the rest of the class who did not dare to question or argue with her because she was a very confident and outspoken, tall girl. A sweet girl that made me look forward to the end of the working day and going to school. I wished I were less tired and less hungry. If she knew what I did during the day she probably wouldn't talk to me, I thought, let alone sit next to me. I loved her clothes; they looked so fine and smelled so good, smelled of comfort, of security, of a normal, comfortable family. I looked at myself and compared to her I looked like a tramp. My clothes were so worn out, more like rags. My shoes were shiny, but I couldn't let her see the soles. I had to be careful about that.

I wasn't surprised when, a few weeks later, she changed her mind and another boy sat next to her, a normal boy, not a hungry, skinny boy badly dressed. I sat at the back, on my own on a bench where I could see her from a distance. She was probably a year or two older than me, or so she looked, with curly dark hair. She had a fully developed body, her face like those found in Rubens's paintings and she had an outgoing personality, carefree, not girly.

So, compared to my feelings of inadequacy, my hunger was not too bad. I knew I could go on like I used to, back when I looked longingly in restaurants' windows. They exhibited the dish of the day on beautifully made plates so you would be tempted to walk in just by the look of the food. I found this display totally unfair to people like me who could not afford a fraction of what was on the plate. You wanted to break the restaurant window, grab the food and run away. I remember feeling quite upset about this. For one thing, I hated my stomach for feeling so hungry at the sight of something so 'trivial'. Then I would feel sad and ashamed of myself for needing something that did not belong to me, something that I was not meant to have. Inside, the people were eating so avidly, looking so dependant on their food, as though it was a matter of life or death. But, wasn't that what it was all about, a matter of life or death? Wasn't that exactly what was going on at the fruit and vegetable market, where people had knife fights so that at the end of the day they could have something to put in their mouths? Wasn't it a fact that I was prepared to steal food for my brother on the days when I thought I would be unable to earn enough money to buy some?

★　★　★

Then, I could not choose whether to eat or not. Now, I was choosing not to eat in protest, to make a point. I must have learned to repress hunger because we were on our fifth day of not eating and most of the strikers felt terrible, with all sorts of symptoms. There were three that had already given up; they felt that they could not go on without eating. The first three days were the hardest for me, after that it seemed that I could go on forever. And I mean forever, until I died. A matter of life or death. So many times near the edge.

The sixth day of the hunger strike must have been a Sunday, a day when the prisoners were allowed a visitor. Not for us though, the ones on hunger strike were not allowed visits. I felt quite poorly that morning. Although I had drunk plenty of water, I could not urinate and the pain was excruciating, so much so that I could not stand without help. It took me an eternity in the toilet leaning against the wall to pass a few drops. I got better later on, staying in bed until just past midday when two or three comrades came rushing into the room.

'Luis,' they shouted, 'your daughter is down there. We can see her leaping and hopping in front of the gate.'

I managed to get to the barbed-wire fence. There my sister stood with my brave little four-year-old. I could see her in the distance, standing out and performing for the prisoners. She would open her arms and then close them in the manner of giving herself a hug, or embracing somebody who wasn't there.

'Political prisoners, here, this hug goes to all of you!' she would shout. When she saw me she started to give the imaginary hugs to me, shouting, 'I love you, papa! Take care of yourself, papa! Be brave, papa!'

I noticed that some of the prisoners had tears in their eyes watching her, while others were responding to her 'hugs' with hugs of their own.

After a while I took out my white handkerchief and placed a little rock in the middle, I threw the hanky with the rock high into the air. The stone detached itself from the hanky, letting it fall gently in the breeze, like a miniature parachute.

'This is for you my love!' I shouted.

Soon there were at least a dozen little parachutes in the air saluting little Dalia for her uniqueness and her bravery. We carried on like this, one after the other, the prisoners throwing hankies and embracing. This activity, in our state, left us exhausted after a short while. Suddenly an old man with a laden donkey appeared in our field of vision. When Dalia saw the donkey, she immediately cried that the donkey was bringing best wishes for 'all the political prisoners on hunger strike.' Later that evening my daughter was the focus of conversation among the exhausted prisoners, making some sob with emotion.

The seventh day of the hunger strike brought more intimidation from the camp administration and we saw our numbers being reduced even further as more strikers felt unable to continue, while a couple were taken ill. But we realised that our action was having an effect on the government and they became desperate for the strike to end. Thanks to the prisoners' families and the relatives of the 'disappeared', the news of our hunger strike had reached the four corners of the world. The pressure put on the government by the international community was immense. Of course we did not know this entirely, only little pieces of information reached us from our rudimentary and precarious connection with the outside world via two or three of the non-striking prisoners. But we could judge something of the effect from the enthusiasm showed by the relatives who came in numbers for visits and from the exasperation shown by the camp's administration.

The Commandant would visit us in good humour and spirits, cracking jokes and promising delicious meals would be served to us immediately after the strike had finished. For our part we carried on, tirelessly explaining to him and his colleagues our motives and our points of view until we gained his respect for what we were doing. He was a reasonable man but we understood that things were out of his control.

We eventually finished our hunger strike after the Chilean Cardinal, Raul Silva Henrique, came for an interview with the striker's representatives together with the Red Cross and representatives of the Centre for European Migrations. The government promised an enquiry into the 119 'disappeared' mentioned in the Brazilian and Argentinean newspapers. We had lasted ten days with nothing apart from water.

Unsurprisingly, there was a short honeymoon period in the camp. We had special food for two days but after that everything reverted to 'normal', until those cars started to arrive; the distinctive cars of the secret service. They were unmarked cars but there was no mistake about it, there were secret policemen inside. At first they talked to the guards, then to the Commandant, and finally to the nurse. About a week later I was called to the main gate. Due to my failing health, an appointment had been arranged for me to have a series of tests at the navy hospital in Valparaiso.

My ill health, caused by torture and made worse by the camp's regime and the hunger strike, did not, usually, attract so much concern from the repressive apparatus. Although the camp's elders told me that the

Commandant had assured them that my temporary removal from the camp was purely medical, I was not convinced. It did not make sense in the logic of the repression. Besides, there were other sick prisoners, some of them with more serious conditions, needing hospital attention. I smelled a rat. However, my comrades assured me that they would send messages to my sister, who was popular among the camp's prisoners for her beauty. I felt that there was nothing I could do but accept whatever was coming. My comrades kindly prepared for me a 'hospital kit' containing a notepad and pen, a couple of books, cigarettes, some money and toiletries. I was the only prisoner in the vehicle, a covered pick-up truck painted in navy colours. After a forty-five-minute journey we arrived at Valparaiso.

I had only been to Valparaiso once before, when I was a kid. The whole family, apart from my grannies and Aunt Raquel, went on holiday to a seaside resort called Quinteros. I must have been eight or nine years old. These were times when we were more 'well off' and my dad rented a cottage by the sea. It was made of wood, I remember, and it had several bunk beds. It was a small cottage, but I loved it. That holiday was one of those rare occasions when dad was kind to mum. They seemed happy and like a normal couple. But we ran out of money. My father was frantically trying to ask his work to send him more but everything was awkward because there was no bank in the little town and all communication had to be made by telegram. In the end the money did not arrive and the holiday had to be cut short. When we got back home, father found out that the money had been sent to a bank in Valparaiso, since this was the only place with banks in the area. He had to go to Valparaiso to recover the cash. He explained to my brothers and sisters what he had to do and that he would take me with him. We would have to stay overnight in a hotel.

We arrived at Valparaiso early, booked into a hotel, went to the bank and then to the beach. It was still the middle of the summer. My dad was a very good swimmer, and had once saved a young girl from drowning in a river in front of a small crowd, including me and my family. The girl, a teenager, had been carried by the strong current towards a big whirlpool. She had already swallowed a lot of water and was waving her arms desperately. My dad jumped into the water without hesitation and swimming at full speed he reached the girl, quickly grabbing her around the waist and continuing his fast swim to the opposite river bank, reaching it at an acute angle due to the speed of the current but with the girl safely in his arms. Everybody clapped and the girl's mother kissed dad, but he was silent. He became serious and quiet, just looking straight at the giant swirl in the middle of the river, as if to say, 'You wanted to swallow that girl up, didn't you!' As if he was talking to death itself. I felt proud of my dad but I wished I had been the one he had rescued.

That day on the beach at Valparaiso dad jumped from a rock into the sea and floated like a seal. I did not know how to float in water but, seeing the ease with which dad did it, I jumped in with the conviction that I could too, not only because father was in the water to rescue me if necessary, but also because he had chosen *me* to be his companion that weekend. I felt loved and his favourite, therefore I could swim. And I did.

But I didn't get to know Valparaiso very well, so that is why, when the navy pick-up truck took a few turns and then started a steep climb up a hill, I did not know where we were. A heavy gate opened, and then we were inside what looked like the entrance to an old fort. I was taken to an office where a man in plain clothes was seated behind a massive wooden desk. One of the soldiers in charge gave him a sheet of paper.

'What have you done to be brought here?' he asked.

'I was brought to the hospital,' I answered.

He laughed, saying that I should wait for an appointment. In the meantime, I should put the contents of my pockets, my books, the contents of my small bag and my shoelaces on the top of his desk. The rules were as follows: nothing of what I had brought with me would be allowed to stay with me, except for what I was wearing and the cigarettes. A blindfold would cover my eyes although I could take this off once inside my room. There would be three meals a day: breakfast, lunch and tea. My toothpaste and toothbrush would be passed to me for use in the morning and evening and then removed after use. When I heard a knock on the cell door I must put the blindfold over my eyes. I must not try to see nor speak to the person bringing the aforementioned items.

'What about my books?' I asked.

'Not allowed.'

The room was quite big with a very tall ceiling and a large window reaching almost to the top of the room, starting about 1.5 metres from the floor. The window was covered with thick glass bricks, except for a small gap at the very top. There was a small toilet with a basin and a shower. There were about a dozen old metal bunk-beds that appeared to have been dumped in the room. Some of the beds had blankets. There were tiles on the floor. The walls were painted in a light-green colour and had handwriting on them, made with pencil or ballpoint pen, and some engravings made with a nail or another sharp object.

The writing on the walls had been made by people who had been imprisoned there. There were poems describing pain, anguish, love and fear. There were political statements, words of encouragement, denunciations, slogans from the recent times of the Popular Government, and more pain. There were desperate messages to parents, children, loved ones and fellow comrades. But most of all, there were farewells, goodbye messages. 'So and so arrived to this hell on the 7 July 1974.' No date of exit; no time to record their being taken during their sleep. No known destination; 'missing'. In the middle of their dreams their bodies thrown from a helicopter with a piece of rail wrapped around them to the deep, icy waters of the Pacific Ocean. Should I write something on the walls? What for? Who is going to read it? Another prisoner like myself who may not go back to the living to tell the story? Or for another to read it and then realise that by the very act of reading it his or her own fate will be sealed?

It was cold in the room and there was no heating, so I gathered as many blankets from the other beds as I could and buried myself under them. I had absolutely no idea where this place was; I was completely disorientated. It seemed that the window was facing south, but I was not sure. I left the task of reaching the gap at the top of the window until the next day. Soon it would be teatime and I would have to wear the blindfold for the guard to put the tray through the door. There was nothing to do but wait. I paced up and down the room at first, then lay down on the bed, thinking. I could not believe what had happened because, back in the camp, some part of me had believed that I was genuinely going to be taken to a hospital for tests, to diagnose the cause of the intense pain in my kidneys. This never happened. Next day I managed to reach the gap at the top of the window. I could see a tiny bit of beach, a road parallel to the sea, then some buildings followed by a sharp rise towards a hill which was dotted with houses and vegetation. There was a small tram, like a wooden box going up and down the hill. I could hear no sounds from outside; my view was like that of a post-card that changed colours during the day, the objects moving very slowly, with no people visible, like a ghost city.

They kept me there for about fifteen days but it felt like fifteen years. There was nothing to do. Despite my request, the guards did not return my books or my pen and paper. I tried to exercise as much as I could, only to stop suddenly at the distant and now familiar screams of torture coming from deep inside the fort. I tried to think about things, about the past, but everything seemed so disjointed. The future lay just a few minutes ahead as hour after hour and day after day passed. I could hear the sound of vehicles arriving at the gate, which was next to my cell, footsteps, voices that might bring the news of more torment and eventual doom, the certain end of the ones who were imprisoned in that place. My main task was to keep my sanity, but I could not avoid the onset of a deep depression; probably as a defence mechanism.

I was eventually taken back to the camp. Here the mood was sombre. There had been rumours of punishment for the hunger strikers. Sure enough, two days after my return an army bus arrived early in the morning. About six or seven prisoners were called to the gates. We were ordered on the bus and handcuffed to the seats. Inside the bus there were crates of beer, wine and food. After about an hour, we left the main road to Santiago and drove along a dusty road until we arrived at a lake. The lake was called Aculeo. Our hearts sank. This lake was known to be a place of execution, with bodies being thrown into the water with heavy objects to weigh them down.

After the soldiers had unloaded the beer crates and food, we were taken off the bus and lined up by the waters edge. The soldiers, who were already drinking and preparing a fire for a barbeque, were laughing and playing with their rifles. 'This is it guys, this is the end of the road for you; we are going to execute you,' they shouted. 'Would you like your eyes covered or uncovered; you can choose, we don't mind.' We looked at each other. One of the prisoners became very agitated and the others looked at me, as though I had an explanation, an answer to what was going to happen next. I looked at them and said: 'It's OK comrades, they are going to shoot us and it is going to be all right, you won't feel anything apart from a heavy blow to your chest. Look ahead, I guess it is better with our eyes wide open to show them we are not afraid. Look straight at them.'

Somehow, maybe because the soldiers were in a festive mood, drinking, laughing and preparing their barbeque, it seemed to me that they did not hate us; they were going to kill us because they had to; they had been ordered to do it. We were saying goodbye to each other in resignation. At least it was a fine sunny day and this was a beautiful place. Some of the soldiers, four or five, took aim while the others carried on with getting the barbeque ready, as if it was the most normal thing to do while people were going to be executed. Then the soldiers opened fire. The bullets were aimed over our heads though, and the soldiers burst out laughing, but almost immediately their mood changed and they became angry, shouting insults and orders. We were rushed into the bus, handcuffed to the seats, and pushed to the floor to wait for them to finish their party.

Towards evening we continued our journey with the soldiers' mood swinging between merry and hostile, and with the threat of execution reiterated every now and then. We arrived back at Tres Alamos concentration camp in Santiago before midnight. A journey that should have taken two or three hours had taken over eight. We were exhausted, our nerves shattered, but we were alive.

# In exile

International pressure eventually forced the junta to close the concentration camps. Prisoners faced an uncertain future; the best we could hope for was exile. Unknown to me, my sister Lucia had managed to get a Norwegian Amnesty group to sponsor me and they had obtained a UK visa. I was therefore released on condition that I left the country.

I am here now in London after many years of distance and many years of silence. There is no point in talking about something you can't do anything about; something you can't prevent from happening. I could not do anything to protect Diana, or Maria Cristina, or my friends, my comrades, my people, my grandmothers' kisses, their lullabies, their wisdom. I could not protect my body so that my torturers wouldn't commit sacrilege against humanity and against evolution.

It is better to keep silent; as a matter of fact, I have no choice because the words don't come out. I have a partner now, Eugenia, a step daughter, Francisca, and a child of my own, Diana. Eugenia says there is an obscure part of my mind that I never open up. She is afraid of what is in there; she cannot cope with it because when we are intimate, in the dark of night, I might retreat there and be in that time, in that place which is terrifying because I would be someone else. I would be someone trying to survive what others did not survive. I might have done something; I might do something now. I could be with other people, with people who are no more, with dead people. I could be loving dead people; I could be very dark. 'No,' she says, 'I cannot stand to be with you.'

'But we have a child,' I say, 'and children are beautiful. They don't know anything, and they need us, and we can protect them, and I can give my life truly now. It does not matter if you do not love me, really, you can do whatever you want, I will be here for you. Please do not take my child away from me. It is true, I do not know what to do about the darkness, and my sleepless nights, and my nightmares and the silences, but it will go away, I can assure you. With our child I am here, you have seen me, I am not there because our little girl does not allow it; she is my sanity, my hope. I will change for her. I will, I will, I will . . . '

On the other hand, I think I can understand you; it must be difficult for you to be with me. I hadn't noticed, but if it is true what you are saying is wrong with me, then it must be bad for you. You see there are some things I cannot tell you about because I don't want you to know. You see, one of the reasons I got involved with you is because you were not there and you really don't know what happened. They didn't get you, they didn't touch you, you escaped from their paws and I really love that; I cannot tell you how much I love that, how much I love you for that. They wanted you, they wanted to destroy you like they did the others, but you escaped before they could reach you, and I really, really love that. Because they are death and you are life and you escaped from them. But not only that, we have a child, a child I helped, in spite of everything, to bring into this world, in hope, to heal the wounds. Or perhaps to just contemplate her little life and pretend that everything has just begun, that there is no past.

Yes, I know I am here, I escaped too, that is a material fact. I am physically here and you are looking at me and you can touch me. But the truth is I did not escape, they caught me and I am not certain of where I am. I think that sometimes I am here, but sometimes I am there, or part of me is here and part of me is there. You may be right; what you call the obscure part of me, that big dark hole, the silent part, the eyes-wide-open part of me that looks at you with a fixed stare, that is the part that is not here. Now, you may ask yourself, which part is the biggest, or what is left for you, for our little girl, for life.

Sometimes you say that you understand me, that you know what happened and that I should tell you, so you can help me; but I can see fear in your eyes, you really don't want to know, you don't want to hear it. The truth is I do not want you to understand, I don't want you to hear it, I don't want you to help me. Because you escaped, you are alive, they did not touch you and that is your virtue and you are a carrier of life. You don't have to go there, to visit them and their places, to be frightened, to die and then to come back in order to understand, to understand me. No, please remain as you are, where you are or they will have won and I could not cultivate the part of me that is here, for our child, for the lost lives, for a different universe perhaps.

Yes, I understand now, you may have to leave me, you can't wait for me, I am walking too slowly. You see, I am dragging along a heavy shadow. It is full of bodies, beautiful bodies; the bodies and faces of loved ones, of the ones who were all alone when they were tormented. They were cold and had nobody to give them warmth; they were scared and had no hand to hold. It is full of their last words before they were raped, their bodies mutilated, abused and broken, defeated, died. I know their last words and their last sounds, because I was there too, because I accompanied them to the threshold. I can hear them, so clear, all the time, their laments, their calls, their mother's names I can hear, and the names of the children they did not have the opportunity to bear or to hold. It makes me very sad; you see, one of those children was mine. Yes, I can hear their voices and I love them, but I cannot reach them; I try to, but I can't reach them. My struggle is to reach them one day, then I will be able to touch them and caress them and close their eyes. So I have to keep trying, because if I try harder, I may be able to reach them. I may die and be with them.

They are so lonely and they don't understand why they have been treated this way. They have their eyes wide open – the ones that still have them – but they cannot see because their eyes are blindfolded. They search in their minds for a clue to explain the horror. They try to find out where this came from; around what dark corner were these members of our society, fellow countrymen, people, waiting in hiding to commit these crimes? Where did the hate come from, the cruelty, the savagery? It was as if they belonged to a different kind of race unknown to us. Where do they come from? They were not in our schoolbooks, or the mythology of the country, nowhere in the stories of the elders. They speak a weird language, insulting, obscene, monosyllabic and morbid. They do not want to converse though; they shout, they give orders, they swear.

My comrades, my friends, my beloved ones, you do not understand, you cannot understand. You have committed no crime, you have done nothing wrong, you never hurt anyone, your aims have been noble and generous. You were used to dialogue, to high discussion, to having respect for each other, to understanding. What is all this? You were told that if you did something bad you would be punished in accordance with the law. What is this then? There is no sense.

I know you want to die now, you have had enough. But it is so enormously sad, to die in the hands of such nonsensical bestiality, in the hands of such monstrous idiocy. I know you feel responsible and ashamed. Responsible for not having noticed them before, for the failure to prevent this, for not interpreting the signs, for allowing the atrocities to take place. You feel ashamed because you are in the hands of sub-humans, in the hands of mentally derailed people who have found the golden opportunity to act out their pathology, and they are all-powerful. Your hands and feet are tied and you cannot see them. There is nothing you can do to defend yourself, to protect yourself, your families and your people. And they are going to kill you and you will be unable to explain it to yourself, to the generations to come. I know, I know. You will not be found, and more frightening still, you will be forgotten.

You see, they cannot be found, their bodies buried at the bottom of the sea, in the solitary and cold heights of the Andes and in the driest, most isolated parts of the desert. But I survived; the psychotic butchers spared my life perhaps without knowing that their victims would inhabit my body and my soul, trying to break the silence, for as long as I live. The problem is that right now, because there are so many and they all want to speak, so urgently, that they block my throat and my mind wants to go blank. At night it is different because I can give them more attention, more time, and I can talk to them, but I can also see their wounds and their despair. Sometimes they appear to me as if nothing has happened and they talk and talk and laugh, making plans for the future, and we all love each other in a way we didn't do before. And we are safe, and it is the summer and we are not cold, and we are very calm, and we know everything and things are as they used to be, in harmony. This makes it even worse, you see, because when a new day arrives, I am here, lying next to you, and I am angry with you because you have intruded into our space; you bring me to the reality, you spoiled it. I am angry and disappointed with myself because I am not there with them, because I couldn't do anything to protect them, to save them and Diana and the baby growing in her belly.

Reality is a foreign and hostile landscape I do not want to be part of. I prefer to contemplate it from a distance. At other times I just want to get lost in the world of the children. And yes, you keep saying that I do not love you, that I only love the children, that I don't need you, that I only need the children. And I do not know; I don't know what is going on, honestly. There are too many things and I am afraid of trying to explain because I do not know what is going to come out; I don't trust myself because the forces that inhabit me are so powerful that anything can happen. It could come out all very articulate, controlled and sensible, but still, how do I know that it is going to come out that way? People might get frightened and leave, or look at me as if I was from another planet. You see, it happens all the time and in the end one doesn't know what to say. Besides, the bodies I am carrying with me, their voices, they all try to say something at the same time and they get stuck in my throat. I know, it sounds schizophrenic, paranoid schizophrenic, but the truth is that there is no other way to describe it.

But it is also my body, you know, what they have done to it, and then my whole self. It hurts all the time, here in my chest, where the heart is, where the emptiness and the loneliness and the cold live. That is why I cannot talk. I remain silent most of the time. That is why I cannot tell you now, and I think I won't tell you ever. Yes, I know, you feel tired and frustrated and you tell me that one of these days you will leave me. It is very sad and it hurts me enormously. It adds to this great sea of pain inside me, a pain that sometimes seems to be taking me to the grave. But I don't think there is anything I can do apart from tell myself that I may not be able to bear it anymore. Well, if it wasn't there, in their hands, it would have to be now, here; I mean the time to die. What the hell, maybe it was never meant to be; maybe I was never meant to live.

No, you will not know all this, not from my lips anyway. You don't want to know and I don't want you to know. They are secrets and it is better they remain very secret. I can't talk anyway, and even if I could, there is nobody to talk to. I can't trust anybody because nobody is prepared to listen, nobody wants to listen to these kind of things. Did you know that when I tell you I need time to myself, two evenings a week, to go out to meet friends or go to the cinema, in fact I have been on my own, walking the streets of London. I have been thinking or talking to myself, sometimes crying, and most of the time waiting for an answer to come. I have walked and walked; it is the best way because, even if I make noises or I cry, nobody cares, nobody says anything. Sometimes I have come up with the same solution I have heard other people in my situation have arrived at, that is to forget, put it behind you and carry on with your life, to think about the future and try to have a good time, be happy. Even my doctor tells me that that is what I have to do when I have been to see him about not being able to sleep or about my back problem or my kidneys or my stomach or the cramps in my legs and my arms. Believe it or not, I have tried, but suddenly my mind stops and goes away and I am not here anymore, and I get this panic, this fear, this terror inside me, without warning, without explanation. Then everything goes wrong, with you, at college, at work and then I want to be on my own, far away, in some place very far away, I don't know where, but I know it has to be a deserted place, just for me, far, very far away.

It is a trap, you see, and I don't know how to get out of it, or when, if ever, I will. So, I have to live day by day, to take every day as it comes, every half-a-day, every hour, which is another thing that irritates you. That I never plan ahead; I never plan for the future. It is true, as I live very basically: if there is food, I am happy; if there is some money to buy food, I am all right; if the children are happy, that is very good for me. If there are none of these things, then I think of something to do to get some money. I feel that I can do any job, as long as it provides enough to pay for food and heating. And if you are lying next to me at night, that is enough for me. Your body, resting, asleep, alive, warm, and then I don't mind if you have been angry with me, as long as you are there, next to me. Tomorrow may be different. Some kind of magic may have happened during the night and tomorrow may be better. You never know. Wait for me.

It is too late now, you are leaving tomorrow. I do not know what I am going to do or what will become of me. I really want to die now. I am desperate. Sometimes it is frightening, but when I get to this stage, I think about the blow, the blow that will finish me. Because it would have to be a blow, something that destroys my brain instantly. It is very sad, because the other side of me knows I can survive, adapt, modify, try again, work hard. I have done it before. But the road is the problem; the road to survival is paved with so much pain, destitution and misery.

The other problem is the delicate balance, a very fine line between mental sanity and madness. That is a great fear of mine, that I may not be able to come out the other side mentally unscathed. It is like the prospect of travelling through a black hole in space. Nobody knows what might happen: matter disappears, time disappears, and space disappears. If everything disappears, one might disappear as well, because the past may also disappear and therefore one's existence. So if one did not exist, then one cannot disappear. But who knows? In any case, it involves travelling, and that is the problem: getting there. Paradoxically, the thought that I can decide to die at any time is what keeps me going. I say: 'Let's see what happens tomorrow; if it is too bad, I can die.'

She is leaving. She is not only leaving, she is taking the girls with her. She is not only taking the girls with her, she is taking them about 14,000 miles away to Chile, even further, since I am not allowed into Chile. What made me believe that it was all over? That it was possible to relax? To release the spring for a while, letting it rest? Was it those eyes? That smile? Who knows, it could have been anything really. After what happened any gesture resembling love, care and understanding would have done the trick. The wounds were too great, too raw, too badly in need of healing. Anything to remind one that life has not ended, that it could have been just a bad dream; that the eyes that were imprinted in one's brain could be found somewhere else. That it was possible to rebuild. That children could now be born, that they had just been waiting for a better moment, for this moment.

Nobody told us. Did somebody know? I had a suspicion back then, during the Villa Grimaldi days, that after what they had done, it was probably better to die. It was difficult to visualise life, as we knew it, continuing along an uneventful path after what had happened. Deep down, in the ancient part of myself, a voice was saying that, after what they had done, life was no longer viable. It was a very strong voice, as strong as the one saying that I must go on. The ancient dilemma was there, once more, with its tremendous clash of forces, 'to be or not to be'. Or was it simply the desire to get to the bottom of things, to find out what was there, beyond one's own threshold, where things end, just before death?

It is time again to pay for trying, for believing, for dreaming, for wanting to dream the impossible. The difference from before is that now there is less certainty that there is anything in reserve to pay with. On the contrary, there is more conviction now that this is the end of it all. There is fear, more fear, a very strange fear, a horrible fear. Death's face is visible again, I can almost touch it, it fluctuates between dark and light, and my brain seethes with a desire to cast my body over a cliff or under a train and achieve complete freedom.

# Primal therapy

16

Only cleaning and restaurant jobs have been available to me so far. Cleaning, always cleaning, cleaning very early in the morning, when the people who are going to enjoy the cleanness, the clean offices, toilets and canteens are still asleep. Cleaning late in the evening, when the people who have soiled the cleanness are already in their homes or enjoying a drink or a meal at a restaurant. People without faces, people one never sees; the smell of people, one gets to know their habits, discarded food wrappers reveal their diets. Anonymous people who leave behind them a scent of normal life, of secure life, of family life perhaps, a continuum of life, a coherent life, a life that makes sense, a life that belongs to them because it always has. I would like to be one of them, have one of their jobs, a normal job with a normal salary with normal working hours with a normal life, normally dressed with just normal worries.

I am cleaning and I wonder if they ever think about the person who cleans their desks and their toilets, a person who knows a little of their intimacy, a faceless ghost that moves around in silence without disturbing anyone or anything apart from the dirt, the discarded papers, the dirty cups, the spills, the dust, the ashtrays. The tired cleaner, too early in the morning and too late at night with not much sleep in between and very little pay. The refugee-cleaner, from some exotic country. The sleepless cleaner, the cleaner in pain in body and soul. The zombie cleaner who once had a life, a different life, a normal life and now runs from one cleaning job to the next wondering when it will all end, when it will be peaceful, when he can have a bit of rest, a bit of ease in order to gather all the little pieces of his shattered life together.

It looks so near sometimes. Here is the desk and the chair of someone who has a normal life, of someone who does not know this anguish of mine, someone who will never know. I sit in his chair at the desk and think that his job looks simple. I have already seen some documents on the desk. I could do this job, and if I could, my life would change dramatically. I could take that person's place and I could be that person. I would laugh, I would go for a drink after work or to the cinema perhaps. I would not smoke though. I would have no worries and I would be able to talk to my colleagues in the pub about the normal things in life and nobody would ask me about what happened because nothing too terrible or too important would have happened. I would still have loved Diana and we would still be together with beautiful children. 'Haven't you finished yet, Luis!' shouts the supervisor. 'There is still a lot to do!'

Isn't it a good thing that the cleaning cannot be done during normal hours, when everybody is in the office? It is good for the civil servants and the white-collar workers not to see the cleaners because, if they did, they would see a person and then they might begin to think about the cleaner, they might empathise with the cleaner, speculate about the cleaner, none of which is a good thing. More dangerous still would be meeting the cleaner's gaze; that could be unbearable and the white-collar worker could feel threatened by the gaze and react unexpectedly. It could be disturbing to remind office workers of the existence of these sorry people who observe them with big eyes-wide-open. The cleaner may have a university degree but can find no other job because he or she is a foreigner. Let the refugee do the dirty work in secret, without showing himself.

★  ★  ★

After years of studying, cleaning and washing up I began to think about what to do next. After being separated from my daughters, there were very few alternatives, only two in fact: to get better or succumb. I decided to give life another chance, but this time it would be different. I would attempt wholeheartedly, I would keep going until the end and I would use all the resources at my disposal. Still, I knew, it was going to be a lonely journey. It was just me and nobody else. I would have to do it on my own, all the way.

I had already started to look for answers, from books in the local library and books in the big bookshops in central London, where I could read a little each visit before an assistant came to ask me if I had found what I was looking for. Fortune smiled on me one day. Helen Bamber, an Amnesty International staff member, whom I had met years before when I participated in a hunger strike in protest against Pinochet's atrocities, lived near where I lived. We used to meet quite often on the number 45 bus on our way to Muswell Hill. She always asked me how I was, and I always said that I was OK. But Helen Bamber, a veteran in the field of dealing with survivors, was not one to be fooled so easily. She never believed me and suspected that things were not nearly OK.

We met one day and she told me that the work she was doing with Amnesty International, with a small group of doctors and other professional volunteers helping survivors cope with the aftermath of horrors they had endured, had to stop because AI thought it was incompatible with their aims. She would continue with her work at another place lent to them by a well-wisher. She also told me there was a small fund available from Amnesty to help survivors pay for treatment.

As I tried to find in psychology books some understanding of what had happened to me and what the effects might be, I realised that another phenomenon was taking place. I discovered that there were other, stronger forces in my personality that dictated behaviour which, although exacerbated by the experience of torture, seemed to pre-date this. I realised that I had not arrived at the torture chamber empty-handed, that I got there with 'emotional baggage'. I did not arrive there clean, a trauma-free being. Because, if torture had taken me back to the primaeval being, it must have taken me back to the child first. And this, I thought, may explain the wide differences of behaviour patterns exhibited by different victims, and it may also explain the ability to survive too.

Among the books I was able to read in bookshops, I came across one called *Children Under Stress* by Sula Wolf, a Scottish psychologist, a magnificent book about the traumas of childhood. In the bibliography I found *The Feeling Child* by Arthur Janov, the American practitioner who became the creator of primal therapy. I became very interested in his theories and, after careful reading, decided that primal therapy was the answer for me. With some small financial help from the AI fund I was able to start the therapy.

It was an extremely arduous and painful journey that took me to the edge of the abyss many times, when I had run out of all strength and I wished I had never been born. It was a lonely, extremely lonely journey. Loneliness never experienced before, not even in my worst times at Villa Grimaldi. It went on for weeks and months, a year and then two. I had to remember and relive every aspect of the torture regime and in so doing I began to realise that, no matter how much in denial I was about the effects of torture on my body, the memory of the incredible pain inflicted on me was still present, locked in every cell. The screaming was the same but now I was fully conscious of what was happening at a cellular level. This, my system allowed to happen because, in the therapy setting, it understood that it was safe to release the memory. What my brain had to repress during torture in order to survive, this time was allowed to be felt in its totality. It was the scream of the cells in my legs, my feet, my lungs, my heart, my damaged kidneys, my testicles, my arms, my eyes, my mouth, my skin, my guts.

I could understand why I used to have cramps in my legs and my stomach. I could make sense of the almost permanent pain on the right side of my abdomen, but most of all I could see the source of my fears and my nightmares. The black hole of fear, which, without warning, would erupt at any time, leaving me soaked in sweat. There was no need, any more, to try to understand the theories that state that the memory of pain in the human body is not only stored in the brain but that it is, perhaps with a more devastating effect, stored and locked at a local level. It will remain there, unless relived and integrated, eroding the system until the day we die. It is, understandably, very tempting to pretend that one can trick the body and the mind, live in denial and follow the popular approach of 'Forget about it . . . put it behind you . . . get on with your life . . . keep yourself busy . . . stop being a victim.'

# Facing my demons

17

I am happy. I am married to Sara and have two sons, Pablo and Orlando. I have an MSc in Sociology, Psychology and Counselling and am a registered Immigration Representative. I am no longer a victim. Justice, however, remains a fantasy until a friend contacts me saying that a Chilean lawyer working with the Human Rights Office in Santiago needs to talk to me following the appointment of a judge to investigate Diana's kidnapping in 1974. Although a written statement of evidence at the Chilean embassy would have done, this would have been a long and difficult process and the lawyer suggests that if I could travel to Chile to give evidence in person it would be better.

Some time before, talking to Helen Bamber at the Medical Foundation, she had asked me if I had ever thought about the possibility of being called to give evidence against Miguel Krassnoff. I had expressed my doubts that such an event would ever take place in Chile. In any case, I had assured her that I would face the situation with dignity, although the prospect of it sent a shiver down my spine.

'These are very stressful and painful situations to face, Luis; it can be terribly devastating. In fact I have witnessed many of these confrontations in my life and I can tell you, it is not a pleasant experience'.

So, here I am now, with an aeroplane ticket sent to me by the Human Rights Office in Chile, twenty-eight years after the events, with the so-much dreamed of and dreaded fantasy becoming a chilling reality. A confrontation, in front of a judge, with the man, Miguel Krassnoff, who, according to his own confession to me at the time, assassinated Diana, tortured me for nearly three months until he got tired of it and caused me so much pain that it will be engraved on my bones until my death.

Helen, as usual, offers me support. Sara, my wife, is extremely worried that I will not come back, that I will be killed. I have no doubts that, whatever the consequences, I have to go.

It is a painful farewell from Sara and my sons at Heathrow on the night of November 30, 2002. It is impossible to sleep on the aeroplane in 'ordinary' class, the airline insisting on reminding me of the wooden box I was placed in by the torturer I am travelling to face. If the night is a nightmare, the next day is like a dream. The plane is flying low over an immense darkness of green foliage. This must be Brazil, I think, and there is the Amazon below. It is not long before we land at Rio de Janeiro airport. It is nearly nine years since I last travelled through Brazil on my way to Santiago. I have four hours to wait for my connecting flight.

The airport and its workers look clean and it is a sunny day outside. I sit in the vast, floodlit waiting room. I haven't seen so many Latin American faces in a long time. They are familiar faces, intriguing too. It is summer here and despite the air conditioning it is quite warm and people are lightly dressed in bright colours. There are flights to all over Brazil and to all the other South American countries. I look at the screens with names that come from a distant past, some of which I only knew from books of South American writers like Bello Horizonte, La Paz, Cochabamba, Quito, Bahia, Bogota, Montevideo, Cuzco, Asunción. I look at the faces going to those destinations and a strong desire to approach them overcomes me. I want to hear their names, the mixture of old native languages and Spanish. I want to know about their places and their lives. A man is talking on a public telephone, I recognise his Chilean accent. I want to listen. Is he phoning home? It is a strange feeling that overcomes me. On the one hand I look at these people with fascination and nostalgia. It gives me a light pressure in my chest. I want to go back to the times of my childhood, to the country of my grandmothers, to their warmth, sense of security and well-being. On the other hand, I can feel the people's indolence and apathy, which one gets so accustomed to, and an overwhelming sense of loneliness and of abandonment. People just like them witnessed the most horrendous crimes being committed in front of them, on their doorstep, and they witnessed them without a murmur, as if saying 'You are on your own now, don't look at me; there is nothing I can do, I can't help.'

These feelings get mixed up with fear. At the moment, I am at Rio's airport waiting for a connecting flight that will take me to Santiago to a confrontation I was convinced would never materialise. A few years ago, during one of the many trials these criminals had been acquitted from, I had been asked to travel to Chile to give evidence. But shortly before I was due to leave, the prosecuting solicitors telephoned me to say that they felt compelled to cancel my trip because they, and the authorities, could not guarantee my safety. Miguel Krassnoff was still in service in the army and he knew I was travelling from London to give evidence against him.

Just like twenty-eight years ago, I feel absolutely on my own, unprotected, uncared for, ignored in a sea of people, but on a mission for justice, to make a point, to defy, to bring to account, on behalf of the people, the silenced, the abused, the fearful. I am once again swimming against the current, on my own. I feel like shouting aloud, 'Listen, all of you, look at what I am going to do and why. Listen to my voice. Understand that they wanted me dead. But I am not, and I am going to face them!'

Finally my flight is called. My flight is with a Brazilian airline but the gate next to mine is for a Chilean airline flight to Santiago. Very few people board that plane, which leaves half an hour earlier. My flight seems to be full. There is something sinister about the people boarding the Chilean plane. They all look like secret police agents to me. The men are all in suits as are the women. They look rich, business like, right wing. I do not like them. Am I prejudiced? On my flight people wear colourful clothes and look cheerful. They talk. They are noisy. They look relaxed. They are not secret agents, that is for sure. I like them.

After a few hours we cross the Andes from Argentina. This part of the flight always overwhelms me. I feel a pressure in my chest. It is the power of the mountains. They are majestic. Their tall peaks are sharp and covered in snow and very close, as if at any moment one of them will scratch the belly of the plane. I can feel it in my own belly. The mountains go on forever and I cannot take my eyes off them. Suddenly, to the right of the plane, an enormous white wall of mountain seems to dwarf us. It is Aconcagua, at over 6,000 metres tall the highest mountain outside the Himalayas. We will soon start our descent towards Santiago, leaving behind the awesome Andean mountains with their hundreds of turquoise-coloured lakes untouched by man.

There is a cloudless sky over Santiago and it is one o'clock in the afternoon. We finally land and I wonder what the next minutes will bring. The arrivals area is packed with passengers from the last three planes and there are long queues to the immigration control desks. The process is painfully slow and without air-conditioning the place is extremely hot. Who will be there waiting for me? My brother Arturo will be there without a doubt. He is the self-appointed official airport collector for our family, relatives and friends. Will my eldest daughter Dalia be there? Or my younger daughter Diana?

After nearly an hour, I arrive at the desk. My Chilean passport is taken for inspection and checked against a computer database. The man looks again at the passport, then at the monitor, then at me. I start to get scared. All the images of detention, questioning, waiting, and imprisonment flash through my mind.

'There is a problem, sir.' My fears are confirmed.

'You will have to come with me, sir.'

I am taken through corridors to a small office. No fancy furnishings or paint on the walls here, just reinforced concrete without windows. Dim light, a desk, a worn-out chair and a computer on top of another desk.

'Take a seat, sir.'

'What seems to be the problem?' I ask.

'I do not know, sir, I have to investigate.' The immigration officer leaves the room with my passport and comes back a minute or two later with another man who is wearing what looks like a black Colt .45 pistol around his waist. I notice that the immigration officer is now wearing a similar gun. They want to intimidate me, I think, but I am a bit surprised that, after all these years of so-called democracy in Chile, the immigration officers are still military personnel, fully armed and probably belonging to the secret police.

After a few minutes of fiddling with the computer and giving each other conspiratorial looks, they start the questioning. 'What was your last address in Chile? Why did you leave the country? What other names did you use to have? What are you coming to Chile for? How long are you staying? Where are you staying? Do you know such and such a person? Do you know where she is?' Fear. Those names are the same names they used to ask me about when I was first detained, back in 1974. I have been back to Chile three or four times since then to visit my daughters and to say goodbye to my dying mother. But they have never asked me about these names. This is information that has been put there recently. It is true, I have not been back to Chile since my mother's death eight years ago, but why put this information there now, twenty-eight years later?

They are still in control, they want to show it, and they want to punish me. But what for? Luis, I say to myself, have you forgotten Pinochet's detention in London for over a year? What did you do then, Luis, if it was not to appear on almost every TV channel in the world, campaigning for him to be extradited for trial in Spain for crimes against humanity? So, my complete file has been transferred to immigration control.

'Look, I have been away from the country for twenty-seven years and I do not know what you are talking about.'

'You have to cooperate, sir.' A glance at their pistols. They are turning nasty now. One of them goes away with my passport. I hear the noise of telephone calls in another room. The temperature is rising inside this room. My temperature is rising, and probably theirs too.

Images are flashing through my mind. What are the prospects? I could be denied entry and sent back on the first available plane; they could detain me until Monday, when the bureaucracy opens for business again, the civil police, the courts, etc., or, worse still, they could act by themselves and hand me over to their friends, the ones that entered the information about me there in the first place. The memories stored in my body are beginning to be awakened. I can feel it in my stomach and in my chest. Getting into emergency mode, into fighting mode, protective mode, all at once. It knows how to do it; it remembers from long ago. The tightening of the muscles of the stomach, the chest, the arms and legs. Thinking and perception are more acute, I feel more focused. They mustn't notice. Do not show it, I say to myself. No faster breathing, no sweating of the hands. You have to seem in control, look calm. This is a silly mistake.

An hour has passed since I was stopped. There is nothing to do, nothing to look at, only the desks, concrete floor, walls and a dim light. Ha! He is also here, the Chilean immigration officer. A white shirt, tie, grey trousers, brown leather belt with the gun hanging from it. His black, short hair, his round face with dark skin and high check bones. He is probably in his late twenties, shorter than myself. From the army, maybe a sergeant. He is enjoying this. He has the power and, to me familiar, militarily brain-washed behaviour common to Chilean military personnel. He is the typical concrete-mind type. He is silent, but he is saying at lot:

'I have orders, I am loyal. I want to please my superiors with a bit of extra brutality and abuse. I may get promotion. I have got a gun, and that gives me more power and protection.'

Now nearly two hours have passed. The other man comes back with my passport. They look at each other conspiratorially. They talk to each other, looking at their computer again. The one with the passport in his hand looks at me as if to say, we do not know what to do with you. I decide to go on the offensive. I cannot show complete submission. I am not going to be easy prey.

'What is going on?' I say. 'This is taking too long, you are wasting my time. There are people waiting for me out there.'

'We understand that you are required to appear before a magistrate, and we advise you to get in touch with the courts before you leave the country or you will have problems.'

'OK,' I say, 'tell me which court and I will do that, but now let me go because this is out of order.'

'Yes, sir, we will let you in the country. Follow me.'

The first hurdle is over, but I fear that there may be more in store. Goodbye to the security of England, I have just entered Chile. I feel unprotected and at the mercy of sinister forces.

I can see the tall, familiar figure of my brother Arturo among the crowd. Then I can see my daughter Diana, with a young man. She is smiling and her eyes are filled with tears. I can also see my daughter Dalia and her little boy. Bizarrely, there is also a band in typical Chilean costume singing folk songs of welcoming. It is not for me they are playing, of course, it's for a sports team that has just arrived. But I tell my brother and daughter that they shouldn't have bothered anyway. They laugh. I feel relieved and comforted. We embrace and tears roll down our cheeks. A warm feeling fills my whole being to see my loved ones and I choose not to answer their questions as to why it took me so long to get out of the airport; there will be time for that later. Of the various offers to stay the night, I opt for my elder daughter's. I really want to stay with her. For some strange reason I want to be close to her, the one who, twenty-seven years before, I had traded in defiance inside a torture chamber, offered up to the men I was going to meet again in a few days.

After a brief conversation with the human rights lawyers, arrangements are made for me to meet the judge in charge of the investigation and prosecution. I also learn that the hearing or cross-examination will take place in closed chambers. My first meeting, with the judge alone, will be the next day at nine o'clock in the morning, scheduled to finish at noon.

The next day I feel confident. After asking for directions to the Human Rights Office, I set out on the half-hour journey, by metro, to the centre of Santiago. I feel uneasy when I find out that the Human Rights Offices are in the Ministry of Interior building, just across the road from the presidential palace. It seems unbelievable to me that a human rights office could be situated in a building that, to me, represented the headquarters of the efficient, repressive, killing machine of the Pinochet regime. Across the road the rebuilt presidential palace looks blindingly bright in the early morning sunshine. The sight of the palace guards in their impeccable green uniform of the 'carabineros' gives me a slight chill, a reminder of the camp's guards of nearly thirty years ago.

I meet the lawyer who is a slender woman in her fifties. She is formal and her demeanour is that of a person who, after years of fighting and campaigning for justice and bringing the perpetrators and those responsible for crimes against humanity to trial, has seen and heard too much. She speaks in a matter-of-fact manner, unimpressed by any more stories of airport interrogations. She will try to find out what the problem was at the airport.

'You see,' she explains, 'under the prevailing Pinochet constitution, the government cannot dismantle the old security systems, and this includes the personnel. Most of them are still accountable to supporters of the previous regime in high places in the military and the civil service. The government has tried to counter-balance this by creating new departments attached to the old. The civil police, who are under army control, are in charge of airport security, immigration control, as well as embassy personnel abroad. Another department, created by the government and accountable to the president, works alongside the civil police, but its powers are limited and its work, more often than not, is obstructed by the old establishment. I will ask, anyway,' she concludes without conviction.

The run-down taxi struggles through the congested streets of Santiago, soon reaching areas unknown to me. Magistrates Court No. 8 is a fairly new brick and concrete building with a garden in front of it. It is situated in a very wide avenue with a central area between the roads. Across from the courts, about one hundred yards away, is one of Santiago's jails, the

Capuchinos. I am surprised to see my twenty-two-year-old daughter Diana waiting between two other familiar faces. Without knowing the arrangements inside the court I panic at the prospect of having my daughter inside the courtroom. She says that she wants to keep me company. I tell her that I do not know if she will be allowed inside the courtroom.

'It does not matter,' she says, 'I'll wait outside.'

'My love,' I say, 'I do not know how long I will be in there.'

'It doesn't matter,' she says, 'I'll go and come back later.'

I have never told my daughters what happened, apart from the historical facts, and I am certain that I never will. It is something that I cannot bring myself to talk about, even to my children or my closest family.

The lawyer leads me through a security door to a corridor with offices on both sides. Another surprise: the judge's room is a small, windowless office with three doors. There is a big desk for the judge and a smaller one, for the typist or actuary, next to it. There are two chairs in front of the judge's desk. There are bookshelves behind the judge's chair and on one of them there is a framed photograph of a young woman with a baby in her arms. The judge is a woman in her late forties, pleasant-looking with a soft voice. Without formality she extends her hand across her desk and welcomes me. We shake hands and she indicates that I should take a seat in one of the chairs. The actuary is a young, good-looking man, in a suit and tie.

The judge confirms my name, date of birth, address and occupation. Immediately after this, she starts to read a witness statement I made in court at the time I was in the Tres Alamos concentration camp in Santiago. I had volunteered to give evidence that I had seen certain detainees in the concentration camp, people the authorities denied had ever been arrested. They had been kidnapped and had subsequently disappeared. I was taken to the court in a police van together with two other detainees. We were handcuffed and plain clothes DINA agents with machine guns accompanied us. The statements were taken by actuaries, but the legal processes resulted in nothing, since invariably the civil courts declared themselves 'impotent' due to the fact that Pinochet had granted amnesty to the accused.

The statement is very brief and lacks the names of the agents I had identified. The judge asks me if I would confirm the statement, adding that she understands I had given evidence in difficult circumstances, being a prisoner at the time and with one DINA agent at each side. I do not know whether the judge knows this as fact or whether she is just being sympathetic. I remember having been told that this judge used to be a right-wing sympathiser of the military regime but that, since she had been appointed as one of the judges with the 'exclusive remit' to investigate crimes against humanity, her views had changed and she had shown increasing interest and energy in her investigations.

She starts by asking me questions about what had happened twenty-seven years before. Once more I start to talk and she asks me a question now and then.

I enter a state of trance. I am no longer in the present. I am back in time and the images of the people and the situations became more and more vivid. When my memory fails, the judge reminds me of a name or a nickname, or corrects me. When in doubt, she asks her assistant to bring so and so's file, although most of the information is already in her head. When we finish I am exhausted. My mouth is completely dry and my muscles ache, but she is still composed, showing no signs of tiredness. We have been working non-stop for six and a half hours. I keep repeating, still unable to comprehend, 'They shouldn't have done it, they shouldn't have done it. Why did they kill them Magistrate, why?' She makes me sign every single page of the long statement. She then proceeds to decide which of the accused I am going to confront. There will be five of them spread over three weeks. Later, I learn that I will have to give evidence in front of another judge.

'When you see them here, Mr Muñoz, you will be able to say whatever you like, within a framework of respect, of course,' she tells me.

'Of course,' I agree.

She also makes me sign a warrant stating that I will appear for the cross-examining sessions in front of her.

'I will be here, Magistrate, you can be sure of that,' I say.

When I step outside the building, there is nobody there. The court is closed and the street deserted, but for a group of men, casually dressed, on one street corner. Suddenly fear strikes me. I do not know where I am; this is not safe. I have to get out of here. I see a taxi standing under a tree a few yards from the court gates. I walk towards it but before I reach it the taxi drives away. This is a set up, I conclude. I look at the group of men talking at the other end of the road. They are still there, and they are staring at me. I decide to go back into the court building, but I can only go as far as the front garden, since the doors are closed.

What to do? There is not a telephone in sight and I haven't got a mobile. Suddenly I notice that one of the houses next to the court building is actually a small grocery shop. I go inside, hoping that the shop is not part of the plot. It is dark inside. I ask the woman assistant how I can get to the city centre. She looks at me as though she does not understand my question. I remember the judge telling me that I do not have a Chilean accent anymore. I repeat my question and this time the woman tells me that I have to go to the metro station. It will take me about ten minutes, she says. I thank her and leave the shop slightly calmer.

The street looks beautiful. There are identical, one-storey terraced houses lining the street, each one of them with an identical, beautiful tree in front, but not a soul in sight. My memory recalls something and my body reacts by tensing every muscle. My nose smells something familiar, something old. It is danger. This is the road. They were waiting for me. It was after Diana disappeared from my life forever. I had to meet a comrade walking down this street, the same deserted street. It was the beginning of December as well, in 1974. The same smell came to me then, the smell of danger warning me to 'Run, brother, run.' Sure enough then, in 1974, I could see their shadows in the long, empty street. The noses of their cars protruding oddly from behind a tree trunk. Their dark smell filled my nose and I followed my senses. I did not enter the street, and I saved myself for another day.

I cannot enter the street this time either. My body will not allow it. My body is back in December 1974 and my legs will not oblige. I go back to the shop and walk to the next street, which runs parallel to an elevated motorway. At least this is open space, and there is heavy traffic on the motorway. They will not ambush me in an open space. I walk nervously and quickly until I reach a petrol station. There is a telephone box there and I hurry towards it, reading the operating instructions, finding the right coins, but who am I going to ring? My daughters. Ring Diana. Yes, I have got grown-up daughters now, they live here, they are from here, they know. It is not 1974, no, but the criminals are still at large. The telephone does not work and I have used all my coins, and it is like an oven inside the telephone box. I had better walk. I can see a low, grey building that may be the metro station. I eventually reach it and find a public telephone. I get some change and phone my daughter Diana. Yes,

Diana, she is called Diana, yes, like Diana. I named her Diana when she was born, in London, in 1980. Diana's telephone rings and rings, but there is no answer, she is not there.

I am now sobbing in a corner of the metro station. Slow down, Luis, I say to myself. Don't lose it Luis. Use the telephone. Phone Dalia. Who? Dalia, your other daughter, remember? The one that is older. The one you seldom see. The one that was only three when they were going to take her to the torture centre to make you talk, to torture her in front of you.

'Bring her bastards! Bring her to see what happens. Bring her and if necessary I will pay with my blood and her blood that is my blood, my flesh!'

They shouldn't have done it, Magistrate. She always says that she needs me so much, that it is so painful for her to live without me, without her dad, even now, to talk to me, to be friends. But she has two little boys now, and she is responsible, and she wouldn't leave them. And she doesn't know, that her beloved dad nearly carried her to the torture chamber. I understand, Magistrate, I beg your pardon. 'Within a framework of respect.'

Dalia answers her mobile phone. 'Where are you, dad? How was it, dad? You are on the right line, dad. Take the metro and get off at Tobalaba. I'll be waiting for you there . . . I have work to do there . . . see you then.'

I feel better now. Why is it that Dalia makes me feel calmer, safer? Is it because I find that she is resourceful, that she knows what to do? Or is it because she has always been there, her whole life? She was very fond of Diana. She was just over two years old when the coup happened. I remember how frightened she was and how she told me that she did not want to be near the *malinares* (military in her own vocabulary). 'My daddy is in prison because he does not agree with the military,' she once told her nursery teachers. It may be that there is a hardness that brings us closer together in spite of time and distance.

I have a sandwich and a drink while we walk to her meeting. She is a drugs company representative. She looks beautiful, her big eyes shining, her lovely smile, long honey-coloured hair. Men turn around to look at her in the street. The security guards hurry to open the glass door of the building and greet her enthusiastically. The concierge stops his telephone conversation to look her up and down, smiling.

218

My little girl is a woman, I say to myself. I don't believe I have ever seen her before as a woman, a desirable woman to other men. I feel uneasy about the whole situation, embarrassed even. If I lived in Chile, I would have got used to the idea, I suppose, that my little girl is a woman liable to be treated like any other woman by men. I wonder how she must feel to be complimented by men almost all the time. I have been in England for too long, I realise. A sudden tiredness invades me and I try hard to fight back. I need to lie down and sleep, as though somebody had injected me with a powerful drug. I decide to wait for Dalia on a bench in the building's front garden. Confusion comes back to me again. Where am I? What is this place? What am I doing here? I just want to fall asleep. When Dalia comes back I tell her that I am too tired, I will go to my brother's to rest. I fall asleep on the bus and miss my stop.

I get off the bus still confused. My youngest brother, his two teenage children and our aunt live in the house that was once our family house. We moved there when I was eleven and the appearance of the neighbourhood has not changed much since I left. The acacia trees have grown taller and some of the chalet houses have extensions. Apart from that everything is pretty much the same. As I recover my sense of orientation, I cross the big avenue and walk the short distance to *our* road. How many times in my life have I walked this distance to the iron gate of the house? I like the journey, for most of the time I have loved this short walk from the world outside to the neighbourhood world and then the family world. I can hear the sound of the metal wheels of the roller skates again. We used to play hockey on roller skates. We formed a team and closed the street to traffic, which at the time was negligible, for training and important matches. We became youth champions once.

Luis Palominos, who lived in another street, used to play, as well as his elder brothers. Luis Palominos was younger than me, but he was good. Years later I met him in the Party. We had to do a job together. We remembered our hockey times and laughed while trying to agree who was the best player. After the coup, we met again a couple of times, in our effort to organise the resistance. But, after I had managed to avoid detention for longer than expected, it was at a place where I was due to meet him that I was finally caught. 'I will never be caught alive comrade, you can trust me,' he had once said, when he learned that Diana had been caught. But about four days after my detention I saw him again at the torture centre, when I was still in the common room among eighty other prisoners. Although he could hardly walk, he came to me at the other end of the big room.

'I come to apologise comrade for having given you away. I had your details on a piece of paper and when they got me I tried to eat it. Realising what I was doing, they made me eat an entire broadsheet newspaper. I do not know what it has done to me, comrade, but I feel terrible in my stomach. They also tried to break my legs.'

'Do not worry, comrade,' I responded, 'you did the best you could, I'm sure. Besides, I was convinced that it was only a matter of time. I managed to escape many times before; sooner or later I would have ended up here or dead. No hard feelings, don't worry, let's carry on doing our best.' He became more cheerful, optimistic and chatty.

Luis Palominos did not make it. He was one of the many taken away on Christmas Eve 1974, inside the infamous refrigerated trucks. His name is one of the thousands on the lists of the 'disappeared'.

My uncle Rene, my father's youngest brother, made the iron fence and gates of our house. He was a good blacksmith. Aunt Raquel unlocks the gate for me. She is happy to see me and talks while I lie on the sofa, but I cannot hear her. I fall into a deep sleep wrapped in a cotton cloud of sweet memories of childhood in the neighbourhood, Uncle Rene, and grandmother.

★　★　★

Marcelo Moren Brito. I did not know his name at the time, only his nicknames: el Ronco (the deep-voiced one) or El Oso Salvaje (the wild bear). It was a thunderous voice, it could be heard all over the torture centre shouting, swearing, giving orders to torture someone or calling one's name for interrogation. He was the boss. I could only see his hands through the gap in the blindfold; they were fat, huge hands. One punch with those hands could send anyone rolling down onto the floor, more so if you could not see where the blow was coming from and your hands were tied at your back.

I do not recognise him when the judge asks me if I know the man sitting next to me in front of her desk. I only know him because she has already told me that my first cross-examination will be with him. This is an old man, with almost white hair, obese, with a slight hump on his back. He has very small eyes, his mouth is pointed and he is always looking at the floor. More astonishing for me is the fact that this man is quite short. The image of him I had formed in my mind was that of a huge man, judging from his unusually deep voice, big hands and high rank, in charge of the torture centre at the time. I keep looking at his hands. There is no mistake, those are the same hands. The same hands that had inflicted so much punishment on so many victims; the bloodied hands, merciless, heavy hands. I never thought I would see those hands again.

'I have never seen this person in my life,' he declares after the judge asks him if he knows me. The same voice! An instant flashback overtakes me. The unbearable heat inside the wooden box that I was kept in, and then suddenly being taken out of the box and led to the windowless room that was the torture chamber. The same voice: 'Do you know this princess? We have reason to believe that you know this beauty.' When they lifted my blindfold all I could see was that the small room was full of men. Down near the floor, lying on a metal bed connected to the electricity supply was the naked body of a young woman. Her legs were spread out and her ankles wired to the bed. Her hands were also wired to the metal. Her face was half covered by a wide black blindfold. I could see her lips and her chin. I could not see her hair. She was slim and pale. She looked like a statue, paralysed by terror, holding her breath.

Maybe I knew her, maybe I didn't, but that was irrelevant because I had already decided that I would never identify her. I spat out my response in anger,

'NO! I DON'T!'

'Take him away, he is lying again.' I was punched, pushed to the floor and dragged back to the wooden box.

'This bloke is lying, Magistrate. What's the name of this bloke?' thunders 'the voice'.

'Don't be rude, sir, you have to show more respect, and you cannot take notes here,' says the judge.

'This is the same man, Magistrate. I would never forget those hands, that voice and that vulgarity,' I say.

I cannot believe what I am experiencing. It is as though my previous life had ended and I have just entered the realm of the absurd. I wish that somebody else were here with me, somebody to be a witness to these happenings because I am not sure it is real. I need somebody to record what is taking place so I can be reminded that it is true, that I was there, and that I did say what I had said. To record that 'the bear' was not really a bear but a mouse, an angry and frightened mouse with a pointed mouth. A defeated, insolent old man who had only a small dog for company, I was told, and who was constantly afraid of casual encounters with the mothers of the disappeared.

That night I stay in the house of a friend I met at the torture centre. He is now a councillor and university lecturer. He has a beautiful house at the foot of the mountains. The next day is a Saturday and my friend suggests that I accompany him to a meeting with his constituents at the town hall. Afterwards he will take me for a visit to Villa Grimaldi Memorial Park. The torture centre has been transformed into a 'Park for Peace', since most of the old buildings were demolished by the colonel who 'bought' the Villa when it was no longer used as a torture centre.

It is a beautiful summer morning, the kind of morning like so many hundreds of mornings of my childhood and of the other half of my life. The air, the sounds, the *cordillera* all seemed so painfully familiar. The stillness is telling me, like before, of the day to come, the predictability of the day, with no sudden change in the weather. This is a summer day in Santiago, and the likelihood is that it will remain summer until at least the end of February.

But it is disturbing for me too. The ease with which my senses recognise and get used to the environment gives me the impression that I have never left the place; that I am just starting from where I left off; that my body and my senses belong there. It is at this precise point that a sort of dislocation inside begins to occur: the reality of life in exile starts to be questioned. The powerful bonds that were formed during my years in Chile since my birth have not been, and will never be, replicated in England. No matter how much I travel up and down the island of Great Britain, admiring its beauty, making sense of its capricious weather, searching for its soul. No matter that I have encountered love and have founded a new family with children born in the UK. No matter how much I admire the culture, the openness, the determination of its people, and countless other things I have assimilated and incorporated in myself, all that entire life, so patiently reconstructed and crafted over more than twenty years. That life can disappear in a few days, or maybe even hours.

My friend and I arrive at the town hall, which is a new colonial-style, two-storey building with a curved, red-tiled roof. Inside there is a big square patio with a garden and a fountain in the middle. The offices and meeting rooms are arranged around the patio with a wide corridor and

222

veranda surrounding the whole perimeter. We go into a meeting room where about twelve people are sat around a table. They are being addressed by a government officer from the Ministry for the Welfare of Children. I am invited to sit at the table and participate if I want to. I sit down and observe. This contributes even further to my uneasy feeling about the whole situation. The meeting, with the women and men participating, is a carbon copy of so many meetings I attended during the Popular Government era; the voices, the gestures, the faces, the officer's responses, everything is the same. Has time stood still up to this moment? Am I watching a film?

I start to feel really bad, until I cannot bear it any longer. I decide that I cannot stay in the room, so stand up and walk outside. It is as if I am losing my sense of reality. Since my arrival, the detention at the airport, the interrogation, the interview with the judge, seeing family and old friends, everything has been taking me back nearly thirty years. Like a time-traveller who has been to the future and has just come back to find that nothing or very little has really changed. The only problem is that there is a big chunk missing, and this is really hurting. Where is Diana? And Maria Cristina? And Nano? And Anita Maria? If nothing has happened and I have never been in exile; if I have just been mad, or in a dream, then where are they? If they were here things would make sense, but they are not.

I stand at the veranda contemplating the Andes, dotted with big houses here and there. Women are watering the garden below and cleaning the fountain. Their voices have a familiar accent and they chat idly. An enormous sadness invades me. Wasn't this exactly what was wanted? That a whole chunk of life and history be eradicated from us forever? They buried it with lies, fear and silence. I tried to uncover it with a life in exile, with work, studies, therapy, failed relationships, children, more pain, more studies, more therapy, more work and many attempts to reconcile myself with life and the world.

But Pinochet was in detention in London for over a year. I was there. I campaigned for his extradition to Spain to face trial for his crimes. I gave countless interviews and participated in a number of forums, on radio and TV, broadcast all over the globe. I shouted in Parliament Square and in front of the House of Lords. Still, it did not seem to be credible.

My friend comes out of the meeting, puts an arm around my shoulder and asks me what is the matter. I tell him that I am feeling very bad.

'I think I need to cry,' I say. 'I am too full of things; it is too much.' It is the only way I could show how I was feeling.

He took out his mobile phone. 'This friend is a psychiatrist, he knows what is going on and has experience with people like us,' my friend says.

The psychiatrist sees me in half an hour at a nearby community health centre. He is a young man in his thirties, very affable.

'What is the matter?' he asks me.

I explain briefly what has happened and why I am in Chile. I am usually reluctant to talk about the subject to people younger than me, thinking, in this case, that he was probably an infant when all these things happened, as if what I have to tell him is going to hurt him. But this time I do not care, I just let it out.

What comes out is that I want my comrades and friends back; I want the murdered and the disappeared back; I want my loved ones back. I cry and I sob and I scream.

'It does not make sense. I want it back!' I cry. 'I want to make sense of it; their absence here and now does not make sense!' I go on.

I tell the young psychiatrist that on the coming Monday I have to confront, in cross-examination, Miguel Krassnoff, Diana's murderer, the murderer of so many, my captor and tormentor.

I tell him that I know Krassnoff is denying everything, denying even having ever seen the victims and witnesses in that place. I say that I always believed he could not deny me, but that now I have my doubts. I explain that I do not know why, but I feel that if Krassnoff denies me totally, I will feel completely defeated and a failure. The doctor asks me, in a soft tone, why I would be a failure. I say that I will have failed the dead, the victims, my loved ones and their relatives.

'You know it is not your fault and it is not your responsibility. You are doing a noble and courageous thing; that is all you can do. You are not the criminal, he is, and you are not the judge.'

He prescribes some medication to help me relax and sleep. I decide not to take it.

I cannot sleep at my daughter's house. She has a dog that, when it barks during the night, makes me think that someone, probably a hit-man, is trying to enter the house. When the dog is silent, it is probably because the hit-man, sent by Krassnoff and his associates, has killed the dog. I realise I have started to feel paranoid; or have I?

On the Sunday I have a meal at my brother's house, with Aunt Raquel and my brother's children. The next day, at ten in the morning I will face Krassnoff. I have already decided against the tranquilizers; I wanted to be fully alert for the encounter. I get up early in the morning and leave my daughter's house at eight. The morning is like every other summer morning I remember. I walk to the nearby metro station, looking every now and then to see if anyone is following me in the almost deserted street. The metro station is fairly busy. I look at people's faces trying to identify a hit-man or woman, an ex-service person ready to push me in front of the Parisian-style metro. I cannot tell, all the faces look hostile and alien, no sign of the friendly, smiling and open faces of twenty odd years ago.

Inside the modern carriage my feelings do not change. It is like being in a foreign country; I cannot find the Chile of my childhood, my youth and my early adulthood. I feel uneasy. How many people on this carriage know what is going on in the courtrooms of their country? I ask myself. The ones who know, do they care? I remind myself that long ago I had decided that this was a lonely battle and that I should carry on looking over my shoulder.

I have to meet the lawyer at the Human Rights Office at nine fifteen. Although I am not a coffee drinker, I need a strong one today, so I have an espresso. Then I buy a bottle of water, arriving early at the office. We get a taxi to the court. When I enter the judge's room, she is already there, and then the actuary arrives. The judge asks me to sit in one of the chairs in front of her desk. I choose the chair facing the door; I want to see Krassnoff from the moment he enters the room.

One or two minutes later Krassnoff enters with a smile that is more like a grimace. He looks at me, his eyes opening wide, then greets the judge and sits down. I feel as if hot water has been poured over my head and is slowly travelling down my body. He recognises me, I think. He won't be able to deny me now. Krassnoff is dressed the same way as when I last saw him twenty-six years before: navy blue jacket with brass buttons, grey trousers and a tie. He has changed, of course, but not much. He has put on weight, his face is broader and wrinkled, but he is the same man. He chain-smokes, I am told.

The judge, experienced in these kinds of situations, notices Krassnoff's half-smile and stare when he sees me.

'You do know this man, don't you?' she asks him.

'He looks very familiar to me; I might have seen him before,' he answers.

The judge turns to me very quickly asking me, 'Mr Muñoz, do you know this man?'

'Yes,' I reply, 'his name is Miguel Krassnoff Martchenko, aka Captain Miguel, aka Crazy Horse, and a former schoolmate of mine.'

He looks at me with surprise on his face, then a smile and he lifts his left index finger to his temple in a gesture of recognition.

'Of course you know him,' the judge says looking at Krassnoff. 'His name is Luis Muñoz, you have met him before and I am going to read to you his statement related to those encounters with you,' she adds.

The judge then proceeds to read a statement I have forgotten I made while still in prison. The family of a 'disappeared' comrade I met in Villa Grimaldi contacted me once to tell me that they were trying to bring charges against DINA for the abduction and disappearance of Anselmo Radrigan and others. This kind of action was unheard of at that time, less so that a prisoner would dare to give evidence against his captors in court. I agreed. I remember that I was taken to the court in a sealed van, and of course I had to give my statement with an armed guard on each side of me. Before reading this particular statement of mine, the judge reminded Krassnoff of the conditions under which this statement was given, leaving no doubt that what I had done then was not just an act of courage but that I was, even then, accusing him.

The reading by the judge takes about half an hour. During this time Krassnoff shows great distress in his chair, with an energetic shaking of his legs and constantly fiddling with his wristwatch and his glasses, cleaning them with his handkerchief again and again. He never looks at me, though I am sitting two feet away from him. As I have purposely situated my chair at an angle so I can half face him and the judge, I keep staring at him, trying to capture his every reaction to the detailed statement of his murderous actions. He becomes more and more nervous, his initial smile completely replaced by the contortion of his face muscles that I know means that he is in a rage. This time, though, he has to contain it, with my stare fixed on him. In contrast to his unsettledness and shaking, I am calm, taking a long time to have a sip of water from my bottle and unscrewing and screwing back the bottle cap.

After the judge has finished reading the statement, she asks him what he has to say about it. He looks at the actuary sitting next to the judge at the keyboard. The actuary perks up on his chair, as though he knows the ritual from before. I remember what people have told me about Krassnoff, 'He dictates to the actuary, in a military fashion.' 'I would like to make a correction,' he says. 'The person I associate with these statements is not this [sic] sitting next to me. That person I remember went to live in Spain, gave an interview to the *Cambio 16* magazine, where these allegations were published, but this I do not recognise and do not remember having seen in the past,' he says, slowly, allowing for the typing.

I know exactly who he is referring to because my friend Ariel in Geneva had told me a week earlier what had happened. This comrade, who I briefly met before I was captured, was already in Villa Grimaldi when I arrived there. Soon it became obvious to me that he was 'collaborating' with his captors. After incredible acts of betrayal he traded Party information and comrades for his life and that of his wife. They were both sent to Spain, at that time still under Franco's rule. He now lives somewhere in Brazil. He was called to testify early in 2002, but the day before he had to confront Krassnoff, he collapsed with panic attacks and begged to be put on the first plane back home.

It is obvious that Krassnoff knows this and is trying to backtrack on his admission that he has seen me before. The judge then makes what is to me an astonishing move. She turns to me and asks,

'Mr Muñoz, did you go to Spain?'

'No,' I say, 'I went to England.'

She astonishes me even further when she asks,

'But you gave an interview to *Cambio 16*, did you not Mr Muñoz?' I suddenly realise what the judge is doing; she is giving it to me on a plate.

'Yes,' I respond, 'I did give an interview to *Cambio 16*.'

'You see, Mr Krassnoff?' she says turning to him. 'This is the same person; what do you have to say?'

I can hear a big cry inside me: 'I'VE GOT YOU, YOU STUPID BASTARD! YOU WON'T BE ABLE TO DENY ME NOW!' I know he cannot say anything to contradict me or to question my response. How can he without incriminating himself, without engaging? But, he knows better; he is well trained and he has been doing this for years. He has to admit defeat and he looks at me as if to say, 'OK, one–nil.'

'But I don't think I have met this person at the time in question,' he answers. The judge looks in her thick file, opens it somewhere and shows him a page. 'You have admitted, haven't you, sir, that you have met these people in Villa Grimaldi?' I look, and I can see my name scribbled on a kind of form. He nods.

Krassnoff resumes his dictation: 'I remember that in my capacity as an analyst at that place this person reminded me that we were at the same school when we were both thirteen. We participated in the occupation of the school demanding a new building because the infra-structure was not good. The following year I left for the military academy. But I totally deny that what has been read to me took place or that I participated in the events described.'

Turning towards me the judge says, 'Mr Muñoz?'

My time has finally arrived, I think. To a certain extent he is now at my mercy. But my experience of having represented clients in the county courts and immigration appeals in England comes immediately to mind. Although the judge has previously reminded me that I can say anything I want, 'within a framework of respect', at the end of the day she will be the one making the decision to send him, or not, to prison. I have to be a convincing, consistent and reliable witness. I have to convince her, if she is not already convinced, that he is guilty, that he is a criminal, a sadistic murderer and a liar. I must not forget that during my enquiries about the judge, before travelling to Chile, I was told that although she is very conscientious, professional and sympathetic, she comes from a very right-wing family, supporters of the dictatorship who do not believe in the charges made against the regime.

I turn in my chair towards her, looking straight into her eyes. 'Magistrate,' I say. 'It is difficult for me to express what I feel about what is happening here in this room today. Here we have,' I gesture towards Krassnoff with my hand, 'one of the most vicious criminals in the land who, when he committed his crimes, was invested, and indeed invested himself, with the title of a brave, courageous, honest and selfless Chilean soldier. What we see here now Magistrate is a liar, a dishonest coward trying to save his miserable skin when required by law to take respon-sibility for his despicable actions. I could perhaps understand, Magistrate, his fear if he was under duress, but I can see no chains on his feet, no cables around his wrists. I can see no metal bed here, Magistrate, connected to an electricity supply and nobody has a machine gun. Nevertheless, Magistrate, our brave soldier, Captain, Colonel Krassnoff is denying in fear, lying in fear and shaking like a leaf.' I say all this turning and glancing around the room as though looking for the implements of torture. 'He told me he shot my wife, Magistrate. He tortured me, Magistrate. He starved me, he hanged me, and did the same to hundreds of others, many of whom died.'

'Mr Krassnoff?' the judge asks after making sure the actuary has typed every word I have said. Addressing the actuary in front of him across the desk, he begins,

'I totally deny that what this person describes took place; I was only an analyst. I have never met the person he describes as his wife, Ms Diana Aron.'

The judge interrupts him and asks,

'Did you look for, find in the street, shoot and subsequently kidnap Diana Aron Svigilsky?'

'I emphatically deny it, and as far as I can remember my relationship with Mr Muñoz at the time was cordial,' he responds, looking at an empty space in front of him and nervously moving in his chair, as if the lie is underneath him, making it uncomfortable to sit.

It is my turn again. 'Magistrate, this man is trying to make a mockery of justice here. Is his fear of having to pay for his crimes so great, because the evidence is so overwhelming, that he has to resort to dirty tricks due to the fact that he cannot, as before, trample over the rule of law? What kind of stupidity is this? Allow me to explain to you, Magistrate, if I may, what *cordial* meant.' And once again I give details of the torture methods I was subjected to at Villa Grimaldi. '"Cordial relationship". Do you think this is a joke?' I add, addressing Krassnoff.

His dictation starts again: 'At that time we had to fight against terrorists and terrorist acts that were aimed precisely at the judiciary. It was they who violated the law and conspired against the state. These were dangerous people. As a soldier I carried out the duties I was entrusted with to prevent acts of vandalism and chaos.' He dictates word by word, allowing an excessive time for the typing. It is clear that he is trying to turn around what I am saying, trying to be 'clever', but cleverness has, obviously, escaped his grasp a long time ago.

'With all due respect, Magistrate,' I begin again, 'I think that this man needs to be reminded of certain facts.' I then turn around in my chair to face him. By now I am angry, really angry, so I shout the words at him, slowly but loud and clear. 'You are accused of murder, torture and kidnapping in this court; you are the convict; you are the one on bail; you are the one who is lying through his teeth to save his skin. Not me, not Diana, not Maria Cristina, not Nano, not Anita Maria and so many others you murdered. Because you could not put them on trial, because there was nothing you or anybody could accuse them of, because they were all innocent. How many bombs did they plant? How many of you were killed or even injured by this "dangerous enemy", these terrorists? Do you understand, Miguel?' I shout. 'Pure and simple butchery; that is what it was. Butchery by psychopaths like you. You are an assassin, a murderer, do you understand? And it is not a joke. Magistrate, he thinks it is a joke. More than that, you have committed crimes against humanity as a whole, you are a mass murderer, you have committed genocide, and you are guilty! It is true, you did not kill me. I slipped through your fingers. There was probably an internal battle between the murderer and the sadist, and the sadist triumphed. It was just his sadism that kept me alive, Magistrate; the perverse curiosity of the psychopath, just to see what happens.'

His legs are shaking; he is compulsively taking his glasses off, cleaning them and putting them back on. Then he does the same with his wrist-watch. Smoking is not allowed in court. The judge repeats my sentences like an echo, dictating to the actuary, 'You – are – a – mass – murderer.'

Krassnoff retreats. 'I am not a murderer. I was an officer of the Chilean armed forces serving my country, and just carried out my duties. I would like to add that due to my personal intervention the life of this person was spared.' He wants to finish now, I think. A very short statement, using the ammunition I had given him: my life. Does he want me to soften my stance? Be careful not to provoke me?

'Magistrate,' I carry on, in a very calm, sad tone. 'It is extremely sad what has happened, what they have done. And it was so completely unnecessary; they had all the power, totally unopposed power, but still, these "brave soldiers" had to commit all kinds of abuse against defence-less men and women of all ages until they had their hands stained with blood. But this individual, Magistrate, did not stop there. In his psychotic mind, this coward had to go even further. One day, he and one of his accomplices, the infamous Maximiliano Ferrer Lima, came to me and declared that, because I had not given them what they wanted and I had not 'cooperated' with them, they would bring my three-year-old daughter, as they had done with others, to be tortured in front of me.'

Krassnoff looks uncomfortable with my statement. He is shaking all over and makes a gesture with his right hand and a sound with his tongue, as if saying, 'This man has gone too far.' I turn around in fury, facing him; the floor is mine now and I take it.

'You don't like it, do you? You don't like to be reminded of your crimes, of your abuses, do you? It's ugly now, isn't it? But you did like it then; you enjoyed it then. But not now, no, you don't like it now, more so because this is not your style, is it! Your style is with your machine guns, with your accomplices protecting you, with me tied to an electrified metal bed, naked, blindfolded; with me hanging from a pole semi-conscious; that is your style, "brave soldier"! But here, in front of the Magistrate, in front of the law, without your weapons, without your generals, it is not nice, is it?' I shout.

'My little daughter, Magistrate,' I continue.

'Did they bring her, Mr Muñoz?' the judge asks me.

'No, Magistrate, they did not.'

'Why not?' the judge asks.

'By then, Magistrate, I think they did not believe they could break me even with my little girl on the electrified bed,' I said in a defeated, sad tone. 'This "innocent analyst" – because they were all analysts, weren't they, Magistrate? – what were they analysing? One can only guess. In his case, I am sure that after shooting innocent people, raping, torturing and killing, he went on to "analyse" the effects of his brutality on the human body and psyche. Although I do not believe that his brain could go that far.'

'My comrades,' I continue in a sad tone, now fully submerged in a catharsis, no longer in the court, no longer in the present anymore, 'my loved ones, Magistrate, how old were they, these "dangerous terrorists"? María Cristina, twenty-one; Diana twenty-three; Nano twenty-five; Anita María, twenty-four. It was a concerted plan to annihilate us, not because we were armed, Magistrate, not because we were a military threat of any kind, but because we had a dream. Because we sang and danced in the streets holding hands with the ordinary people, with the workers, with the mothers and the children of the dispossessed, offering our lives for a better future for all. They assassinated the dreams of a generation of young Chileans to satisfy the twisted desires of the psychopaths that they are.

'They assassinated the dreams of a generation of. . . .' repeats the voice of the judge, like an echo from another world, dictating to the actuary so he won't miss a word.

I am exhausted, I want to cry, but just like twenty or so years before, I will not give him a drop of my tears. Krassnoff has nothing else to add, his legs are shaking violently.

'You may leave now, Mr Muñoz", says the judge.

It is twelve thirty. I have been there two and a half hours. The lawyer is waiting outside. She wants to know how it has gone; I am speechless, unable to talk and unable to grasp what is going on. Everything is so strange. There is a part of me that feels elated because I have done it, I have given evidence, I have confronted Krassnoff, I have said what I wanted to say to him and, more importantly, he cannot deny me. He has admitted he knew me, that we were together in the same school when we were twelve and thirteen and that he used to live near where I lived. He has admitted I was one of his prisoners at Villa Grimaldi, although he attempted to deny it at first. The rest, what he did to me and Diana's killing, just adds to the mountain of other testimonies and evidence against him amassed by the judge over two years.

'What would you like to do?' The lawyer asks me. 'We can go back to the office if you like.'

'I need a drink,' I say. 'Let's go back to the city centre.'

We get into a taxi. Near her office we have fruit juice and I realise I want to be on my own. I walk through the crowded streets of Santiago, my city, or the city that used to be mine, and I want to rediscover it. I want to immerse myself in the city, to mix with the crowds, the streets, the traffic, rubbing off the skin that made me feel foreign, alien. Soon I notice the buildings, the ministry of justice, the bookshop and stationers where I worked for a time. I go in, looking intently. Yes, I was here many years ago, I worked long hours here, I was tired here.

'What are you looking for, sir?'

'Oh, yes, a notebook please, a small notebook.'

It is all the same, but I still feel like an intruder, an intruder into a dream. I go out, the slabs of the pavement look very worn, and they are probably the same as they were thirty years ago. People pass me by, bumping into me without even noticing me, as if I do not exist, I am a ghost. But I did go to that café, I remember, and I once bought a coat for my brother over there.

I carry on walking until I reach Santiago's main square, which is surrounded by the old buildings of the cathedral, the post office and the two old commercial galleries with their traditional arches. The square is full of people and on one side there is something new, about a dozen tables and chairs with people, mostly men and boys, playing chess, looking very professional and very serious. I stay there for a while, fascinated, looking at their faces; this did not happen thirty years ago. Where do these people come from? I ask myself. The concentration in their faces. Whose idea must this have been? This is a reflection of a Chile I do not know: serious, pensive, calculating, looking ahead, in silence, oblivious of what is going on around them, with an individualistic pursuit.

I remember that I have promised to send postcards back to England, so I go to the central post office across the square. The square, Plaza de Armas (Square of Arms), is where all the protests and marches used to gather, or at least tried to.

I can see myself at seventeen, running from the tear gas, ducking the police batons, going around the block and coming back to the Plaza shouting abuse against the finance ministry and its new economic measures. I am running again from the tear gas and water cannons, this time holding Maria Cristina's hand, more than twenty years ago.

The pretty girl selling postcards at a kiosk treats me like a foreign tourist, of which there are plenty here. I can't avoid it, I have changed, I am different, and these people do not consider me one of their own. The girl is pretty, very pretty, and she smiles at me and tries to help. It is then that it hits me. That smile, her face, her attitude, her mode, her eyes, her voice, the way she moves and gestures with her hands. I recognise her, the girl from my youth, the university student, the girl from the neighbourhood, the girl at the café across the faculty, the Party comrade. I cannot carry on any longer; something hurts at the base of my head and I need to fall asleep.

With great difficulty I manage to board a bus to my brother's house where, surrounded by vines, a huge avocado tree and other flowering plants and bushes, which make it cooler, I fall asleep on the sofa as though under the influence of a powerful drug.

Roberto, my councillor friend, invites me that evening to a gathering at a rustic restaurant where the city ends at the foot of the mountains. There is going to be music by a famous Chilean band and other singers. The proceeds will go to the Villa Grimaldi foundation, to help rebuild the centre and maintain the remembrance park. I make my way to the restaurant, which is a lovely place. Roberto has told me that I will be taken care of at the door by a woman called Viviana. It is quite dark in the restaurant and I do not recognise the people there, though I am supposed to know them. A nice looking woman in her forties, dressed in a long white dress, approaches me, asking if I am Luis. She takes me into the main area and sits me at a long table next to a woman. I am introduced to the others who are eating tapas and drinking wine, but nobody seems to recognise me. I start a conversation with the woman next to me; the man sitting opposite her seems to be her husband. Then the singing starts.

It is not until the end of the first part of the concert when Roberto, who after arriving late with his wife is sitting at another table, calls out my name and a few faces turn around to look at me and a bald man sitting at the front of the table stands up and comes to embrace me. I recognise him too and call out his name while we embrace. We first met at Villa Grimaldi, but I remember him taller, with a beard and more hair. He used to sing beautifully in the camp. We have spent almost an hour staring at each other without recognition. Two or three other men also come to greet me, finding no words to utter, only a few tears. It has always been the same pattern; it is almost impossible to talk, I believe, for fear of the other's reaction, the worst being 'I do not talk about it' or 'That is in the past'. Everybody is holding tears back as if they are shameful, as if shedding tears means to undress again, to be naked in front of the torturers again. It is therefore assumed that nobody wants to talk about it or the painful memories may overflow. Everybody seems to know what I have come to Chile for, but nobody dares to ask me. Only my brothers seem interested, but then their pain and anger is only too visible.

At the end of the evening, Viviana, who has by now told me that she was my daughter's teacher at primary school, suggests that I sleep at her place. Roberto encourages her. I panic. I have no desire to share the night, or any night for that matter, with a woman, but I am miles away from my daughter's house and there is no public transport at that time of the night. I decide to wait until the joke is over, if it is a joke, but Viviana comes back to me in the milieu of the guests leaving the place.

'You stay with me then,' she says. I do not answer. Luckily, it only takes a few glances between Roberto's wife and me for her to understand the situation. I make my way towards her through the crowd.

'I think Roberto has planned this a bit,' I tell her. 'But I can't stay with her; I would feel awful.'

234

'I understand,' she says. 'Roberto is quite stupid sometimes. You come with me, stay with us. We have no room in the car though. We will have to walk. It's not far but it's very dark. Roberto offered quite a few people a lift home.'

We walk together with her grandson through the dark and unpaved road up the mountain. I am so relieved. Was Viviana lonely? Was it just the old songs and the sweet wine and a shadow of the lost past that I represented for a few moments? I do not know.

I have a sleepless night, the scene at the court repeating itself in my head time and again. Next day, two or three old friends contact me to enquire about what happened at the court, and when I tell them, to my surprise, they warn me that I have to be careful for the rest of my stay in Chile. 'They are dangerous people, and they are free to do as they please.' There have been allegations that the so-called 'Comando Conjunto' (Joint Command) that used to operate in conjunction with the official repressive apparatus is still in existence in defiance of the decree that dissolved it.

It is true, nobody can prevent them from attacking me. There must be a lot of volunteers among their supporters inside and outside the armed forces. The men at the airport are definitely sympathisers with the previous regime. Remember that the Pinochet constitution prevents any subsequent government from removing from the civil service any personnel who had been appointed when Pinochet was in power; thus, diplomatic personnel, apart from the ambassador and the consul, cannot be replaced. The same applies to the immigration staff at the airports. Didn't they beat a human rights lawyer unconscious just a couple of weeks ago?

There is a possibility that I could be attacked, I think, but, on the other hand, it does not matter now; I have already testified against Krassnoff, and I am quite sure he will be found guilty and sentenced. If I have to die now, so be it. I feel sad for Pablo, Orlando and Sara back in England. Especially for Pablo and Orlando, as they will not understand. Sara has told me, over the phone, that Pablo has already asked her, 'Who made daddy go to Chile?' When I have only a little more than a week of my visit left I decide that I will feel safer if I have a car rather than rely on public transport, so I manage to hire the smallest car available. For some reason, being inside a tin on wheels gives me a sense of security.

There is a long weekend coming so I ask Roberto if I can stay in his flat in Valparaiso for two or three days with my daughters. He is happy for me to use it and it proves a powerful experience. Memories of my stay at Valparaiso once when I was a boy of seven or eight and then again when I was in the Puchuncaví concentration camp flood back.

I drive there on the Saturday morning with my daughter Dalia. Diana and Francisca travel up by coach on the Sunday evening at the same time as Dalia leaves on the coach to go back to Santiago. Dalia and I sing all the way to Valparaiso, through the countryside and across the coastal mountain ridge. At one point we get lost and drive along the old road, which is very steep with sharp bends. Ours is the only vehicle climbing up the winding road when suddenly I have to look twice to make sure I am not seeing things. Very slowly a fully grown spider and her family are crossing the barely used road. This particular spider is the size of a large male human hand; it is quite tall, hairy and the colour of a lion's mane with distinctive black, round eyes. It does not look real at all, resembling a cuddly soft toy more than a ferocious spider. The previous time I had seen one of these creatures was high in the Andes when a friend and I decided to spend Christmas in the open. As I woke up one morning inside my sleeping bag, I saw the same scene unfolding before my eyes: a mother spider followed by about five little ones a few centimetres from my face. As I was moving, they stopped for a few seconds and then carried on walking. When I used to tell this story nobody would believe me because people expected me to be terrified and I was not.

At Valparaiso I have the privilege of spending time with my daughter on my own, something I have been unable to do for too many years. We talk and sing (she has an incredibly beautiful voice and knows how to sing) into the early hours. We laugh and cry, too, reluctant to go to sleep, in a desperate attempt to recover two decades of missing and longing. Late the next morning we go for a walk to a beach. It is misty and the sea is rough, but it is a warm day. Later we go to a restaurant for lunch. This is a picturesque place, traditional, where the waitresses wear old-style aprons and hats. Soon we become the waitresses' centre of attention, probably because we are an unusual couple; a man in his early fifties with a young woman in her late twenties.

After we have eaten we go for a drive by the coast. I have not felt so happy in a long time. I needed this time to stop. In a square of the beautiful city of Vina Del Mar, my attention is captured by a group of singers. They are singing old songs, sambas from when I was young. They are good singers and we sit down to listen. The day I leave Chile, at the airport, Dalia hands me two CDs, one with the songs we listened to in the car and the other the original Argentinean group who sang the sambas. The next day I take Dalia to the coach station in the afternoon and collect Francisca and Diana.

My next cross-examination is with the sinister Maximiliano Ferrer. This ex-torturer is better trained. He just denies everything, apart from the fact that he was present at Villa Grimaldi at the time, but that his role was as an 'analyst'. He denies having seen me there and says that there was no contact between the prisoners and staff at the centre.

My statements, though, are relentless and methodical. This, plus the judge's ability, finally breaks his resistance; he contradicts himself and has to lie. The judge tells him that she is tired of his tactics and of his lying time and again, assuming that she is stupid. However, I get the impression that there is not as much evidence against him as there is against Krassnoff and the others. Then I remember something.

'Magistrate,' I say. 'With all respect, you are a woman and I would not want to offend you, and I am not sure whether this is an appropriate thing to reveal, but the words that this "innocent analyst" used to refer to a woman and a woman's body when she was naked and tied to the metal bed and he was torturing her, may be significant.'

'You can speak, Mr Muñoz,' the judge says.

But I find that I cannot bring myself to say the words and it takes me some time before I can speak at all, my memory and my whole being being transfixed in the scenes at the torture centre, in extreme pain and sadness. Then the words come; the barrage of abuse flows from my lips as it had from his: 'Bitch, disgusting, smelly, bloody cunt, whore, cocksucker . . .'.

The next accused, who I have to see three days later, is a man who was a young sergeant at the time. The second or third day after I arrived at the torture centre, this man, who they used to call 'Troglo', perhaps referring to his looking like a troglodyte, asked a guard to lift the blindfold from my eyes so that I could see he was wearing my clothes stolen from my house. He lived up to his nickname, behaving worse than a troglodyte with the prisoners. His real name, though, is Barcalay Zapata. At first, when the judge asks him if he knew me or had seen me before at Villa

Grimaldi he emphatically denies it. After the judge reads the part of my statement relating to him, his memory is refreshed, and he suddenly remembers having seen me at the centre, but denies that he ever wore my clothes, stating that he is a modest man and would never wear other people's clothing. He also denies using my clothes and my glasses to impersonate me in order to capture a comrade who was supposed to meet me; information about the appointment having been obtained from another captured comrade. The meeting was, unfortunately, successful. The comrade had been given my description with emphasis on my jacket, trousers and dark glasses. He fell into the trap and his name is on the long lists of the 'disappeared'.

Zapata denies that he used to boast about his ability with the AK47 assault rifle and his accuracy when aiming at his victims' heads. He tells the judge that he could not drive, making my statement that he was often at the wheel of the pick-up truck used to take victims to their deaths a complete invention.

The judge quickly turns the pages of a file in front of her and, stopping at one, she says, 'Hang on a second, I have here, in your own writing, profession: driver. When it is for your convenience you say you were a driver; now it's not convenient and you say you can't drive. What do you take me for sir? When are you going to start to tell the truth?'

Zapata was a vicious assassin working in the team under Krassnoff. His disregard for people's lives was astonishing and he is here now sitting next to me, all humbled in front of the judge, playing the 'friendly chap' card, minimising what has happened and what he did. It is just nauseating.

I decide to go on the offensive. 'Soon after I was taken to Villa Grimaldi, you told me that after you and Krassnoff had shot Diana in the back, you took her to Grimaldi where, although badly wounded, she was interrogated and tortured, but that she did not give you our house address. You told me that you got to our house anyway after a few days, because you knew it was in the vicinity of where she had been shot. It took you two days to empty the house, keeping for yourself my clothes and some of the furniture. You also told me that you shot comrade Riveros in the head; that although it was from quite a long distance you managed to kill him. Another comrade tried to 'escape' and you pushed him in front of a passing bus. He died a few minutes after that. How can you be such a shameless coward now, telling me and the judge that none of this ever happened, acting the innocent?'

He gets agitated, telling the judge he finds it difficult to understand me, that I speak a language typical of those working for international human rights organisations who, from the very beginning, have been broadcasting fictional accounts.

'Why don't they leave us alone, so we can get on with our lives and they with theirs abroad?,' he says.

'That is because from the very beginning the world has known of the atrocities you committed,' I replied. 'And I want you to get this clear: I am not interested in your miserable life, all I am interested in is that you, and the ones you are protecting, pay for your crimes; because that is what you are, a criminal, a murderer, and murderers should go to prison.'

He decided to back down. Addressing the judge, he started in a lamenting voice, 'Magistrate, you do know me, I have been here many times and confronted many people who have accused me of this and that and the other, but when we have finished, they have no longer been angry, and we have shaken hands and in some cases even had a coffee together.'

'They were not angry perhaps because they were afraid,' I interrupt. 'But I am not afraid of you, disgusting worm, and I would certainly not shake your assassin's hand. Without the machine gun and on your own you are nothing, just a coward!' I thought that I had overstepped the mark of the 'framework of respect' the judge had warned me to keep in our first meeting. I was angry and almost lost my composure. But, to my surprise, she warned Zapata that he was fantasising about shaking hands and cups of coffee with witnesses. After that, she dismissed him, reminding him that he was on bail and had to sign on.

The judge asked me to take a break and relax. A few minutes later she called me back. 'The next person is Osvaldo Romo. You know him; he is in prison, and has been for the past seven years. He is not well and he is, in a way, 'cooperating'. He is different to the others, so I want you to calm down and use your professional experience when dealing with him'.

'I understand', I said.

The actuary removes the chair next to mine and replaces it with a metal one. Noticing my surprise, he explains: 'He is incontinent, you see, and sometimes wets the chair.'

With much noise and scuffling, a door opens, a door I have not noticed before, opposite the main door to the room. An armed guard in combat uniform and a black beret enters first, followed by an obese man in shorts, a T-shirt and a leg covered in bandages. He is, without a doubt, the ferocious 'Fat Romo'. It has never been established if he was a military man. After he was extradited from Brazil, where he had gone with his family for a new life of anonymity, the military was quick in declaring that Osvaldo Romo had never been a member of the armed forces. At the beginning Romo denied any participation in the crimes he was charged with, in spite of the overwhelming evidence from hundreds of testimonies to the contrary, and claimed that he was an army officer. He hoped that the military would back up his story, but he was too much of a liability and an embarrassment, and that was why he had been sent to live in Brazil under a new identity in the first place.

Osvaldo Romo was a typical 'lumpen', a term used in sociology to describe people who are not involved in the economic process of a society; they are neither proletarians nor peasants. They are often unemployed; they live in the margins of the city and at the margins of society. These people are supposed to develop their own ideology which despises and rejects both the proletarian and the bourgeoisie ideologies and values. Due to their living conditions and degree of isolation, they can be volatile and explosive, that is why they are easily drawn to any political cause. Typical of this kind in Latin America are those that populate the shantytowns around big cities.

Romo was one of these people. During the Popular Government, he established himself as a homeless activist in a shantytown in the south-west of Santiago. It is not known whether he was already working for military intelligence then or if he was recruited later. He was obviously unemployed, but never complained about not having money, which made him a good candidate for being on the payroll of one of the agents or provocateurs funded by the CIA, of which many were prominent right-wing journalists, landowners, petty criminals and 'lumpens'.

It seems that Romo's only purpose as an agent and a provocateur was to mingle, as much as possible, with those working in the shantytowns, so as to get to know the composition of the organisations working there, their membership, structures and names, hundred of names and personal details of those comrades passing through their makeshift towns, many of them students. Of course, Romo refused to become a member of any of the parties, preferring to join a small, unknown, populist, and now non-existant party, which was founded with the sole purpose of taking votes away from the Popular Front during the presidential campaign.

Even before the coup, Romo had started to actively and publicly campaign against the Popular Government and in favour of military intervention. Soon after the coup he joined the army intelligence service in the capture and killing of coalition party members and the MIR. He then claimed that he was, and had always been, a member of the Chilean armed forces, a sergeant, on commission before the coup. The army strongly denies this, stating that he was a civilian, 'occasional collaborator'.

In any event, Romo was, and still is, a psychopath. It may be the case that sometimes he has been a 'functional' psychopath, when there has been a functional outlet or role for him, like a shantytown provocateur, but a psychopath nonetheless. His behaviour as a hunter, torturer, rapist and murderer of hundreds of comrades can only be described as bestial. As a member of Krassnoff's team, who all stood out for their bestiality, he had participated in the capture and torture of almost everyone of the nearly four hundred prisoners that were 'processed' during the three months I spent at Grimaldi.

With more pretence than real difficulty, Romo enters the room aided by a second armed guard, and is helped to sit down. He does not look particularly old, nor infirm. If anything, he looks more demented, greeting the judge and the actuary as if they are old chums of his, complaining about his ailments, 'Diabetes is the worst,' he claims, as if being humble and familiar with the judge will save him from being found guilty. He looks at me and I am struck by his eyes: big, round, black, mad eyes. His eyes resemble the eyes depicted in caricatures of mad people, the iris constantly turning around in the socket, seemingly unable to look straight at one point. The same eyes from my most horrific memories from the torture centre. 'It does not matter that you see me, that is why I am lifting your blindfold; everybody knows me here and I am not afraid. Tell me where the money is,' he would say, before hitting you with the open palm of his huge hands in both ears at the same time, rendering you deaf for several days. Or, 'That whore has just bled on my hand when I was trying to touch her there; I just wanted to put an electrode inside her.'

'Do you know this man, Mr Romo?', the soft, authoritative voice of the judge asks.

'Err . . . no, I do not seem to recognise him,' Romo responds, giving me an oblique glance, without lifting his head.

'His name is Luis Muñoz,' continues the judge.

'Oh yes, he is Diana Aron's partner, now I remember him. I have seen him on television, he spoke from London when Pinochet was in detention there; yes I know him, he was in Villa Grimaldi, and he used to live in Villa Macul . . .'

Nothing can stop him from talking. I later find out that he was desperate to talk, to fill all the gaps, to prevent anyone else from saying anything because what they would like to say would inevitably condemn him. He has even written a book containing his account of the events, exonerating himself from his participation in the crimes.

'Yes, I believe that Diana is dead now,' he continues.

'But you were there, Romo,' I interrupt. 'You were there when she was captured, when she was hunted down, when she ran and Krassnoff and you shot her; you were in the pick-up truck.'

Romo does not argue, instead he starts to hit himself hard in the face with both hands while his mad eyes wander in circles in their sockets. The guard tries to prevent him from hitting his face by holding his arms. The judge reprimands him and reminds him that he has promised not to do it again, as nothing will be gained from it.

'But listen to what he is saying, your honour, that I did it when I did not do it,' Romo says in an imploring voice.

I then realise what the judge had hinted at before. Romo no longer has a defenceless victim at his disposal, to beat up, to perform his necessary acts of brutality against. Now when he gets angry the only physical object available to him is himself. From then on, every time I implicate or accuse him directly, Romo hits himself hard in the face. I decide to use a different tactic and a different approach. If Romo has been trying to protect himself from being implicated in the crimes, he will not, I assume, protect his accomplices. Also, Romo had been on trial since his extradition from Brazil, individually for many cases of the disappeared, with overwhelming evidence against him. He has been sentenced, individually, for every case, with many more cases to come; he cannot escape. Krassnoff and the others, on the other hand, are fighting tooth and nail, denying everything to get off the hook. I will make Romo work for me, I thought. He was there, in every single case; he knows who else was there and knows exactly what happened. Not only

242

that, Romo has been shown to have a prodigious memory, with a keen eye for detail.

'Romo,' I begin. 'When I was first brought to Villa Grimaldi, on the second or third day, Krassnoff told me that Diana had been shot on the eighteenth of November 1974 and that she was still alive and cared for in a clinic. That must have been the twelfth or thirteenth of December 1974, because I was captured on the tenth. What do you have to say about that?'

Romo does not hit himself this time.

'I believe that Diana was shot in the street. It could have been Krassnoff who shot her. But when I was at the Villa one evening, Sergeant Perez, yes, it was Perez, arrived in the pick-up and said, "I bring a dead one." He opened the back door and showed us the dead woman: it was Diana Aron.'

This partial version of events, where Romo takes himself crudely out of the picture, could bear some truth in that Diana, badly wounded, might have been taken to one of the clandestine clinics they kept, in an attempt to keep her alive for interrogation. These attempts may not have been very 'thorough', and ultimately she was either killed or died of her wounds. Her body was then taken to Villa Grimaldi for 'disposal'. It has recently been discovered that hundreds of bodies were taken by helicopter out to the cold and deep waters of the Pacific Ocean, tied to pieces of rail track and dumped into the water. The helicopter pilots and assistants could not hold their silence anymore and talked, in secret, to an investigating judge.

I have made some progress: Romo has confirmed, beyond doubt, Krassnoff's participation in Diana's kidnapping, torture and murder. I look at the judge who is busy looking at the PC screen, dictating what has been said to the actuary. She looks back at me and, noticing that Romo is not looking, tells me in a very low voice to carry on talking, that I am doing just fine.

I talk Romo into telling me about other assassinated comrades, putting emphasis on Krassnoff and the others' participation in the crimes. Romo is unhesitating, bringing in names and places I did not know. He is particularly angry about an army officer who, according to Romo, committed most of the crimes and who, up to then, had escaped prosecution, apparently by going to live in Miami. The 'conversation' goes on for what seemed like a century, with Romo hitting his face only once

243

more. I do not want, though, to let him go that easily, whether he hits his face or not.

I bring him back to Maria Cristina, to how beautiful she was, to where she was captured, to when, after weeks in captivity, he took her to my father and younger brother's house. He remembers all this with incredible accuracy.

'Yes,' he confirms, 'she was very beautiful.'

'Nice body too,' I add.

'Yes, nice body,' he agrees.

'She must have been wearing a short one piece, wasn't she?' I venture.

'As a matter of fact, yes, she was wearing a very short piece. How do you know?' he asks.

'I was with her when she bought it,' I reply. 'We went together to the boutique. For interrogation purposes, I guess they would have taken her clothes off, wouldn't they?' I say tentatively.

'Oh yes, certainly,' is his reply, his mad eyes circulating furiously.

'If she was naked, blindfolded and handcuffed,' I say in a calm manner, 'it would have been inevitable to touch her body; I mean to tie her to the metal bed and then to attach the electrodes, don't you agree?' My heart is hurting and I am unable to look the judge in the eye.

'Yes, I suppose so, yes,' Romo says cautiously.

'And then, of course, you know the genitals are the most painful part of the body to receive electric shocks. Well, it did happen to me, you see, my penis and anus. For women it was their vaginas, don't you agree Romo?'

'Oh yes, definitely,' he says, looking at the judge who carries on dictating. 'You did touch her, didn't you, Romo. Not only that, Romo, you raped her, you and the others!' I am shouting now.

'No, no,' he says hitting his face hard. Good, I thought, do it for me.

'You told me in Villa Grimaldi that she had a nice arse and a great vagina. Zapata told me too, boasting that both of you raped her. Didn't you, didn't you, murderer?' I am exhausted, Romo is sobbing, his face red from his own slapping, the guards holding him. The judge looks at me amazed.

'I didn't do it, Magistrate, you know me, Magistrate, I would have told you,' Romo says, almost imploring the judge and naming names of 'others' who might have done it.

'I remember, Romo,' I say in a calm voice, 'I remember a very beautiful black pistol you used to have.'

'Yes, I do remember,' Romo interrupts. 'That was a Colt .38, a gift from Captain Krassnoff after we killed Miguel Henriquez,' he volunteers enthusiastically, his face lit up like a child remembering a beloved toy.

'And you are saying that you never used the gun on our people; you carried the gun all the time and never used it, is that what you are saying?' I ask him, showing genuine incredulity.

'Well, I did use it in self-defence,' Romo said meekly.

'So you did use it then?' I continue.

'Yes.'

'Who were the ones who did most of the shooting? Was it Krassnoff? Zapata? Ferrer? Tulio? Because a lot of people died after being gunned down at that time, didn't they, Romo?'

'Well, yes, they did most of the shooting,' he says.

'All right then, Romo, so Maria Cristina, Marcelo Salinas, Jorge D'Orival, Diana Aron, you saw them all in Villa Grimaldi, did you not, Romo?' He nodded. 'So how come,' I continue, 'they were reported later as dead in Brazil and Argentina?'

'I do not know. I was not supposed to know who was in charge of the prisoners after that. I have already given the judge the names of the people I know could be responsible, but I can give you the names again, I can write them down, if that is OK with the judge.' He wrote the names down on an envelope I still have.

'Romo,' I venture again, 'you know, I am quite certain that the decisions on whether a prisoner should live or die were taken by officers there at the torture centre. Discussions must have taken place among the officers when the decisions were taken. You see, perhaps prisoners were not eliminated there, but the decisions were made there, were they not?'

'I believe you are right,' Romo replies.

'Now then, who would be in a better position to take those decisions than the officers who knew the most about the prisoners, the ones who interrogated them? Because what we are working on here with the judge is to find out what happened, what is the truth, don't you agree?'

'Oh yes, of course, that is what I have been doing over the years, telling the truth, cooperating, but then the judge put me behind bars,' laments Romo.

'Did they ever ask you for your opinion about any prisoner in that respect – to let them live or to "eliminate" them? Because I overheard conversations, you see, between Max Ferrer and Krassnoff; and then somebody approached you to ask your opinion; what do you think?'

'Yes, they did a sort of classification, but I did not know the exact purpose of that at the time. Some were not too bad and others were classed as bad, others as of no major interest, etc.,' Romo said.

'Have you any idea how I was classified, because, you see, I was there for a long time and got to know a lot, names of officers and prisoners. Even if I was not classed as dangerous, I became dangerous for "knowing too much". Why did they not kill me? What was your opinion in the matter? After all, Krassnoff had confessed to me he had shot Diana in the back, and I do know that Ferrer wanted me dead.'

'I really don't know,' Romo answers, and then he adds, perhaps to gather some sympathy. 'Maybe because you were a nice guy who came from a nice family.' I decide that his comment does not deserve an answer.

The judge is busy with the actuary typing all that has been said, Romo and I remain in silence for a long time. I want to cry out loud in pain. How futile everything has been, I think without comprehending, unable to accept that this mad, stupid, ignorant beast, sitting there, only a few inches from me, saw my lovely Diana die; raped and crushed sweet Maria Cristina; shot Anita Maria and Nano dead; pierced my ear drums, gave me a heart attack and fractured my ribs with a pole and my feet with a hammer. Who knows how many more atrocities there were on top of those that he had already been found guilty of? And I was 'a nice guy from a nice family'.

After what seems to me like a long, long time, the judge looks at me inquisitively, as though I am in charge of the proceedings and she is only taking notes. I suddenly 'come back' from Villa Grimaldi, as if I had been transported there yet again.

'Romo,' I say, 'tonight I am going to meet, for the first time in twelve years, Anita Aron, Diana's sister. She will surely ask me what happened to Diana. So what should I tell her?' He looks at me in a pensive manner and for the first time in the past two or maybe three hours he does not move to answer. A hint of coy cleverness appears in his eventual reply 'Tell her that Diana is dead; she is dead,' he says, not daring to add anything else, as if for once he understood that more pain would be better avoided this time. The judge tells Romo she has finished with him for today and, looking at the guards, asks them to remove him from the room. He looks at me as if he is puzzled, trying to find something in me, an almost imploring look, and then says: 'I wish you well, Luis.' I take this as an insult and look at him with hate. Without answering I turn around towards the opposite door and leave the room.

The judge has asked me to wait to see a detective who has been investigating the incident at the airport. All he can say to assure me is that it will not happen again when leaving Chile. He gives his name and telephone number confirming that his superior had also been informed and has given instructions to immigration at the airport. After this he leaves the room. The judge is standing in front of the desk, looking beautiful in her summer outfit, as though she has made an effort for this, our last encounter, in a difficult situation. I gather myself and my thoughts and say,

'Magistrate, I would like to thank you for what you have done. I think you are a remarkable woman and a person who deserves my utmost respect and admiration. The work you do is an example to humanity.' She looks down and, in a soft voice, full of modesty, says, 'Thank you.' Then she adds, 'I only hope that one day we can meet in different circumstances; for now I just sincerely hope you have a happy Christmas and New Year back in England.' We shake hands; I am full of mixed emotions. I tell myself 'Luis, it is time to go.'

# Rebirthing

# 18

The boys: yes, two lovely innocent boys over there, in England, waiting to play football with me, their dad, in the garden or in the park. Growing fast, there are many football games waiting to excite them. I seem like another person, another dad in another time, but it is me all the same. I was there next to Sara, my wife, when Pablo was born in 1997 at the hospital's birthing pool, holding him against my chest until he seemed to be part of me. Hungry after practically having lost my daughters I felt a strong urge to carry him around everywhere I went. In a hospital toilet I thought was empty I shouted like an animal, letting out the joy and the pressure of becoming a father again, the father of a boy: 'MY BOY!' Then suddenly a man came out of a cubicle and looked at me in fear.

'An only child is a very lonely child,' repeated Sara a year or two after Pablo was born, knowing that I was reluctant to have more children. When I look at Pablo and Orlando now, playing together, I feel so happy that there are two. Orlando appears to have created himself without our 'intervention'. We cannot recall having engaged in 'reproductive' activity at the supposed time of his conception. Not only that: Orlando decided to 'come out' on his own. When Sara and I were watching the news at nine o'clock, she calmly stated that she thought she was going to give birth that night. She was having contractions and a few minutes later she asked me to phone the midwife at the local hospital.

The woman at the other end of the line asked me how often Sara's contractions were. By that time there was one every two minutes or so. In a very calm voice she told me that unfortunately the midwife would not be able to arrive for at least forty-five minutes. In the next few minutes, Sara's contractions became more frequent. I phoned the hospital again and when the same calm voice asked about the contractions and dilatation, I could already see a tiny bit of Orlando's head. The woman on the phone said: 'Well Mr Munoz, you know what you have to do? Keep the baby warm, wrapped up in a towel or something, OK'

'Yes, of course,' I said, and slowly put the phone down.

Sara was already on all fours on the bedroom floor, which I had covered with an old duvet, panting heavily but avoiding making loud noises. 'I have to save energy,' she said courageously. I positioned myself to receive the baby. I had been at the births of my daughters, a friend's son and Pablo but this was going to be a completely different experience. We were on our own, with Pablo fast asleep in the room next door, but Sara, this admirable woman who is my wife, was incredibly calm and in control. 'The head is out, but still covered in the membrane', I reported to her. Silence; only Sara's heavy breathing, the baby's head facing up, resting in my hands. I was transfixed looking at this face resembling that of a bank robber with a stocking on his face. Not a movement.

Suddenly, as Sara pushed again, in one movement the baby rotated ninety degrees, exiting one shoulder and an arm first, then the other, and suddenly the rest of the body was out in my arms together with the fluids released by the breaking of the sac. 'It's a boy!' I shouted to Sara who was facing in the opposite direction. 'Count its fingers and toes please; are they all there?' she whispered. The baby lay calmly in my arms, not breathing. I wrapped him up in a towel, but did not worry as he was still attached to his umbilical cord. He opened his eyes for a couple of seconds; still no breathing. I would wait for a few more seconds, and if he still did not breathe, I would suck the mucus from his nose and then blow gently in his mouth. His eyes opened again, this time slowly moving around inside their sockets, looking at me. Suddenly, when I was about to make contact with his nose, he whimpered and his chest started to move up and down. I was enormously relieved.

I knew there was no need to cut the umbilical cord yet. I also remembered that Sara's blood was rhesus negative, and that if the baby was positive, she would need an injection to prevent her body going into shock. Therefore we would need to get a blood sample from the cord.

For a moment I could not believe what had happened. I had directly participated in the miracle of human birth and I was feeling very small, almost embarrassed at my smallness, while the baby seemed to be invested with a wisdom beyond imagination. I felt that was the way he was looking at me: with the eyes of ancient wisdom, slowly blinking, overwhelmingly calm, as if questioning my entire life during the few minutes of his own.

The midwife arrived well after our baby's first forty-five minutes of life and after the delivery of the placenta. We had wrapped him in soft blankets, in our love and in our admiration. After taking a blood sample from the cord, she stated that because 'I' had done everything, I should cut the umbilical cord and handed me the surgical scissors. The whole process had lasted a little over two hours, when finally we were all together back in the bed, together with Pablo, who, having woken up, jumped into our bed to discover a tiny foot hanging from Sara's chest. 'A baby!' he cried. Orlando still looks at me with those same eyes: when I reproach him for some mischievousness, he says nothing, just stares calmly straight into my eyes, defiant and making me feel ashamed and inadequate because of my petty, ill-tempered behaviour.

★   ★   ★

'Mama, who made dad go to Chile?' Five-year-old Pablo had been asking. He missed his dad so much. They were all there at the airport: Sara, Pablo and Orlando, waiting for a long time because there was no space for the plane to land.

It was wonderful to embrace my loved ones, my dear little boys full of love for their dad. 'Who made dad go to Chile mum?'

And then, back to work, to appeals in court, to clients suffering from neurosis and depression, because that is what I do: I represent asylum seekers in their appeals during the day and practise psychotherapy two evenings a week. But Anita, Diana's sister, had warned me: 'Be careful, when you get back to England. It's going to hit you. You might have been functioning on adrenaline here, but once you are there things will be different.'

It was a few days before Christmas and, as usual, we would spend time with my wife's sister in Shropshire, and New Year's Eve with her parents in the Wirral. I felt the force of the clash between my two worlds, with devastating effect. It was difficult even to move around familiar people. I did it like a robot, following instructions to move, eat, to hold, smile and answer questions. I just had a constant need to cry without having the space to do it. I also felt tired all the time; given the chance I would have slept every time I sat down. The festive mood in the people surrounding me seemed totally incongruous to me.

Going back to work, I was eager to tell my colleagues what had happened in Chile, what I had done, but I realised people were only marginally interested, if at all. On the contrary, I sensed resentment because they had been working hard until the end of the year while I had been 'having a good time in an exotic place'. My manager listened to me for a few minutes, then just interrupted me to update me on work and tell me that I had to attend an appeal hearing in Leeds a few days later.

It is hard work taking a case from the initial asylum application, to refusal, then appeal and hopefully success. But more often than not the applicant gets refused and subsequently loses their case at the appeal stage.

I went to Leeds the night before the appeal of a lawyer fleeing persecution in Kurdistan feeling cold and anxious at the prospect of being 'grilled' by a judge. I developed an inexplicable and excruciating pain on my right arm for which I needed strong painkillers. As it happened, a crucial witness was not called and the judge agreed to adjourn the case to allow time for the witness to be called. After the hearing I started to feel increasingly worse. I dreamt a lot during the night and then could not go back to sleep, increasing my tiredness during the day. The pain in my right arm had not gone.

My dreams were not nightmarish, they were incredibly sad and real. I would wake up crying, wanting to be with the people in my dreams who were, invariably, Diana and the rest of the comrades and friends I had lost in Chile. The people I had been talking with the judge about became real in my sleep. Maria Cristina would ask me, time and again, not to leave her alone, begging me to take her away with me. I would try to reach her running through a muddy field while my feet got heavier and heavier, making my efforts more difficult.

I was about to leave the doctor's room, after complaining about my aching arm, when I decided to tell him I was having problems sleeping. I briefly told him what I had done four weeks before. I kept talking about what 'I had done', as though I had gone to Chile and committed a terrible act. I had, but only against me. A terrible act. I had gone and awakened the dead and I was with them. I saw them every day for three weeks, and they were so lovely, it felt so good to be with them, my lovely dead ones.

I went to all the places we used to go, the houses we used to frequent and live in. The places where we used to eat, hold hands kiss. And now they don't want to leave, they do not want to leave me. 'Don't go!' they cry. 'Don't leave us alone, don't sleep without us, don't eat without us, and don't laugh . . .' And I just cry, and I can't sleep, I can't eat, and I can't laugh, and I do not want to leave them. 'What a terrible loss,' my heart keeps saying and hurting in my chest.

This went on and on for months. Now 'they' let me sleep most of the time, and eat and laugh and love. 'They' are more playful now, and when they make themselves present in the form of a particular smell, a voice in the street, a face, another person or a landscape, it is both sad and longing. And I feel an impulse to tell someone 'Excuse me, you remind me of . . .' But the words are sucked back in, where they belong, in a world of silence where they have long been sentenced forever.

New beginnings: Luis and his eldest son Pablo.

# Postscript

Diana Aron was beautiful, extremely intelligent and very generous. But the most fundamental thing of all is that Diana, like so many of the young people of that generation, had the chance to choose, and she chose to share the destiny of the overlooked people of her country. Diana came from a wealthy family in Santiago. She could have chosen to go with the flow; to do what her brothers and sisters did, and follow the route of her normal life. She could have accepted the demands of her family to leave the country. 'What ever you choose', they said. Diana chose to stay in Chile to work together with others, to organise and minimise the impact of the barbarism that fell on the Chilean people.

Diana chose to hold on with all her strength to her dream, without giving importance to the price of her audacity. And she continued to dream of a free country, with popular rights already won, with a radiant future for the poor, the workers, the peasants and the young Chileans. Diana dreamt the impossible trying to reach the possible.

I had the privilege to love that woman, and also had the privilege to be the one who received her love in the sphere of our intimate lives. But beyond all else, Diana loved her people, and decided to prove her love with an incredible constancy.

Diana, in my dreams you come and go, sometimes sweet, sometimes sad. In my daily routines you appear, in the look of another woman, in a voice, in the smell of perfume. In those moments I stop and try to find you amongst the crowd, as if you would be in Santiago. I know it is useless, that I might seem crazy, but it is an instinct stuck to my skin. Without being aware I turn my head when I recognise your voice, your laughter, your eyes in a London street.

*Postscript*

Forever my heart will remain pierced by those strokes. It is as if the dagger of your absence, which I carry in my breast, would enter a bit deeper into my broken heart when I hear you, until I have no more strength left. Then I will stop, with eyes wide open, trying to find you amongst the crowd.

★   ★   ★

Miguel Krassnoff, Marcelo Moren (the Bear), Osvaldo Romo (Guaton), Manuel Cotreras (Mamo) have been found guilty of the kidnapping, disappearance and probable murder of Diana Aron Svigilsky and sentenced to 15 years in prison. They are also being sentenced to 12 and 15 years in prison for the same crimes against no less than 100 other victims. And the trials continue.

At least my trip to Chile to testify against them was not in vain.